BROKEN WINDOWS BEHIND BARS

TRANSFORMING JAIL OPERATIONS THROUGH ORDER AND ACCOUNTABILITY

SHAUN KLUCZNIK

SHINE
Tampa, Florida
Jodi K Costa, LLC

Publisher: Shine Press
4522 W. Village Dr. #1294
Tampa, Florida 34624
Shine-Press.com | Jodi@Shine-Press.com
Shine Press is an imprint of Jodi K Costa, LLC.

This is a work of professional nonfiction. Case studies are based on real incidents from correctional facilities across the United States but have been anonymized and, in some cases, combined to protect staff, inmates, and institutions. The lessons and conclusions remain authentic to the lived realities of corrections.

Paperback ISBN: 979-8-9937924-5-3
Hardcover ISBN: 979-8-9937924-4-6

For permission requests, ordering information, bulk orders, more information about the author, to book the author for your next event, or media interview, please contact the publisher at:
jodi@shine-press.com

FIRST EDITION

DEDICATION

To the correctional officers, supervisors, administrators, and support staff who walk into the hardest places in America every day.

To those who keep order, protect each other, and never walk past disorder. This book is for you.

CONTENTS

ACKNOWLEDGMENTS

Writing a book on corrections is never an individual effort. It is the product of countless conversations, lessons, and examples drawn from the people who dedicate their lives to this profession.

To my wife, Lindsay, your love, support, patience, and encouragement made this possible. To my daughter, Grace, I hope I have provided you with a good example. To my family, including those who came before me and gave me both challenges and strength, thank you for shaping the person I became.

I thank my colleagues across the country who shared experiences, insights, and lessons that shaped the case studies and analysis found in these pages. Each of you reminded me that corrections is not just about custody; it is about culture.

To Sheriff Al Nienhuis and the Hernando County Sheriff's Office, thank you for allowing me to lead, learn, and grow within one of the most dedicated teams of professionals I have ever known.

To the American Jail Association, thank you for the opportunity to serve and to learn from leaders across the nation who have shown me the best of this profession.

And finally, to the correctional officers and supervisors across this country, the men and women who step into danger daily with little recognition but enormous responsibility, this book belongs to you. You are the real "keepers of the keys."

INTRODUCTION

Broken Windows In Corrections

The Broken Windows Theory was first introduced to the public in 1982, when James Q. Wilson and George L. Kelling wrote an article in *The Atlantic Monthly* describing how small signs of disorder, if left unchecked, create an environment that invites larger crimes. Their example was simple: if one broken window in a neighborhood goes unrepaired, soon all the windows will be broken. Graffiti, litter, vandalism, and loitering were not just nuisances; they were signals. They communicated that nobody cared, that order had collapsed, and that anything was permissible.

The theory was tested and refined in community policing, especially in New York City during the 1990s. Officers began enforcing quality-of-life offenses, fare evasion, graffiti, and public drinking, and they saw major declines in serious crime. While debates continue in academic circles, practitioners recognized a core truth: disorder tolerated becomes disorder multiplied.

Corrections professionals have known this instinctively for decades. Jails and prisons are compressed societies where signals spread at lightning speed. Inmates live in constant contact, observing staff and each other closely. When one inmate refuses lockdown without consequence, soon an entire pod challenges orders. When one officer overlooks a dirty shower, trash piles up across the facility. When a supervisor ignores sloppy counts, inmates recognize the opportunity and test for escape routes.

This book applies Broken Windows directly to the correctional environment. It is not theory for theory's sake; it is a practical manual for jail and prison leaders, supervisors, and correctional officers who must create and sustain order in some of the most difficult environments imaginable.

Corrections is about details. A tucked-in shirt, a clean floor, a locked door, a properly conducted count—these may appear small, but they are the difference between control and chaos. Broken Windows provides the framework to understand why those details matter and how to enforce them consistently.

About the Case Studies

Throughout this book, you will find case studies that illustrate the principles of Broken Windows in corrections. These case studies are based on real incidents from facilities across the United States, but all names, locations, and identifying details have been changed. Some are composites of multiple events. They are anonymized to protect institutions and staff, but the lessons are authentic.

Corrections professionals will recognize themselves in these stories. These are not isolated incidents; they are patterns that repeat in every jail and prison. The purpose of these case studies is not to criticize but to teach. They show how small cracks in order become crises and how attentive staff and supervisors can prevent escalation by addressing details before they spiral.

Corrections as a World of Details

The book is divided into six parts. We begin with the foundations of Broken Windows in corrections: why the theory belongs inside jail walls, how jails function as microsocieties, and how leadership presence sets the culture. From there, we explore staff accountability, inmate management, sanitation and design, security, technology, professionalism, and finally, long-term sustainability.

The intended audience includes correctional officers, supervisors, administrators, trainers, and policymakers. Each has a role in shaping the culture of their facility and the responsibility to enforce order in the details.

Broken Windows is not just useful in corrections; it is essential.

- 1 -

THE BROKEN WINDOWS THEORY FROM STREETS TO CELL BLOCKS

The Origins and Logic of Broken Windows

In the late 1970s and early 1980s, American cities faced crises that seemed overwhelming. Crime rates were high, fear was widespread, and entire neighborhoods appeared abandoned by public order. In New York City, subway cars rolled into stations covered end to end in graffiti. Public parks were littered with trash. Vacant buildings sat with broken windows and kicked-in doors, becoming havens for drug use and vandalism. Many city residents had stopped reporting minor crimes altogether because they no longer believed anything would change.

This was the world in which James Q. Wilson, a respected political scientist, and George L. Kelling, a criminologist, presented a new way of thinking about crime and disorder. In March 1982, they published an article in *The*

Atlantic Monthly called “Broken Windows.” The idea they put forward was straightforward but powerful. They argued that disorder in a community does not remain contained. If small violations are ignored, they multiply. If a window is broken and not repaired, it sends a signal that nobody cares. Soon, other windows are broken. What looks like a cosmetic issue is actually a cultural signal. Disorder tolerated becomes disorder multiplied.

Wilson and Kelling wrote at a time when criminology was heavily focused on broad social explanations for crime. Many scholars argued that poverty, inequality, and unemployment were the root causes. Wilson and Kelling did not deny that those factors mattered, but they argued that the environment people saw around them each day also mattered. A broken window, a wall covered in graffiti, or a corner filled with loiterers sent a message. It told residents that order had collapsed and told potential offenders that rules were negotiable.

Their theory suggested that communities could not wait for large social problems to be solved before addressing crime. They could start by fixing windows, cleaning graffiti, and addressing the smallest signs of disorder. These small actions would send the opposite signal. They would show that rules were enforced, that order mattered, and that authority was present.

The article struck a nerve. It gave residents and police officers language for something they had felt but could not easily explain. Disorder was not trivial. It was contagious. And when corrected, it could be contained.

Broken Windows in New York City

The most famous test of the Broken Windows Theory came in New York City during the 1990s. At the time, the city was struggling with high crime rates, particularly violent crime. The subway system had become a symbol of disorder. Fare evasion was rampant, graffiti covered cars, and commuters felt unsafe.

When William Bratton became head of the New York City Transit Police in 1990, he applied Broken Windows principles aggressively. Officers began targeting fare evaders, removing graffiti, and addressing public disorder in stations. Soon after, Bratton became Police Commissioner and expanded the approach citywide. Under Mayor Rudy Giuliani, quality-of-life enforcement became a centerpiece of policing strategy.

Officers were directed to focus not only on serious crimes but also on smaller offenses: public intoxication, vandalism, aggressive panhandling, and loitering. Graffiti was removed immediately. Broken windows were repaired. Subway turnstiles were monitored closely.

The results were dramatic. Crime rates in New York City fell throughout the 1990s, including declines in homicide and robbery. While scholars still debate the causes of the crime drop, some point to demographic changes and others to economic growth. Many practitioners credited the consistency of Broken Windows enforcement. What mattered most was not the severity of punishment but the fact that small violations were not ignored. Signals of disorder were met with signals of authority.

The public perception shifted as well. Residents reported feeling safer. Visitors to the city noticed cleaner streets and subways. Even those who criticized the strategy for being heavy-handed admitted that the city looked different.

Academic Debate and Criticism

The success of Broken Windows policing in New York City made the theory famous, but it also sparked criticism. Some argued that the strategy unfairly targeted marginalized communities by focusing on minor infractions such as loitering and public drinking. Others questioned whether the drop in crime was really caused by policing or whether larger social and economic trends were more responsible.

Wilson and Kelling's original article had not suggested mass arrests or harsh punishments. They emphasized the importance of maintaining order through presence, consistency, and community engagement. Yet in some places, the application of Broken Windows was criticized for becoming too punitive.

Despite the debate, the central insight of Broken Windows has held. Small signs of disorder send signals. Ignoring them allows disorder to spread. Addressing them sends the opposite message. Whether in cities or correctional facilities, this principle remains true.

The Logic of Broken Windows

At its core, the Broken Windows Theory is about the psychology of signals. People look to their environment for cues about what is normal and what is tolerated.

- A broken window left unrepaired suggests abandonment.
- Graffiti left on a wall suggests nobody is watching.
- Trash piled in a public park suggests rules do not matter.
- Aggressive behavior in public spaces suggests authority is absent.

When rules appear optional, people adjust their behavior downward. A neighbor who once might have called to report graffiti decides not to bother. A shop owner who once might have swept the sidewalk lets trash accumulate. A teenager who once might not have considered vandalism joins in. The cycle continues until disorder becomes the culture.

The opposite is also true. When disorder is corrected quickly, people adjust their behavior upward. A repaired window shows care. A freshly painted wall signals ownership. An officer addressing a small violation communicates authority. People learn that rules are enforced and that standards matter.

This cycle of signals is universal. It applies in neighborhoods, schools, workplaces, and public spaces. But nowhere is it more immediate than in corrections.

From Streets to Cell Blocks

Jails and prisons are microsocieties. They are compressed environments where hundreds or even thousands of people live in close quarters. Inmates observe staff constantly. They notice which rules are enforced and which are ignored. They test boundaries relentlessly.

What might take months to spread in a city can spread in minutes inside a housing unit. Disorder in corrections is not slow. It is immediate, visible, and contagious.

- If one officer ignores an untucked shirt, others will be tested.
- If one sergeant overlooks a refused lockdown, others will soon face group refusals.
- If supervisors tolerate sloppy rounds, inmates learn where blind spots exist.

Broken Windows belongs in corrections because the environment magnifies the impact of signals. Small cracks in discipline quickly become cultural collapse unless addressed. A single ignored infraction can shape the behavior of an entire housing pod. A broken piece of equipment tolerated by staff can invite escape attempts. A sloppy count overlooked by supervisors can lead to breaches that threaten safety.

Case Study 1: The Graffiti Wall

Graffiti is one of the clearest examples of how Broken Windows operates in corrections. At first glance, it may seem cosmetic. It can be dismissed as the work of a bored inmate, a minor distraction in a facility where more serious issues dominate. But graffiti is not simply writing on a wall. It is a signal. In the correctional environment, signals spread faster than anywhere else.

This case comes from a large metropolitan jail that housed more than two thousand inmates. The facility was modern by design but strained by population pressure and staffing shortages. Officers worked long shifts, often rotating between pods with little consistency. The facility's leadership emphasized major security measures such as perimeter checks, contraband sweeps, and emergency drills, but small details like markings on walls and tables were rarely a focus of daily inspections.

It began with a scratch on a dayroom table. An inmate carved his initials into the wood with a makeshift tool, a sharpened piece of plastic fashioned from a food tray. The marking was crude, only a few letters, and it attracted little attention. The officer assigned to the unit saw it during rounds but was dealing with a medical escort at the time. He made a note to report it later, but by the time his shift ended, it slipped his mind.

The next day, the scratch was joined by another. Within a week, several tables carried initials and small drawings. None of them were immediately threatening. They were not gang symbols, at least not at first. But they were visible to every inmate in the pod. They sent a message: staff saw the markings and did nothing.

Inmates pay attention to what staff tolerate. They test constantly to see where the boundaries are. In this pod, the message was clear. Marking property was not being enforced. Soon, what began as scratches became etchings. Inmates began carving deeper, bolder designs. Some brought ink into the process, smearing pen ink or boot polish into grooves to make the symbols stand out.

By the end of the month, entire tables were covered. Walls near the showers displayed crude drawings. Even cell doors had markings scratched into the paint. What had begun as boredom became competition. Inmates compared designs, boasted about who controlled which table, and challenged others to cross out markings. The graffiti had become a visible scoreboard of dominance.

Officers working the unit felt the shift. Where once they had been able to direct inmates with simple commands, they now faced resistance. Inmates laughed when told to clean tables. Some refused outright, pointing to the markings as proof that staff did not care. Control of the dayroom had subtly shifted. It was no longer neutral ground. It had become inmate territory, marked and defended with symbols.

Supervisors walking the unit saw the graffiti but failed to act decisively. A sergeant noted it in passing but prioritized a staffing shortage elsewhere in the facility. A lieutenant included it in a shift report but did not initiate corrective action. Each time leadership walked past the markings without ordering immediate removal, the signal grew louder: staff did not own the space.

Within two months, gang symbols began to appear. What had started as initials and crude drawings evolved into structured messages. Rival groups carved identifiers into tables and walls. Fights broke out over who controlled certain areas. One evening, two groups clashed in the dayroom, and the spark that ignited the fight was an argument over whose markings were allowed to remain on a table.

The facility was now dealing with a problem far greater than graffiti. What had begun as a minor issue had escalated into gang violence. The signals of disorder had multiplied until they became signals of power. Inmates had successfully claimed physical space inside a secure facility, and staff were reacting rather than controlling.

The administration finally responded. A directive was issued for the immediate removal of all graffiti. Maintenance crews and inmate workers were brought in to sand and repaint tables, repaint walls, and strip markings from doors. Officers were ordered to report any new graffiti as contraband destruction of property. Supervisors were required to inspect each housing pod daily and certify that surfaces were clear.

The cleanup took weeks. Each time an area was repainted, new markings appeared within hours. The battle for control was not won with paint alone. It required consistent enforcement. Officers were instructed to stop and correct any inmate observed scratching surfaces, confiscate tools, and issue disciplinary reports. Supervisors were directed to back officers immediately and to document enforcement. Slowly, over several months, the tide shifted. Inmates realized that markings were erased quickly and that consequences followed. The graffiti culture diminished.

The lesson for staff was sobering. What had begun as a minor scratch had grown into a facility-wide problem because it was ignored. The failure was not one of equipment or policy. It was a failure of signals. By overlooking graffiti, staff sent the message that inmates could own the space. Once inmates believed that, they acted on it, and the result was violence.

Lessons from the Graffiti Wall

- **Graffiti is never cosmetic.** It is always a signal of control. Left unchecked, it becomes a visible scoreboard for inmates.
- **Staff silence is consent.** Each time an officer or supervisor walked past the markings without addressing them, the message grew louder.
- **Correction is not one-time.** Removing graffiti once is not enough. It must be enforced consistently and quickly.
- **Ownership is visible.** Whoever controls the markings controls the space. If staff tolerate graffiti, they surrender ownership of the environment.

Graffiti in corrections is a classic broken window. It begins small, often so small that busy officers barely notice. But it spreads rapidly, and once it spreads, it reshapes the culture of a unit. This story illustrates how fast signals multiply and how costly it becomes to correct them once they are embedded.

Case Study 2: The Broken Door

Physical infrastructure in correctional facilities communicates powerful signals. Doors, locks, windows, and gates are not simply pieces of hardware. They are the backbone of security. When they fail, they do more than allow movement—they send messages. Inmates notice instantly when a piece of equipment does not function properly, and they interpret it as weakness. Staff who tolerate broken security equipment communicate, intentionally or not, that safety is negotiable.

This case comes from a county jail in the Southeast that held just over a thousand inmates. The jail was a mixture of old and new construction. Some housing units dated back to the 1970s, while others were built in the past decade. The older sections suffered frequent maintenance problems. Doors stuck. Locks jammed. Cameras flickered. Officers and supervisors had grown used to working around equipment failures.

One of the older units contained single cells designed for two inmates each. The cell doors were solid steel with narrow vision panels. Each door was controlled by a mechanical latch that was supposed to secure when closed. Over time, one particular door developed a problem. The latch did not always engage. Sometimes it clicked into place. Other times, it did not.

The first time officers noticed, they improvised. One officer placed a broom handle across the door as a temporary fix. Another shoved a plastic wedge under the door to keep it closed. Maintenance was notified, but the request was marked low priority. Other issues, such as a broken chiller in the kitchen and faulty lighting in a control room, were addressed first. The door remained unrepaired.

Inmates, of course, noticed. They heard the uneven sound of the latch. They saw the makeshift broom handle wedged against the door. They began rattling the door during rounds, testing its strength. At first, it was a game. They shook the door when officers walked past, laughing when it wobbled. Officers told them to knock it off but did not escalate the issue.

Over time, the inmates' curiosity became intent. One inmate, serving a sentence for burglary, studied the latch carefully. He tested it at night when rounds were less frequent. After repeated attempts, he discovered that with enough pressure, he could force the latch open. The door would swing outward, giving him access to the hallway. He quietly showed his cellmate. Together, they practiced opening and closing the door without alerting staff.

The broken latch had now moved from inconvenience to vulnerability. What had been a maintenance issue was now a security breach.

One evening, during a particularly busy shift, the inmates acted. Officers were dealing with a fight in another pod and staff presence in the unit was thin. The two inmates pushed open their door and slipped into the hallway. They moved quickly toward a service corridor that led to an unsecured supply area. Their plan was to find tools or cleaning supplies that could be turned into weapons.

They did not make it far. An officer on rounds in an adjacent unit noticed movement where there should have been none. He radioed for assistance. Responding staff intercepted the inmates before they could reach the supply area. Both were restrained and placed in segregation.

The incident sparked an immediate investigation. Administrators wanted to know how long the latch had been malfunctioning and why it had not been repaired. Maintenance logs revealed that the door had been reported several weeks earlier. Work orders had been submitted but marked as non-urgent. Staff interviews revealed that officers had known about the issue and had improvised fixes. Supervisors had walked the unit, seen the broom handle wedged across the door, and said nothing.

The broken door had become a symbol. To inmates, it signaled weakness. To staff, it represented a tolerance of disorder. Everyone had seen the problem. Nobody had corrected it. The inmates simply acted on the message.

The fallout was significant. Several officers were disciplined for failing to report and follow up on the issue. Supervisors were reminded of their responsibility to treat broken security equipment as emergencies, not inconveniences. The maintenance department changed its prioritization process, requiring that any malfunctioning lock or door be repaired within twenty-four hours.

The jail also launched a staff training initiative. Officers were taught to see equipment through the eyes of inmates. A door that rattled was not just an annoyance. It was a test waiting to be exploited. A camera with a blind spot was not just a technical glitch. It was an opportunity for contraband drops. Staff were reminded that improvising fixes might work for a moment, but they sent dangerous signals if left uncorrected.

Lessons from the Broken Door

- **Every lock is a line of defense.** When a lock or latch fails, the line of defense fails with it. Staff must treat every malfunction as a serious breach.
- **Improvisation is temporary.** A broom handle across a door or a piece of tape over a latch is not a solution. It is an admission of weakness. Inmates will notice and test it.
- **Maintenance is security.** Administrators must ensure that maintenance requests involving doors, locks, and cameras are treated as emergencies. Security equipment is not cosmetic.
- **Supervisors must act.** Walking past a malfunctioning door without correcting it is as dangerous as ignoring inmate misconduct. Leadership presence is measured in details.
- **Inmates adapt quickly.** A single inmate with time and patience can exploit weaknesses that staff overlook. Once discovered, the knowledge spreads instantly.

This case underscores the Broken Windows principle in its most concrete form. Disorder tolerated becomes disorder multiplied. A door that did not latch properly became a signal of weakness. That signal was tested, shared, and acted upon. The incident could easily have become an escape or a violent assault. Only chance prevented a disaster.

Corrections professionals cannot afford to treat security equipment as background noise. Every malfunction is a window into how the facility communicates authority. If equipment works, it signals control. If it fails and is ignored, it signals neglect. Inmates act accordingly.

Case Study 3: The Sloppy Count

Among the most sacred duties in any correctional facility is the inmate count. Count is not a formality, it is the backbone of security. Every lock, every search, every policy ultimately depends on one principle: staff must know where every inmate is, at every moment. When count is sloppy, the entire security structure begins to collapse.

This case comes from a medium-security state prison that held roughly 1,500 inmates. The prison had a long history, with some housing units built decades earlier. Staff turnover was high, and the facility often operated short of full complement. Officers were expected to cover overtime shifts, and supervisors were stretched thin. In this environment, small shortcuts became routine.

By policy, count was required three times daily, with additional standing counts at night. Each count required officers to visually confirm the presence of every inmate, standing at the cell door, looking inside, and ensuring that each person was present and accounted for. The policy was clear, but over time, practice began to drift.

Officers, pressed for time, began counting from the doorway. Instead of opening the door flap and requiring inmates to stand, they simply glanced at bunks. If they saw a body-shaped outline under a blanket, they marked the inmate as present. Some officers even joked that they could count a unit without waking anyone. Supervisors, equally pressed, signed off on these counts without verification.

The inmates noticed. They always notice.

In one housing unit, two inmates began experimenting. During count, they would crouch in a closet off the main hallway, just out of sight. Their cellmates arranged blankets to look like occupied bunks. Officers walked by, glanced into the cells, and recorded the inmates as present. The ruse worked. The inmates were marked accounted for, even though they were not in their cells.

At first, the trick was for amusement. They moved freely through the unit after count, bragging quietly that they had beaten the system. Soon, however, they used the opportunity for more serious purposes. They coordinated contraband drops, slipping items between cells during count. They explored hallways, noting where cameras did not reach. They tested how long they could remain unaccounted for before anyone noticed.

The scheme went on for weeks. Each successful attempt emboldened the inmates further. They recruited others, teaching them how to stage bunks with blankets and pillows. What had started with two inmates became a pattern across the unit. Dozens of inmates were moving during count, confident that staff would not detect their absence.

The problem came to light only by accident. One evening, officers intercepted a package of contraband in a hallway. The package contained tobacco, pills, and a cell phone. Investigators traced the package back to the unit and discovered that the delivery had taken place during count. Inmates admitted that they had been hiding in closets and dayrooms, slipping through blind spots while officers marked them present.

The revelation stunned administrators. The very process designed to guarantee security had been corrupted. The integrity of the count had been destroyed. The fact that the deception had gone on for weeks raised troubling questions. How many inmates had moved freely during count? What opportunities for violence or escape had been created? The answers were uncertain, but the risk was undeniable.

The investigation revealed several contributing factors. Officers admitted they were rushed. Some acknowledged they had been trained properly but had fallen into bad habits. Supervisors admitted they trusted their staff but had not verified counts themselves. The culture of the facility had shifted from precision to assumption.

The consequences were immediate. Officers involved were disciplined. Supervisors were held accountable. The warden ordered a facility-wide retraining on count procedures. From that point forward, every inmate was required to stand for count, and officers had to visually confirm each face. Supervisors were required to physically walk units during count, ensuring compliance.

The lesson was clear. A sloppy count is not a minor mistake. It is a broken window that undermines the credibility of staff and invites serious breaches. When count is done carelessly, inmates learn that they can move unnoticed. They exploit the opportunity quickly, and once they do, the entire security of the facility is at risk.

Lessons from the Sloppy Count

- **Count is sacred.** It is the foundation of security. Every officer and supervisor must treat it as non-negotiable.
- **Shortcuts destroy trust.** Once staff begin taking shortcuts, the culture shifts. Inmates see it, test it, and exploit it.
- **Supervisors must verify.** Trusting staff is not enough. Supervisors must be physically present during count to ensure compliance.
- **Training is not permanent.** Even when staff are trained properly, habits drift over time. Retraining is essential.
- **Signals spread instantly.** Once two inmates discovered they could beat count, the knowledge spread through the unit like wildfire. Staff must assume that any weakness discovered by one inmate will soon be known by many.

The failure of count in this prison demonstrates Broken Windows in its purest form. A small tolerance for shortcuts became an invitation for disorder. What seemed efficient in the moment created long-term risk. The signal to inmates was simple. Staff are not paying attention. Once that signal was sent, it was acted upon.

Count is the single most important ritual in corrections. It is not tedious. It is not negotiable. It is the ritual that communicates authority, presence, and control. When done properly, it sends the message that staff know where every inmate is at all times. When done sloppily, it sends the opposite message. In corrections, signals determine culture.

Analysis and Application

The three case studies in this chapter, the graffiti wall, the broken door, and the sloppy count—demonstrate that the Broken Windows Theory is not abstract philosophy. It is lived reality in corrections. Each example began with something small, a scratch on a table, a latch that failed occasionally, a count conducted from a doorway instead of face-to-face. None of these issues seemed like emergencies, yet each was tolerated. Each sent a signal that was noticed, tested, and acted upon.

The power of Broken Windows in corrections lies in the speed at which signals spread. In a city neighborhood, graffiti left unchecked may spread block by block over weeks. In a housing unit, graffiti can spread table to table overnight. A broken window in a community might invite trespassers over months. A broken door latch in a jail can be exploited within days. A sloppy count can embolden inmates immediately, allowing them to move during the most critical security procedure of the day.

The lesson is simple but profound. In corrections, nothing is small. Every detail is magnified. Every inconsistency is multiplied. Every tolerated weakness becomes a tool for inmates.

Staff sometimes push back against this level of scrutiny. They argue they do not have time to address every detail. They believe they must prioritize "real" security issues, fights, contraband, and emergencies. The truth is that ignoring details creates those emergencies. The graffiti wall became a gang fight. The broken door became an escape attempt. The sloppy count became a contraband pipeline. Emergencies are often the end result of unattended details.

Leadership in corrections is measured not only by how staff respond to crises but also by how they prevent them. Prevention requires attention to detail. It requires discipline to enforce small rules consistently. It requires supervisors to back officers and officers to own their units. It requires administrators to understand that maintenance is security, professionalism is control, and culture is defined by what staff walk past.

The application of Broken Windows in corrections also explains why staff presence is so critical. Inmates are constantly watching. They learn more from what staff do than from what policies say. An officer who walks past graffiti communicates that rules do not matter, no matter what the handbook says. A supervisor who signs off on a sloppy count communicates that procedures are optional, no matter what training requires. Conversely, an officer who corrects small infractions communicates that order is expected. A supervisor who insists on thorough counts communicates that security is sacred.

Corrections professionals must internalize the principle that signals are the currency of culture. Every interaction, every detail, every action or inaction sends a message. Those messages shape inmate behavior, staff morale, and facility safety.

Tools and Takeaways

This section translates the lessons of Chapter 1 into actionable practices for staff, supervisors, and administrators:

1. **Graffiti is not cosmetic.** Graffiti must be treated as a security issue, not merely an appearance issue. It communicates ownership of space. Facilities should have clear policies requiring immediate removal. Officers must document new graffiti as destruction of property. Inmate work crews should be mobilized quickly to repaint or clean affected surfaces. Supervisors should inspect housing units daily, checking tables, walls, and doors. Administrators must ensure resources, paint, cleaning supplies, and maintenance support are readily available.

When corrected consistently, the signal shifts: space belongs to staff, not inmates.

2. **Broken equipment is security.** Every lock, latch, and camera in a facility is a line of defense. When one fails, the line weakens. Staff must report equipment problems immediately. Supervisors must treat reports as urgent. Administrators must prioritize security-related maintenance. Facilities should implement daily security inspections. Improvised fixes send signals of weakness, while repairs send signals of control.

3. **Counts must be sacred.** Count procedures are the backbone of security. Every inmate must be visually confirmed. Officers must require inmates to stand. Supervisors must physically verify counts. Retraining should occur regularly to prevent habits from drifting. Administrators should make clear that failure to conduct accurate counts will result in disciplinary action. Count is not negotiable. It is the foundation upon which every other security measure rests.

4. **Signals spread instantly.** Inmates share information constantly. A weakness noticed by one inmate will soon be known by many. Officers should train themselves to see housing units through inmate eyes. Supervisors should reinforce this perspective in briefings and conduct walk-throughs not just for compliance but to understand the culture inmates perceive.

5. **Culture begins with staff presence.** Line officers are the first and most important presence in a pod. If they enforce rules consistently, culture shifts toward order. If they ignore details, culture shifts toward disorder. Supervisors must back officers, and administrators must back supervisors. Staff empowerment is key. Officers should be authorized and encouraged to correct small infractions immediately. Culture cannot be delegated; it must be modeled and reinforced at every level.

Reflection

The Broken Windows Theory, born on city streets, finds its most powerful application behind bars. Jails and prisons are compressed societies where signals spread at lightning speed. A scratch on a table becomes a fight. A broken latch becomes an escape attempt. A sloppy count becomes a contraband pipeline.

Corrections professionals cannot afford to dismiss details. In corrections, details are not cosmetic, they are culture. They determine who owns the environment, who sets the rules, and who controls the future of the facility.

Broken Windows reminds us that order is not built by grand gestures. It is built by enforcing the smallest rules, correcting the smallest cracks, and sending consistent signals that staff, not disorder, run the jail.

- 2 -

THE JAIL AS A MICRO-SOCIETY

Jails as Compressed Societies

Step into a housing pod in any jail or prison, and you are stepping into a society. It may not look like the neighborhoods and towns outside the walls, but it functions with the same social mechanics—only faster, more concentrated, and more visible.

A housing unit may hold fifty inmates, or it may hold several hundred. Within minutes of being placed together, inmates begin forming groups, creating informal rules, and testing boundaries. In this compressed environment, signals travel with extraordinary speed. What one inmate does at one end of the pod is known across the unit within the hour. What one officer tolerates in a corner becomes common knowledge by the end of the shift.

Unlike a city neighborhood, where individuals may pass through without ever speaking to each other, a jail unit forces constant interaction. Inmates eat, sleep, and recreate in the same space. Officers walk the same floors day after day, observed closely by those they supervise. The result is a pressure cooker of culture. Signals that might take weeks or months to spread outside can spread in hours or even minutes inside.

This is why corrections professionals must understand their facilities as micro societies. They are not simply warehouses for offenders. They are environments with economies, hierarchies, alliances, conflicts, and rules—both formal and informal. The staff who work within them cannot separate themselves from these dynamics. They are participants as well as enforcers.

When James Q. Wilson and George L. Kelling described Broken Windows in 1982, they focused on city neighborhoods. But if they had walked the tiers of a jail, they would have recognized the same principles at work, only magnified. Disorder tolerated becomes disorder multiplied, and in the compressed ecology of a jail, the multiplication is rapid and unavoidable.

The Ecology of Micro Societies

Every jail and prison develops an internal ecology. Just as plants, animals, and weather interact in an ecosystem, inmates, staff, rules, and routines interact in correctional environments. Each influences the other. Each creates signals that shape behavior.

Informal Economies

Money is restricted in most facilities, but economies always form. Commissary items become currency. A ramen soup, a pack of coffee, or a honey bun takes on exchange value. Informal trades begin, some harmless, others predatory. When left unchecked, these economies expand into black markets involving contraband, gambling, and extortion.

Group Work

Inmates quickly sort themselves into groups. Some are gang-affiliated. Others form by geography, race, or shared background. Within groups, hierarchies emerge. Influencers and leaders direct others, and followers enforce norms.

Staff must understand these hierarchies because they determine how rules are followed, tested, or resisted.

Staff as Cultural Participants

Staff do not exist outside this ecology. Their presence, decisions, and consistency shape the culture as much as inmate behavior does. An officer who enforces rules consistently strengthens staff authority. An officer who is careless or unprofessional weakens it.

Supervisors who back staff reinforce order. Supervisors who overlook misconduct signal tolerance. Administrators who prioritize maintenance and sanitation signal ownership. Those who ignore details signal surrender.

The Dynamics of Micro Societies

Every correctional facility functions as a micro society. Within the walls, inmates and staff interact in ways that mirror, compress, and intensify the structures of the outside world. Understanding these dynamics is essential for applying the Broken Windows framework to corrections. Disorder in micro societies does not stay small. It accelerates because the environment multiplies signals at extraordinary speed.

Informal Economies

The first feature of any micro society is its economy. Even in environments where cash is restricted or prohibited, people find ways to trade. In jails and prisons, commissary items become currency. A pack of ramen noodles might buy a service. A honey bun might pay for protection. A bag of coffee might cover a gambling debt.

On the surface, these trades may appear harmless. Two inmates exchange soups for candy bars, and no harm is done. But informal economies rarely stay benign. They expand. One inmate becomes known as the commissary broker. Others borrow against future deposits. Debts build. Extortion follows.

Officers see the trades. Some ignore them because they appear small. Others dismiss them as unavoidable. But each trade is a signal. It communicates that inmates, not staff, are regulating commerce in the unit. The danger comes not from the first soup traded but from the culture that forms when trades are tolerated.

Once the economy grows, it fuels contraband markets. Tobacco, pills, and even weapons are introduced. Gambling rings form, with commissary used as currency. Fights break out over unpaid debts. Inmate-on-inmate assaults increase, and staff are forced to intervene in crises that could have been prevented if the early signals had been addressed.

The lesson is simple: informal economies are not minor. They are the foundation of inmate power structures. Staff must intervene early, shutting down unauthorized trades before they become markets.

Group Hierarchies

The second feature of micro societies is hierarchy. Humans naturally form groups, and inmates are no different. Within hours of entering a housing unit, individuals align themselves. Some join groups based on race or geography. Others gravitate toward gang affiliations or familiar faces. Leadership emerges. Certain inmates become influencers, controlling access to resources, information, or protection. Others fall into roles as followers.

These hierarchies matter because they determine how culture spreads. When a leader ignores staff authority, his followers often mimic the behavior. When a leader enforces a unit norm, such as quiet during count, compliance spreads. Officers who fail to recognize these hierarchies miss the underlying currents of behavior.

Consider an officer who orders silence in the dayroom. If the recognized inmate leader smirks and continues talking, others will follow his example. If the officer fails to correct the leader, the signal is sent that rules are optional.

Within minutes, the entire pod is noisy. The officer is now shouting to restore order instead of directing with authority.

Understanding hierarchies does not mean staff should tolerate inmate authority. It means staff must recognize how influence operates and act decisively. Correcting behavior at the top of the hierarchy often shifts the entire group. Ignoring leaders while focusing only on followers sends the message that the most influential inmates are untouchable.

The Role of Routine

A third feature of micro societies is routine. Inmates live by schedules: wake-up, meals, counts, recreation, lockdown. Routines provide predictability. When routines are consistent, they communicate control. When routines are sloppy, they communicate weakness.

For example, if meals are served late every day, inmates grow restless. They begin to test boundaries during wait times. If counts are conducted at different times or with inconsistent thoroughness, inmates adjust their behavior accordingly. If officers enforce rules inconsistently—one allowing extra time on the phone, another cutting it short—inmates exploit the inconsistency.

Routine is not about convenience; it is about signals. A predictable, orderly routine communicates stability. A sloppy, inconsistent routine communicates vulnerability. Staff who understand this use routine as a tool to reinforce order.

The Magnification of Staff Behavior

The final and perhaps most important feature of micro societies is the magnification of staff behavior. Inmates watch officers and supervisors constantly. Every action, every expression, every decision is studied. In a compressed environment, staff behavior is magnified.

An officer who cuts corners sends a message that rules are flexible. A supervisor who ignores an officer's mistake sends a message that leadership is indifferent. An administrator who tolerates broken equipment sends a message that details do not matter. Inmates interpret these signals instantly.

The reverse is also true. An officer who enforces rules consistently communicates authority. A supervisor who backs staff communicates unity. An administrator who prioritizes maintenance communicates ownership. These signals are magnified just as much, shaping culture in positive ways.

The danger lies in staff underestimating their influence. Many officers believe their actions are small, that one ignored infraction is inconsequential. In reality, inmates see it, test it, and spread it. Staff behavior is culture. Culture determines safety.

Why Broken Windows Belongs in Micro Societies

Broken Windows Theory explains why micro societies function the way they do. Small signals are not small. They multiply. In a jail, a single ignored infraction can shift the behavior of dozens of inmates within hours. A single tolerated weakness can reshape the culture of an entire housing unit.

Corrections professionals must accept that they are not simply managing individuals. They are managing societies. The health of those societies depends on signals. Enforce small rules, correct small cracks, and the society bends toward order. Ignore them, and the society bends toward disorder.

Case Study 1: The Noise Problem

Noise is one of the most overlooked signals in corrections. At first glance, it seems like background sound. The hum of voices, the clang of doors, the shuffle of movement. But inside a housing unit, noise is culture. It communicates respect or disrespect, compliance or defiance, order or disorder.

This case comes from a regional jail in the Midwest housing about 800 inmates. The facility was relatively new, designed with open-pod architecture and central control stations. Each pod held 60 inmates, with dayrooms surrounded by two tiers of cells. Officers worked inside the pods, positioned on the floor rather than behind glass. This design emphasized direct supervision, where staff presence was intended to control behavior through proximity and relationships rather than physical barriers.

At first, the model worked well. Officers were visible, inmates adjusted to their presence, and noise remained manageable. But over time, standards slipped. A new generation of officers rotated into the facility with less experience and confidence. Supervisors were stretched thin, covering multiple pods at once. Noise enforcement began to weaken.

It started subtly. Inmates raised their voices during recreation, and officers allowed it. Television volume crept higher, and nobody adjusted it. Arguments carried across the dayroom, but staff did not intervene unless they turned physical. Soon, the pod was loud almost constantly. Officers had to shout to give commands. Radios struggled to cut through the din.

Noise became the new normal. And with it came signals.

For inmates, noise was power. Talking louder than staff showed dominance. Refusing to quiet down when ordered showed resistance. Groups gathered around tables and raised their voices in defiance, daring officers to confront them. New inmates entering the pod quickly recognized that the rule of noise belonged to the population, not the staff.

For officers, noise was frustration. They shouted to be heard, but shouting rarely worked. Some gave up, retreating to control stations where they could at least communicate with each other. Others avoided confrontation, believing that addressing noise would only escalate tensions. Supervisors passing through quickly told officers to "keep it down in here" but did not stay to ensure compliance.

The shift was cultural. Noise was no longer background. It was a visible, audible sign that inmates controlled the environment.

The consequences escalated. With noise unchecked, arguments turned into fights before officers could intervene. Commands during lockdown were ignored because inmates claimed they "did not hear." Announcements from supervisors were drowned out. Radios failed to carry over the volume, slowing response times. Noise became not only disorder but also a direct safety hazard.

One incident illustrated the danger. During evening recreation, an officer ordered inmates to return to their cells for count. The pod was so loud that most inmates ignored him. Some claimed afterward they did not hear the order. Others openly laughed, enjoying the spectacle of an officer shouting without compliance. The officer called for backup. By the time additional staff arrived, the unit was on the verge of open defiance. The incident ended without violence only because supervisors flooded the pod and ordered lockdown with overwhelming presence.

The administration investigated and discovered that noise violations had been reported in logs for months, but no decisive action had been taken. Officers admitted they did not feel supported when trying to enforce noise control. Supervisors acknowledged they had prioritized other issues. The failure was cultural. Staff had tolerated a signal of disorder, and that signal had multiplied.

The solution required a deliberate reset. The administration issued a facility-wide directive: noise standards would be enforced consistently. Television volumes were set at fixed levels. Inmates were prohibited from shouting across pods. Officers were required to address noise violations immediately, beginning with verbal corrections and escalating to loss of privileges if needed. Supervisors were directed to support officers and remain in pods during high-noise times such as recreation and meal periods.

At first, the reset met resistance. Inmates mocked officers, deliberately raising their voices. Officers struggled with the discomfort of constant confrontation.

But supervisors remained present, backing officers consistently. Over time, the culture shifted. Noise levels declined. Commands became audible again. Radios could be heard. The dayroom returned to a manageable level of sound.

The lesson of the noise problem was not about decibels. It was about signals. Noise communicated ownership. When staff allowed noise to dominate, inmates interpreted it as permission to own the pod. When staff enforced noise consistently, the signal reversed. Order belonged to staff.

Lessons from the Noise Problem

- **Noise is not background;** it is a signal of who controls the environment
- **Tolerance is contagious.** Once noise is tolerated, other forms of disorder follow quickly.
- **Enforcement requires support.** Officers cannot confront noise alone; supervisors must be present and consistent.
- **Culture is audible.** A loud pod is often a defiant pod; a controlled pod is usually a safe one.
- **Resets are possible.** Even when disorder becomes the norm, consistent enforcement can reclaim the culture.

Noise in corrections may seem minor compared to violence or contraband, but it's significant. It is a clear example of how Broken Windows operates in a micro-society. The sounds of a housing unit communicate its culture. Staff must decide whether that culture belongs to them or to the inmates.

Case Study 2: The Commissary Hustle

Every correctional facility has an economy. Even when cash is restricted or prohibited, people find ways to trade. Commissary items: soups, coffee, candy bars, hygiene products - quickly take on value. The danger is not in the existence of value but in who controls it. When inmates run the economy without staff intervention, commissary becomes the foundation of disorder.

This case comes from a county jail in the South housing about 600 inmates. The jail offered a modest commissary program with weekly orders delivered directly to housing units. Inmates could purchase food items, writing supplies, and limited hygiene products using money deposited by family members. The system was intended to provide small comforts while reducing pressure on facility-provided meals and supplies.

At first, the commissary system functioned smoothly. Inmates received their orders, consumed their items, and occasionally traded with cellmates. Officers observed some bartering but did not consider it a priority. The trades seemed small: a soup for a honey bun, coffee for a bag of chips. Staff were more concerned with contraband searches, fights, and medical calls. Commissary trades were dismissed as harmless.

But inside the pod, the trades were not harmless. They were signals.

Inmates quickly recognized who had commissary and who did not. Those with outside financial support accumulated items. Those without became borrowers. Informal credit systems formed. One inmate became known as the "store man." He loaned out soups and coffee in exchange for repayment plus interest the following week. Borrowers who failed to repay were pressured by their peers. At first, the pressure was verbal. Soon it became physical.

Within months, the commissary economy dominated the pod. Inmates who controlled commissary items wielded power. They decided who ate extra and who went without. They decided who had the privilege of coffee in the morning and who had to beg. They extended credit, collected interest, and enforced debts. Staff saw the trades and knew about the hustles, but they continued to dismiss them as inevitable.

The consequences escalated. Gambling rings formed, using commissary items as currency. Inmates bet soups and candy bars on card games, then fought over unpaid debts. Extortion appeared. Stronger inmates demanded commissary "taxes" from weaker ones, threatening violence if they did not comply. The store man became untouchable. Officers gave him orders, but he carried himself with the authority of someone who ran the pod.

One incident exposed the depth of the problem. An inmate who owed commissary debts was assaulted in the shower by three others. The attack was brutal, leaving him with broken ribs and a concussion. Investigators discovered that the assault had been ordered by the store man as punishment for unpaid debts. The commissary hustle had turned into organized extortion.

The administration responded by restricting commissary privileges facility-wide. Items were reduced to essentials, and limits were placed on quantities. Staff were instructed to monitor trades more closely and to confiscate items being exchanged. The store man was moved to segregation, and his network was disrupted. But the damage had been done. The culture of the pod had shifted, and rebuilding order required more than confiscations.

Staff were retrained to recognize commissary as more than comfort. It was currency. Officers were instructed to intervene in trades, shut down unauthorized stores, and document violations. Supervisors were directed to back officers in enforcement, making it clear that commissary belonged to the facility, not to inmate entrepreneurs.

The lesson of the commissary hustle is clear. Small trades are not small. They are signals of who controls the economy. If inmates run the economy, they run the pod. If staff enforce commissary rules, staff run the pod. Ownership of the economy is ownership of the culture.

Lessons from the Commissary Hustle

- **Commissary is currency.** Every item has value, and value fuels power. Staff must recognize commissary as the foundation of inmate economies.

- **Small trades multiply.** What begins as a soup-for-a-snack trade quickly becomes loans, interest, and extortion if left unchecked.
- **Store men are power brokers.** Inmates who control commissary control others. Allowing store men to operate undermines staff authority.
- **Violence follows debt.** Unpaid commissary debts almost always lead to fights, assaults, or extortion.
- **Enforcement requires consistency.** Officers must address trades immediately. Supervisors must support them. Administrators must set clear limits on commissary.

The commissary hustle illustrates Broken Windows in economic form. A single trade tolerated becomes a network. A network becomes a market. A market becomes a power structure. Staff who ignore small trades are not avoiding conflict. They are inviting it.

Case Study 3: The Shower Dispute

Sanitation in corrections is more than hygiene. It is order. Cleanliness communicates care, discipline, and ownership. Neglect communicates abandonment. When showers, toilets, or dayrooms fall into disrepair or filth, inmates read the signal instantly. If staff do not own the environment, inmates will. And when inmates own it, conflict follows.

This case comes from a state prison in the Northeast housing nearly 2,000 inmates. The prison was divided into multiple housing units, each with its own dayroom, cells, and shower facilities. The showers in one unit had been deteriorating for years. Tiles were cracked. Mold spread along grout lines. Drain covers rusted and shifted. Water pressure was inconsistent, leaving some stalls nearly unusable.

Staff knew the showers were in poor condition. Maintenance requests had been filed repeatedly. Administrators, facing limited budgets, prioritized security upgrades such as cameras and perimeter fencing. Showers were categorized as quality-of-life issues rather than security concerns. The result was predictable. Inmates began treating the showers as contested space.

It started with disputes over functioning stalls. With only two of six showers offering strong water pressure, inmates jockeyed for position. Fights broke out over access. At first, the fights were minor scuffles, shoves, curses, and threats. Officers intervened, but their responses were inconsistent. Some ignored the conflicts, seeing them as inmate issues. Others tried to enforce order but lacked backing when discipline was challenged.

Soon, the disputes hardened into rules. Stronger inmates began controlling access to the working showers. They claimed stalls, demanded payment in commissary for usage, and restricted weaker inmates to the broken or moldy stalls. Hygiene became a privilege controlled by inmate authority. Those who could not pay or resist went days without showers. Sanitation declined, odor spread, and tensions mounted.

Staff walked past the conditions daily. Some expressed frustration but felt powerless without maintenance support. Others accepted the situation as inevitable. The signal was clear: staff did not own the showers. Inmates did.

The conflict escalated when a group of younger inmates attempted to challenge the control system. They demanded equal access to the functioning showers. The controlling group refused. A fight erupted in the dayroom involving more than a dozen inmates. Officers responded but were overwhelmed until backup arrived. Several inmates were hospitalized, and multiple officers sustained injuries during the struggle.

The investigation revealed that the root of the violence was not simply inmate aggression. It was disorder tolerated. Broken showers, ignored maintenance requests, and inconsistent staff intervention created an environment where inmates established their own rules. Once those rules were challenged, violence was inevitable.

The administration finally acted. Emergency maintenance crews were dispatched to repair the showers. Tiles were replaced, drains fixed, and water pressure restored. The facility instituted a strict shower schedule, monitored by staff, ensuring equal access for all inmates. Officers were trained to view sanitation not as cosmetic but as security. Supervisors began inspecting showers daily, documenting conditions, and holding maintenance accountable for timely repairs.

The cultural shift was noticeable. With showers functional and staff enforcing order, disputes decreased. Inmates no longer controlled access. Staff presence in the shower area communicated ownership. Hygiene improved, and tensions declined.

The lesson of the shower dispute is not about plumbing. It is about signals. Dirty, broken showers told inmates that staff did not care. Inmates filled the vacuum with their own rules, and violence followed. Clean, functional showers told inmates that staff owned the environment. Order followed.

Lessons from the Shower Dispute

- **Sanitation is security.** Broken or dirty facilities are not quality-of-life issues. They are direct signals of neglect that breed conflict.
- **Ownership must be visible.** When staff tolerate filth or disrepair, inmates claim the space. Staff must enforce cleanliness and maintenance consistently.
- **Maintenance is authority.** Delayed repairs communicate weakness. Prompt repairs communicate control.
- **Hygiene is dignity.** When inmates are denied clean, functional showers, tensions rise. Providing equal access reduces conflict and improves morale.
- **Culture is physical.** The condition of showers, toilets, and dayrooms communicates the culture of the facility as much as staff behavior does.

The shower dispute shows how Broken Windows operates in the most basic aspects of daily life. Cracked tiles and broken drains may seem small compared to weapons or escapes, but they are not small. They are signals. And in a micro society, signals are everything.

Analysis: The Ecology of Order

The case studies in this chapter - the noise problem, the commissary hustle, and the shower dispute - illustrate a reality that every corrections professional must face: jails and prisons are not warehouses. They are micro societies. They contain economies, hierarchies, disputes, and informal systems of control. Within those systems, signals spread at lightning speed.

Each case began with something that appeared minor. A pod that grew louder by the day. A commissary trade dismissed as harmless. A broken shower tile left unrepaired. None of these issues looked like emergencies. None seemed as urgent as a fight, a medical call, or an attempted escape. Yet each was the beginning of a cultural shift.

Noise unchecked became defiance. Commissary trades became extortion. Broken showers became violence. The common thread is not the specific issue but the principle: in micro societies, disorder tolerated becomes disorder multiplied.

Why Micro Societies Amplify Disorder

In free-world communities, signals travel gradually. A broken window in a neighborhood may stand for weeks before others notice. Graffiti may spread slowly from wall to wall. Neighbors may ignore a problem for months before disorder becomes visible.

In correctional facilities, signals spread instantly. Inmates live in constant proximity. They talk, observe, and test boundaries relentlessly. A single act of tolerance by staff is noticed by dozens of eyes at once. Word spreads within hours. Before long, the entire pod knows what is allowed and what is ignored.

This speed of transmission makes corrections uniquely vulnerable to Broken Windows effects. Small signals that might remain localized in a city become facility-wide in a matter of days inside a jail. Staff cannot afford to walk past disorder. It is not contained. It is contagious.

The Magnification of Staff Presence

The second factor that amplifies signals in micro societies is the magnification of staff behavior. Inmates watch officers and supervisors constantly. Every word, every action, every inconsistency is scrutinized. Staff may believe their actions are small, but in the compressed world of a jail, those actions are magnified.

When an officer ignores noise, the message is not limited to one inmate. It is communicated to the entire pod. When a supervisor fails to back an officer, the weakness is broadcast instantly. When an administrator delays maintenance, every inmate sees that staff do not own the environment. These signals are magnified, repeated, and acted upon.

The reverse is also true. When an officer enforces small rules consistently, it strengthens staff authority across the pod. When a supervisor backs that officer, it reinforces unity. When an administrator prioritizes sanitation, it communicates ownership. These signals, too, are magnified. They spread order instead of disorder.

Ownership Defines Culture

The third factor is ownership. In every micro society, the question of ownership must be answered. Who owns the pod? Who owns the economy? Who owns the showers? If staff answer those questions with consistent enforcement, staff own the facility. If they hesitate, ignore, or tolerate, inmates claim ownership.

The commissary hustle demonstrated this clearly. Staff tolerated small trades, believing them harmless. Inmates claimed the economy, and soon commissary became the foundation of extortion and violence. The shower dispute told the same story. Staff tolerated broken tiles and poor maintenance. Inmates claimed the showers, and soon they controlled who bathed and who did not. Ownership cannot remain neutral. It belongs either to staff or to inmates.

Tools and Takeaways

This section translates the lessons of micro societies into actionable practices for officers, supervisors, and administrators. These are not theories. They are tools to be used daily to build and sustain order.

1. Treat Economies as Security

Commissary, trades, and informal markets are not background activity. They are the economic foundation of inmate power structures. Staff must:

- ☐ Enforce rules against unauthorized trading immediately.
- ☐ Confiscate items being used as currency.
- ☐ Shut down store men before they gain influence.
- ☐ Monitor gambling and intervene before debts escalate.

Supervisors must back officers when they act against inmate economies. Administrators must set clear limits on commissary orders and ensure distribution is controlled by staff, not inmates. A facility that ignores its economy invites inmates to run it. And when inmates run the economy, they run the culture.

2. Control Noise Before It Controls You

Noise is not harmless background. It is a signal of who owns the environment. Officers must:

- ☐ Correct shouting and loud arguments immediately.
- ☐ Regulate television and music volumes consistently.
- ☐ Enforce quiet during counts and lockdowns.

Supervisors should remain present during high-noise periods and back officers who enforce noise control. Administrators should provide clear policies and support for staff, recognizing that noise management is not optional. A facility that controls noise communicates discipline. A facility that tolerates noise communicates weakness.

3. Sanitation is Security

Broken showers, dirty dayrooms, and unsanitary toilets are not quality-of-life issues. They are signals of ownership. Staff must:

- ☐ Inspect sanitation daily, noting any signs of neglect.
- ☐ Require inmates to maintain cleanliness through assigned duties.
- ☐ Report maintenance issues immediately and follow up until resolved.

Supervisors must hold officers accountable for sanitation enforcement. Administrators must prioritize maintenance requests involving hygiene facilities. A facility that owns sanitation communicates control. A facility that surrenders sanitation communicates abandonment.

4. Use Routines to Communicate Authority

Routines are signals. Consistent schedules for meals, counts, and recreation communicate order. Sloppy, inconsistent routines communicate weakness. Staff must:

- Conduct counts at the same times with the same thoroughness.
- Serve meals predictably and fairly.
- Enforce recreation schedules consistently.

Supervisors must monitor routines for consistency and correct deviations immediately. Administrators must provide resources to support predictable operations. A facility that controls routines controls culture.

5. Support Officers in the Details

Line officers are the frontline owners of micro societies. They cannot be left to enforce details alone. Supervisors must:

- Back officers when they enforce small rules.
- Remain present in housing units, not just passing through.
- Address officer mistakes quickly but privately, so inmates see unity.

Administrators must model attention to detail during walk-throughs, reinforcing the message that small rules matter. A facility that supports officers creates confidence. A facility that leaves them isolated creates fear and inconsistency.

6. Remember That Signals Spread Instantly

Every action or inaction is a signal. Staff must recognize that what they walk past today will shape behavior tomorrow. Officers should train themselves to see units through inmate eyes. Supervisors should emphasize signal awareness in roll calls. Administrators should review incidents through the lens of what signals were sent and received. The speed of signal transmission in micro societies means that prevention is always better than reaction.

Reflection

Micro societies inside correctional facilities function by the same rules as neighborhoods outside. But they operate at a faster speed and under higher pressure. Disorder spreads instantly. Ownership is contested constantly. Culture is determined by signals, and signals are determined by details.

Noise, commissary, and showers may seem like small issues compared to weapons or escapes. But they are not small. They are the foundation of culture. A facility that owns them communicates order. A facility that ignores them surrenders control.

The Broken Windows Theory teaches us that small cracks create collapse if left unchecked. In corrections, those cracks appear in noise, trades, and sanitation. The staff who close those cracks create safe, orderly environments. The staff who ignore them create facilities where inmates rule.

Corrections is about details. Details create culture. Culture determines safety. The ecology of order depends on signals, and those signals are controlled by staff presence, consistency, and ownership.

- 3 -

LEADERSHIP AS THE FIRST SIGNAL

Leading By Example, Setting The Culture

Every correctional facility communicates culture long before a word is spoken. The uniforms, the cleanliness of the pod, the way counts are conducted, the consistency of routines—all of these are signals. But above all, the most powerful signal comes from leadership.

Leadership is the first and clearest message inmates and staff receive about whether order matters. A warden who walks a facility, stops to correct details, and engages staff communicates that standards are non-negotiable. A sergeant who conducts rounds in housing units, backs officers, and corrects disorder shows that small rules matter. Conversely, a captain who remains in the office, reviewing reports but never leaving the desk, sends the message that paper is more important than presence. Inmates and staff interpret these signals instantly.

Corrections is a profession defined by example. Officers watch supervisors for cues on what will be enforced. Inmates watch staff for cracks they can exploit.

A rule written in a handbook has no power unless enforced in practice. A policy means nothing if leaders do not model its importance. Leadership is not about issuing memos. It is about modeling behavior in ways that staff and inmates cannot ignore.

Leadership is also the key to culture. Culture in a correctional facility is not created by words on posters or values in a mission statement. It is created by what leaders do and what they tolerate. Staff take their cues from supervisors. If supervisors overlook details, officers quickly learn to do the same. If supervisors enforce details, officers gain confidence to enforce them as well.

The Broken Windows Theory explains why this matters. Disorder tolerated at the leadership level multiplies through staff and into inmate culture. If leaders accept sloppy counts, officers will conduct sloppy counts. If leaders ignore graffiti, officers will overlook graffiti. If leaders tolerate unprofessional behavior among staff, inmates will see division and exploit it. Leadership is the first broken window or the first repaired one.

The opposite is also true. Leadership that enforces details consistently builds cultures of order. A sergeant who insists on proper rounds communicates to officers that thoroughness matters. Officers, in turn, communicate to inmates that rules are enforced. A warden who inspects showers and demands repairs communicates that sanitation is non-negotiable. Inmates, seeing consistent enforcement, adjust their behavior upward.

In corrections, leadership is presence. It cannot be delegated. It must be seen, heard, and felt daily. Leaders who remain behind office doors surrender the culture to staff habits and inmate influence. Leaders who walk the floors, correct details, and support officers create the culture themselves. The first signal of order always comes from leadership.

The Power of Example

Corrections is not primarily a profession of words. It is a profession of actions. What officers, supervisors, and administrators do communicates far more than what they say. In a jail or prison, the eyes of two groups are always watching: staff and inmates. Both mirror what they see from leadership.

Officers Mirror Supervisors

Line officers take their cues from the supervisors who direct them. A sergeant who checks rounds carefully and asks questions sets a standard that officers follow. An officer in that unit will walk the pod with confidence, knowing the sergeant expects precision. The same officer in another unit, supervised by someone who rarely inspects or asks, may drift into shortcuts.

Supervisors are the first mirror in corrections. They reflect the values of the administration downward to staff. They enforce consistency or allow inconsistency. They reinforce details or erode them. Officers do not only listen to what supervisors say in roll call. They watch what supervisors do in practice.

Consider two sergeants in the same facility. One spends roll call emphasizing professionalism, then walks the housing pods daily, checking counts, inspecting cells, and backing officers when inmates test limits. The other spends roll call reading announcements but rarely leaves the office during the shift. The difference in culture between their units is obvious. In the first, officers enforce rules with confidence, knowing they will be supported. In the second, officers hesitate, knowing they will be questioned if inmates complain but not supported if they act.

Supervisors must recognize that they are always setting an example, even when silent. If they allow unprofessional behavior among staff, that behavior spreads. If they tolerate sloppy documentation, accuracy declines facility-wide. If they dismiss officer concerns, morale sinks. Officers mirror supervisors, for better or worse.

Inmates Mirror Staff Presence

Just as officers watch supervisors, inmates watch officers. Inmates study staff constantly. They note who enforces rules, who overlooks them, and who can be pressured. They also note who carries themselves with confidence and who hesitates.

Inmates quickly learn to mirror the presence of staff. In a pod where officers walk with ownership, enforcing details consistently, inmates adjust their behavior upward. They tuck in shirts, keep noise manageable, and comply with lockdowns. In a pod where officers walk past infractions, inmates mirror that indifference. They test boundaries, grow louder, and challenge rules openly.

This mirroring is not accidental. It is strategic. Inmates know that culture is shaped by consistency. If they sense inconsistency, they exploit it. If they sense confidence, they adjust to it.

One officer's behavior can set the tone for an entire pod. An officer who begins the shift with strong presence—greeting inmates firmly but professionally, inspecting cells, and enforcing sanitation—communicates order. Inmates may resist at first, but over time, they conform to the consistency. Another officer, beginning the same shift with casual posture, ignoring noise, and avoiding confrontation, communicates disorder. Inmates mirror that as well, growing louder, messier, and more defiant.

Leadership Is the First Broken Window

The Broken Windows Theory explains why leadership by example is so powerful. A supervisor who overlooks a detail becomes the first broken window. Officers see the tolerance and mirror it. Inmates then see officers tolerating it and mirror them. Disorder multiplies from the top down.

The reverse is also true. Leadership that corrects details becomes the first repaired window. Officers see the attention to detail and mirror it. Inmates then see officers enforcing rules consistently and mirror them. Order multiplies from the top down.

This is why leaders at every level must understand that their actions ripple outward. A sergeant correcting an untucked shirt is not nitpicking. They are setting a cultural tone. A lieutenant walking pods and enforcing sanitation is not micromanaging. They are owning the environment. A captain conducting surprise count checks is not creating extra work. They are reinforcing sacred rituals.

Leadership always multiplies. The only question is whether it multiplies order or disorder.

The Silent Lessons of Leadership

Not all leadership lessons are verbal. In fact, the most powerful lessons are silent. Inmates and staff both learn from what leaders walk past.

When an administrator walks a unit and ignores graffiti, the silent lesson is that graffiti does not matter. When a supervisor hears an officer curse at an inmate and says nothing, the silent lesson is that unprofessionalism is tolerated. When a sergeant sees sloppy paperwork and signs it anyway, the silent lesson is that accuracy is optional.

These silent lessons shape culture as much as active directives. They may even shape it more because actions carry more weight than words. Leaders must constantly ask themselves: What silent lessons am I teaching?

Consistency Builds Credibility

The final element of example is consistency. Officers and inmates both respect leaders who are consistent, even if they disagree with decisions. A sergeant who enforces rules firmly every day builds credibility. Officers know where they stand. Inmates know the line will not move.

In contrast, inconsistency destroys credibility. A lieutenant who enforces noise control one day but ignores it the next communicates confusion. Officers hesitate, unsure what will be supported. Inmates test constantly, searching for cracks.

Consistency is not about perfection. It is about reliability. Leaders who are consistent in enforcing details, supporting staff, and modeling professionalism create stability. That stability is mirrored downward to officers and outward to inmates.

Reflections on Example

Corrections is a profession of example. Officers mirror supervisors. Inmates mirror staff presence. Leadership is the first signal that determines whether a facility bends toward order or disorder. The Broken Windows Theory teaches that small cracks multiply if ignored. In corrections, those cracks often begin with leadership.

The power of example cannot be overstated. Leaders who walk the floors, correct details, and support staff communicate order. Leaders who remain behind desks, overlook details, or tolerate inconsistency communicate disorder. Staff and inmates mirror whichever example they are given.

Leadership in Daily Practice

Leadership in corrections is not measured by what appears on paper. It is measured by what happens in housing units, hallways, control rooms, and yards. Policies matter, but they are only as strong as the daily practices that enforce them. Culture is built shift by shift, detail by detail, action by action.

This is why leadership must be lived, not just spoken. The presence of supervisors in daily routines sends stronger signals than any directive. Inmates and officers alike pay more attention to what leaders do than what they say.

The details of leadership in practice, from how roll calls are conducted to how supervisors walk the floors, determine whether the facility bends toward order or disorder.

Roll Call: The First Moment of Culture

Every shift begins with roll call. Too often, roll call is treated as a formality—a place to read announcements, issue assignments, and dismiss staff to their posts. But roll call is far more than that. It is the first moment of culture each day.

When a supervisor enters roll call late, unprepared, or indifferent, the signal to staff is clear: the shift is not important. Officers leave with the same attitude, and their presence in the pods mirrors the disorganization they observed. Inmates notice that lack of presence almost immediately.

Contrast that with a supervisor who arrives early, prepared, and professional. They greet staff by name, review assignments clearly, and set expectations firmly. They emphasize the importance of details: sanitation checks, count accuracy, and enforcement of rules. They use the moment to recognize staff who corrected disorder the day before. Officers leave with clarity and confidence. Inmates see the difference by the way officers carry themselves into the units.

Roll call is not just a logistical task. It is a leadership tool. It sets the tone for the entire shift. Supervisors who own roll call own the culture.

Walk-Throughs: Presence as Ownership

Walk-throughs are another routine often overlooked or minimized. A sergeant or lieutenant may pass through a pod briefly, nod at officers, and leave quickly. But this kind of pass-through does not communicate ownership. It communicates obligation. Inmates notice. Officers notice.

A true walk-through is deliberate. The supervisor moves slowly, inspecting details: Are shirts tucked? Are cells orderly? Are showers clean? Is graffiti visible? Are officers enforcing rules? They ask questions not to catch staff, but to reinforce presence. They pause to speak with inmates, not to negotiate, but to remind them that leadership is engaged.

When walk-throughs are consistent and thorough, they communicate ownership. Inmates know leadership will appear at any time and check details. Officers know their enforcement of small rules will be supported and verified. Culture bends toward order.

When walk-throughs are rare, quick, or indifferent, they communicate abandonment. Inmates learn that leadership does not see or does not care. Officers feel isolated, left to enforce rules without support. Culture bends toward disorder.

Corrections as Signals

Small corrections made by supervisors carry outsized weight. When a lieutenant corrects an untucked shirt, it communicates more than a dress standard. When a captain orders graffiti removed immediately, it communicates ownership of the space. When a warden points out a sloppy count sheet and demands accuracy, it communicates that sacred rituals will not be compromised.

These corrections are signals. They ripple outward. Officers see them and mirror them. Inmates see them and adjust their behavior. The opposite is also true. When leaders overlook small details, the ripple communicates tolerance. Officers mirror that tolerance. Inmates exploit it.

Leadership in practice is not about speeches. It is about small corrections made consistently. Each correction is a message. Together, they define the culture.

Support in Conflict

Perhaps the most critical element of daily leadership is support. Officers in housing units face constant testing. Inmates challenge rules, resist orders, and probe for weakness. When an officer enforces a detail—noise control, sanitation, uniform compliance—they are immediately tested. If the officer stands alone, unsure whether supervisors will back them, hesitation creeps in. That hesitation is noticed instantly by inmates.

Supervisors must make it clear through action that they support officers who enforce rules. When an officer corrects disorder, supervisors must appear, reinforce the command, and document the action if necessary. Even when inmates complain, supervisors must stand with staff. If mistakes are made, corrections can be addressed privately later. Publicly, unity must be absolute.

Support in conflict communicates confidence. Officers who know they are backed enforce rules consistently. Inmates who see supervisors supporting officers adjust to authority. The opposite is equally true. Officers left unsupported hesitate. Inmates exploit the hesitation.

The Visibility of Administrators

Administrators—wardens, majors, captains—often believe their influence lies in policies, budgets, and meetings. While these responsibilities are real, cultural influence is magnified most by visibility. When administrators walk housing units, inspect showers, ask about sanitation, and observe counts, they communicate that even the smallest details matter.

An administrator who remains in the office, focusing only on paperwork, cedes cultural authority to the habits of staff and the influence of inmates. An administrator who walks the floors regularly sends a different message. They model ownership for supervisors, who mirror it for officers, who mirror it for inmates. Culture cascades downward, beginning at the top.

Leadership Presence During Crises

Crises reveal culture. A fight breaks out, a medical emergency occurs, or an escape attempt is discovered. In these moments, leadership presence determines whether staff respond with unity or hesitation.

When supervisors are visible and consistent in daily practice, staff are confident in crises. They know what is expected. They know they will be supported. When supervisors are absent or inconsistent in daily practice, staff are uncertain in crises. They hesitate, unsure of the response.

Crisis response is the fruit of daily practice. Leaders who own the details during calm periods create cultures that respond with order during emergencies. Leaders who ignore details during calm periods create cultures that collapse under pressure.

Reflections on Daily Practice

Leadership is not abstract. It is not limited to titles or offices. It is lived in daily practice. Roll calls, walk-throughs, small corrections, support in conflict, and visibility in crises are the building blocks of culture.

The Broken Windows Theory reminds us that disorder tolerated becomes disorder multiplied. In corrections, the first tolerance often comes from leadership. A sloppy roll call tolerated leads to sloppy enforcement. A quick walk-through tolerated leads to unchecked disorder. A lack of support tolerated leads to hesitation.

Leaders must treat every daily practice as a cultural signal. Each roll call is an opportunity to set the tone. Each walk-through is a chance to communicate ownership. Each correction is a message. Each show of support is reinforcement. Leadership lived daily is leadership that builds order. Leadership absent daily is leadership that abandons order.

Case Study 1: The Absent Captain

Leadership in corrections is presence. Staff know it, inmates know it, and culture proves it. When leadership is absent, even unintentionally, order begins to erode. This case from a large urban jail illustrates how one absent captain reshaped the culture of an entire facility without raising his voice or issuing a memo. His absence itself was the signal.

The Setting

The jail held over 2,500 inmates and employed several hundred staff. It was a challenging environment: high turnover, frequent overtime, and a steady flow of inmates awaiting trial. The facility was divided into multiple divisions, each overseen by a captain. Beneath the captains were lieutenants and sergeants who managed daily operations in the housing units.

One captain, a veteran of twenty years, had developed a reputation for running his division "from the office." He handled paperwork efficiently, met deadlines, and attended meetings, but he rarely walked the housing units. His lieutenants and sergeants seldom saw him on the floors. Officers could not recall the last time he had entered a pod.

On paper, his division appeared functional. Incidents were reported. Counts were completed. Reports were submitted. But the culture inside the units told a different story.

The Signals of Absence

In the absence of visible leadership, lieutenants drifted. Some walked the floors, others did not. Sergeants varied widely in enforcement. Some corrected noise and sanitation, others ignored them. Officers, seeing inconsistency from above, mirrored it. Enforcement of rules became optional, depending on which supervisor was on shift.

Inmates noticed immediately. They saw hesitant officers and inconsistent supervisors. They tested boundaries more aggressively. Noise grew. Graffiti appeared. Commissary trades multiplied. Sanitation declined. These changes did not occur overnight, but over weeks and months, the culture shifted.

The absent captain did not cause these changes directly. He never told officers to ignore noise or instructed supervisors to overlook graffiti. But his absence communicated indifference. His failure to appear in housing units was interpreted by staff and inmates alike as tolerance. And tolerance is a powerful signal.

The Escalation

The cultural drift culminated in a major incident. In one housing pod, inmates had grown accustomed to loud recreation, frequent trades, and minimal enforcement of small rules. One evening, a fight broke out over commissary debts. The fight escalated quickly, involving multiple inmates. Officers called for backup, but the response was slow. By the time supervisors regained control, three inmates were hospitalized and two officers injured.

The incident itself was serious but not unprecedented. What alarmed administrators was the underlying pattern. Reports revealed that small signals of disorder had been tolerated in the pod for months. Noise complaints were ignored. Graffiti had spread. Commissary hustles were known but not corrected. Supervisors admitted they had not enforced consistently because they felt no pressure from above. Officers said they hesitated to act because they were unsure what would be backed.

When asked about the conditions, the absent captain insisted he had no knowledge of the details. He pointed to paperwork showing that counts were correct, reports submitted, and staffing levels met minimum requirements. He was technically correct. But culture is not measured on paper. It is measured in presence.

The Aftermath

The administration launched a review of all divisions. The differences were stark. Units led by captains who walked the floors regularly showed stronger order. Noise was under control. Sanitation was maintained. Officers enforced rules consistently. Units led by the absent captain showed decline in every detail. Disorder was visible, and inmates had claimed ownership of the space.

The absent captain was reassigned, and a new leader was brought in. This captain walked the units daily, spoke with officers, inspected details, and corrected small infractions. Within weeks, culture began to shift. Noise declined. Graffiti disappeared. Commissary hustles diminished. Officers reported feeling supported. Inmates adjusted to the renewed consistency.

The contrast made the lesson clear. Leadership absence is not neutral. It is a signal of tolerance. And in corrections, tolerance multiplies disorder.

Lessons from the Absent Captain

- □ **Leadership is presence.** Reports and paperwork cannot replace visibility in housing units. Staff and inmates interpret absence as indifference.
- □ **Culture fills vacuums.** When leadership is absent, staff drift and inmates claim ownership. Disorder grows rapidly.
- □ **Consistency begins at the top.** Supervisors mirror captains. Officers mirror supervisors. Inmates mirror officers. Absence at the top cascades into disorder.
- □ **Paperwork is not culture.** A division may look functional on paper while collapsing in practice. Culture is visible only through presence.
- □ **Recovery requires presence.** When disorder takes root, only consistent, visible leadership can reset the culture.

Reflection

The absent captain believed he was doing his job by completing paperwork and attending meetings. But corrections is not an office profession. It is a presence profession. His absence was the first broken window. Supervisors mirrored it, officers mirrored them, and inmates mirrored the officers. Disorder multiplied.

Leadership absence is not silent. It communicates loudly. In corrections, silence is never neutral. It is always a signal.

Case Study 2: The Supervisor Who Owned the Pod

Order in corrections is rarely an accident. It is almost always the product of leadership presence. This case, from a mid-sized county jail in the Midwest, illustrates how one sergeant's consistent ownership of his pod reshaped a unit that had been sliding toward chaos. His example shows what leadership by presence, rather than paperwork, looks like in practice.

The Setting

The jail housed just under 900 inmates, spread across multiple housing units. One unit, designed for 64 inmates, had a reputation as one of the most difficult pods. It was loud, graffiti-covered, and tense. Officers rotated in and out frequently, often requesting reassignment after a few weeks. Supervisors dreaded the unit because every shift seemed to bring new problems: fights, contraband, sanitation failures, and noise complaints.

The pod had become known among inmates as a "free zone." Rules were enforced inconsistently, and officers often walked past disorder to keep the peace. Trash overflowed. Tables bore gang markings. Noise levels were constant, forcing officers to shout over the din. The unit was not in open rebellion, but it was sliding steadily in that direction.

Into this environment stepped a newly promoted sergeant. Unlike many peers, he was not intimidated by the pod's reputation. He believed that culture could be reset through consistent presence. From his first shift, he made it clear to officers and inmates alike that he intended to own the pod.

Establishing Presence

The sergeant began by walking the unit himself, not just sending officers. He moved slowly through the dayroom, inspecting tables, cells, and showers. He corrected inmates directly but professionally. Untucked shirts were addressed immediately. Noise that rose too high was shut down. Graffiti was noted, and maintenance was called to remove it.

At first, inmates resisted. They mocked his corrections and tested him with small acts of defiance. The sergeant did not flinch. He repeated commands, called for backup when necessary, and documented every incident. Officers watched closely. They had never seen a supervisor commit so much personal presence to a pod.

He also changed roll call. Instead of reading announcements quickly, he used it to set expectations. He reviewed what he had seen in the unit the day before, praised officers who enforced rules, and reminded the team that consistency was the key to regaining control. His roll calls were brief but deliberate.

Supporting Officers

One of the most significant changes the sergeant introduced was unwavering support for officers. When an officer enforced a rule, he stood behind them, no matter how small the issue seemed. If an inmate challenged an officer, the sergeant appeared. If an inmate complained, he calmly but firmly explained that staff decisions would be backed. Mistakes were corrected privately later, never undermining authority in front of inmates.

This support changed officer behavior. They enforced rules confidently, corrected noise and sanitation issues without hesitation, and reported graffiti immediately. They no longer sought the path of least resistance because resistance no longer fell on their shoulders alone.

Resetting Sanitation and Routine

The sergeant understood that the physical environment shaped culture. He prioritized sanitation as a signal of order. Officers conducted daily inspections of cells and dayrooms. Inmates were held accountable for cleanliness, and work crews deep-cleaned showers and common areas. The sergeant walked inspections himself to ensure standards were met.

He also enforced routines strictly. Meals were served on time. Recreation periods began and ended predictably. Counts were conducted thoroughly, with the sergeant personally verifying accuracy. Once sloppy routines became reliable. Inmates adjusted to the consistency, recognizing that the sergeant's expectations would not waver.

The Cultural Shift

The shift in culture did not happen overnight, but within weeks the difference was visible. Noise levels dropped. Graffiti disappeared. Trash was emptied regularly. Inmates who had once resisted now complied with orders. Officers, once reluctant to work the pod, began requesting assignments there because they felt supported and safe.

Inmates noticed as well. Some complained that the pod was now "tight," meaning rules were enforced consistently. Others admitted privately that they preferred the stability. Tension was lower, fights declined, and commissary hustles diminished. The pod, once chaotic, became one of the most orderly units in the facility.

The Ripple Effect

The sergeant's ownership of the pod had ripple effects beyond his unit. Other supervisors began walking their units more deliberately, encouraged by his results. Officers across the facility noticed the difference and pushed for similar consistency elsewhere. The administration took note, using the pod as a model for training new staff.

The transformation of a single unit proved a larger point: leadership presence at the supervisor level can reset culture facility-wide. The sergeant had not issued new policies, created programs, or written lengthy memos. He had simply owned his pod, enforced details consistently, and supported his officers.

Lessons from the Supervisor Who Owned the Pod

- **Presence changes culture.** Walking the unit, inspecting details, and correcting disorder communicates ownership.
  Support empowers officers. Supervisors who back officers consistently foster confident enforcement.
- **Sanitation and routine are signals.** Clean environments and predictable schedules communicate order as clearly as written rules.
- **Resistance is temporary.** Inmates test consistency at first, but once they recognize firmness, they adjust.
- **Leadership is contagious.** One supervisor's presence can inspire others and ripple across a facility.

Reflection

The sergeant who owned his pod demonstrated what leadership looks like in daily practice. He was not louder than other supervisors. He was not harsher. He was consistent, present, and supportive. In doing so, he reset a culture that had been sliding toward chaos.

Corrections professionals often search for complex solutions to cultural problems. The truth is simpler. Leadership presence is the most powerful tool in corrections. When supervisors own their pods, staff enforce rules confidently, and inmates adjust their behavior. The Broken Windows Theory explains why: small cracks left unchecked multiply disorder. Small cracks corrected consistently multiply order. The sergeant closed cracks every day, and culture bent toward order.

Case Study 3: The Mixed Messages

Consistency is the bedrock of correctional leadership. Officers and inmates alike adjust their behavior based on what leaders enforce. When leaders contradict one another, the result is confusion for staff and opportunity for inmates. Few things corrode authority faster than mixed messages. This case, from a state correctional facility in the South, illustrates how inconsistent leadership signals can dismantle officer confidence and empower inmates to push boundaries.

The Setting

The prison housed 1,200 inmates in a mix of dormitory and celled housing. Staff turnover was high, and many line officers were relatively inexperienced. The administration relied heavily on lieutenants and sergeants to set the tone. Unfortunately, these supervisors disagreed on enforcement.

Some believed in strict application of policy: noise control, sanitation, commissary restrictions, and consistent lockdowns. Others focused on “keeping the peace” by overlooking minor infractions. Both groups were committed professionals, but they sent different signals. One sergeant might insist shirts be tucked immediately. Another might walk the same pod an hour later and ignore untucked uniforms. A lieutenant might back an officer for documenting a commissary hustle, while another dismissed it as “not worth the paperwork.”

The result was a patchwork of enforcement. Officers never knew what would be supported. Inmates quickly learned to exploit the inconsistency.

The Signals of Contradiction

Officers described the problem plainly: they were caught in the middle. One day they were told to enforce noise control; the next, they were criticized for "nitpicking." One sergeant instructed them to confiscate unauthorized commissary trades. Another told them to "let the little stuff go."

Inmates observed carefully. They challenged rules by citing supervisors who had given different instructions: *"Sergeant Smith lets us do this,"* or *"Lieutenant Jones said it was fine."* Officers hesitated, knowing enforcement might be undercut. The inconsistency communicated uncertainty to officers and opportunity to inmates. Both groups mirrored the contradictions they observed.

The Escalation

The cultural drift began slowly. Inmates became louder, citing lenient supervisors. Officers stopped reporting trades, fearing criticism. Sanitation declined, with inmates claiming "last shift didn't care."

The situation escalated during evening recreation. Several inmates refused to comply with noise control, insisting another sergeant had allowed more freedom. The responding lieutenant, known for leniency, sided with the inmates, telling the officer to "pick battles that matter" and ordered him to stand down.

The officer felt humiliated. Inmates laughed openly, emboldened by the division in leadership. From that point, they challenged the officer constantly, citing the lieutenant's decision as proof that rules were negotiable.

Soon, the inconsistency spread. Commissary hustles flourished. Sanitation declined further. Officers became divided, with some enforcing rules and others giving up. Culture bent sharply toward disorder.

The Crisis

The breaking point came when an officer attempted to enforce lockdown after recreation. Several inmates refused to enter their cells, insisting "different sergeants say different things" and daring the officer to act. Unsure of support, the officer hesitated. This hesitation was the crack inmates were waiting for. Others joined in, shouting and stalling. The unit teetered on the edge of a group refusal.

Backup arrived, and supervisors forced compliance. But the damage was done. The refusal had been sparked not by deep inmate grievances but by leadership inconsistency. Mixed messages had created a culture where inmates no longer took orders seriously.

The Reset

The administration recognized the danger. Supervisors were convened and clear expectations were established: rules would be enforced consistently, and supervisors had to present a united front. Disagreements could be voiced privately, but publicly, unity was mandatory.

Supervisors were retrained together, officers were told explicitly they would be backed when enforcing policy, and inmates were informed that standards applied uniformly. The message was repeated daily until culture began to stabilize.

Over time, noise declined, commissary trades were curbed, and sanitation improved. Officers regained confidence, knowing they would be supported. Inmates adjusted to the renewed consistency. The pod shifted back toward order.

Lessons from the Mixed Messages

- **Inconsistency is a broken window.** Contradictory leadership signals multiply disorder faster than almost any other failure.
- **Officers need clarity.** Without consistent backing, officers hesitate, and hesitation is interpreted as weakness.
- **Inmates exploit division.** Inconsistent leadership provides ready-made arguments to resist rules.
- **Unity must be public.** Supervisors can disagree privately, but in front of staff and inmates they must present one standard.
- **Resets require clarity.** Once inconsistency spreads, only firm, repeated unity can repair culture.

Reflections: Leadership as Culture-Building

The three case studies—the absent captain, the supervisor who owned his pod, and the mixed messages—demonstrate that leadership is not measured by reports, policies, or titles. It is measured by presence.

- The absent captain showed that absence becomes a signal. Paperwork may be complete, but failure to appear in housing units communicates indifference. Supervisors mirrored absence, officers mirrored supervisors, and inmates mirrored officers. Disorder multiplied.
- The sergeant who owned his pod showed that consistent presence reshapes culture. Correcting details daily, backing officers, and enforcing sanitation and routine communicated ownership. Officers mirrored confidence, and inmates adjusted upward.
- The mixed messages case showed that inconsistency erodes authority. Contradictory supervisors create hesitation, giving inmates opportunity to exploit divisions. Culture bends toward disorder until leadership resets with clear and consistent standards.

Taken together, these cases reveal a central truth: leadership is the first broken window—or the first repaired one. Absence, inconsistency, or contradiction creates cracks in discipline that multiply disorder. Presence, consistency, and unity create signals that multiply order.

Leadership Is Not Rank—It Is Example

Rank or title does not define leadership. It is defined by example. A sergeant walking the floors with presence can have more cultural influence than a captain in the office. A lieutenant backing an officer in a moment of conflict shapes culture more than an administrator issuing memos from behind a desk.

Inmates respond to presence, not titles. Officers are motivated by supervisors who model enforcement, not by policies alone. Leadership is example, not position.

Why Presence Matters More Than Paper

In corrections, every detail of leader behavior is magnified. Paperwork has little influence compared to the daily signals staff and inmates observe. Presence communicates ownership. Absence communicates tolerance. Leaders who remain in offices send the message that small details do not matter—and inmates act on those messages immediately.

The Role of Unity

Consistency among leaders is essential. Inconsistent supervisors create hesitation and opportunity. Unity does not require private agreement on everything, but publicly, leaders must present one voice. Unity removes hesitation from officers and opportunity from inmates. When officers know they will be backed, they enforce rules confidently. When inmates see consistency, they stop testing boundaries.

Leadership as the First Signal

The Broken Windows framework explains why leadership is so powerful in corrections. Leaders set the first signal. Officers mirror supervisors. Inmates mirror officers. Culture mirrors leadership.

- ☐ The absent captain demonstrated neglect as a signal.
- ☐ The sergeant who owned his pod demonstrated consistent ownership.
- ☐ The mixed messages case demonstrated contradiction's corrosive power.

Leadership is always the first window—broken or repaired.

Tools and Takeaways

This section translates leadership principles into practical tools for administrators, supervisors, and officers.

1. **Walk the Floors Daily**
   Presence cannot be delegated. Every leader—from sergeants to administrators—must be seen in housing units daily. Walk slowly. Inspect details. Speak with staff. Observe inmates. Look for graffiti, sanitation, uniform compliance, and routine. Correct immediately.

Presence communicates ownership. A leader who walks the floors owns the culture. A leader who avoids the floors surrenders it.

2. **Own Roll Call**
   Roll call is not paperwork; it's the first moment of culture each shift. Supervisors must arrive prepared, professional, and early. Use roll call to:
   - ☐ Set expectations clearly.
   - ☐ Emphasize details like counts, sanitation, and noise.

- ☐ Recognize officers who enforced rules.
- ☐ Reinforce unity and professionalism.

A strong roll call sends officers into pods with confidence. A weak roll call sends them in with indifference.

3. **Correct Details Publicly, Coach Privately**
   When details are wrong, correct them in the moment, in front of staff and inmates. Untucked shirts, sloppy paperwork, or ignored graffiti must be addressed immediately. These corrections send the signal that details matter.

When staff make mistakes, coach privately. Never undermine officers in front of inmates. Unity must always be visible; correction can be handled behind closed doors.

4. **Back Officers Consistently**
   Nothing destroys officer confidence faster than supervisors abandoning them in conflict. When officers enforce rules, supervisors must stand behind them. Mistakes can be addressed later, but in the moment, officers must know they are supported.

Support communicates confidence. Officers who feel backed enforce rules firmly. Inmates who see supervisors stand with officers respect authority.

5. **Enforce Sanitation and Routine**
   Physical environment is leadership. Supervisors must inspect showers, dayrooms, and cells daily. Sanitation is not cosmetic—it is culture. Routines must be enforced consistently. Meals, counts, and recreation must run predictably. Sloppy routines communicate weakness. Consistent routines communicate order.

6. **Present a United Front**
   Supervisors must never contradict one another publicly. Disagreements must be resolved privately. In front of staff and inmates, leadership must be unified. Contradictions are broken windows—they multiply disorder instantly.

Unity communicates clarity. Clarity builds culture. Culture builds safety.

7. **Administrators Must Be Visible**
   Wardens, majors, and captains often believe their influence lies in policy. In reality, their influence lies in presence. Walking units, asking questions, and correcting details communicate ownership from the top. Administrators who remain behind desks surrender culture to middle managers. Administrators who are visible shape culture directly.

8. **Remember That Leadership Is the First Window**
   Every leader sets the first signal. Absence breaks the window. Consistency repairs it. Contradiction cracks it. Officers and inmates alike mirror the signals leaders send.

The question every leader must ask daily is simple: **What window am I setting today?**

Reflection

Leadership in corrections is not complicated—but it is relentless. It requires presence every day, in every detail. It requires unity, consistency, and visibility. The Broken Windows Theory reminds us: disorder tolerated becomes disorder multiplied. Leaders tolerate disorder first—through absence, inconsistency, or contradiction.

The opposite is equally true. Leaders prevent disorder first—through presence, consistency, and unity. The first signal is always leadership. The culture of a facility is a mirror of what leaders enforce—and what they walk past.

Corrections is not about grand speeches or lengthy memos. It is about the daily signals leaders send through their presence. Those signals determine whether order or disorder multiplies. The choice belongs to leadership.

- 4 -

BUILDING A TEAM COMMITTED TO BROKEN WINDOWS PRINCIPLES

Why Teams Matter in Corrections

Corrections is one of the most demanding professions in public service. Officers walk into housing units where dozens of inmates study their every move. Supervisors balance the needs of their staff with the relentless testing of the inmate population. Administrators juggle budgets, maintenance, and safety under constant public scrutiny. No single person, no matter how experienced or skilled, can manage these challenges alone. Corrections is a team profession.

Unlike policing, where officers often work independently in the field, corrections staff operate in compressed environments where their success depends on each other. An officer entering a pod does so with the expectation that backup will come when called. A sergeant enforcing discipline relies on officers to carry out corrections. A warden walking the facility depends on supervisors to mirror expectations. Corrections requires unity. Without it, culture fractures.

The Broken Windows Theory emphasizes that small cracks in discipline create larger collapses. In corrections, those cracks spread fastest when teams fail to enforce standards consistently. One officer tolerating disorder can undermine the work of an entire shift. One supervisor sending mixed signals can undo weeks of effort. A single officer cutting corners during count can compromise the safety of every staff member in the building.

This is why teams matter. Broken Windows cannot be applied by individuals in isolation. It must be embraced collectively. Every officer, supervisor, and administrator must share the same commitment to details. Every shift must mirror the same standards. Every unit must operate under the same expectations.

When teams commit together, culture shifts. Inmates sense unity. They recognize that rules will be enforced no matter who is on duty. Testing slows because boundaries are clear and consistent. Staff confidence rises because they know they will be supported. The facility bends toward order.

When teams fracture, culture collapses. Inmates sense division. They learn which officers can be pressured and which can be ignored. They exploit inconsistencies across shifts. Staff morale declines as officers lose confidence in one another. The facility bends toward disorder.

The power of Broken Windows in corrections lies not only in leadership presence but also in team ownership. Leaders can model standards, but only teams can enforce them daily. A leader may repair the first window, but it is the team that keeps the windows intact.

Recruiting for Detail and Ownership

A correctional facility's culture does not begin on the day staff report for duty. It begins at the hiring table. Recruiting decisions determine whether a facility fills its ranks with staff who can sustain order or with staff who will tolerate disorder. The Broken Windows Theory teaches that small cracks in discipline multiply.

The same is true of hiring. One poor hire tolerated becomes five. Five tolerated become twenty. Before long, culture bends toward disorder not because of inmates, but because of who was chosen to wear the uniform.

Hiring for More Than a Body

Too often, correctional agencies hire for numbers rather than for qualities. Staffing shortages push administrators to fill rosters quickly. As long as an applicant passes a background check and basic testing, they are offered a position. The result is predictable. Staff who lack attention to detail, resilience, or ownership enter the facility. They may fill a vacancy, but they do not strengthen culture.

Hiring must be more than filling slots. It must be about building teams. Administrators must ask not only whether this person can pass the minimum requirements but also whether this person will enforce details when tested by inmates, support peers under pressure, and model professionalism even when tired, frustrated, or provoked.

Screening for Attention to Detail

Corrections is a detail profession. The difference between order and chaos is often as small as whether a door latch is checked, whether graffiti is removed, or whether a count is verified. Staff who lack attention to detail will walk past disorder. Staff who are detail-oriented will correct it immediately.

Recruiters must screen applicants for detail orientation. This can be done through structured interview questions, scenario-based testing, and observation during pre-employment processes. Ask applicants:

- What would you do if you noticed a fellow officer cutting corners during count?
- How would you handle graffiti beginning to appear in a housing pod?
- What small details do you think communicate whether a workplace is disciplined or not?

The answers reveal whether the applicant sees details as cosmetic or as culture. Only those who view details as essential should be advanced.

Screening for Ownership

Ownership is the second quality every hire must demonstrate. Ownership means recognizing that authority is not delegated only from rank but also from personal responsibility. An officer who owns their pod does not wait for a sergeant to tell them to correct noise. They correct it immediately because they recognize the pod is theirs to control.

Recruiters must test for ownership through questions and scenarios:

- Tell me about a time you took responsibility for something that was not technically your job.
- How would you respond if an inmate challenged your authority in front of others?
- What does it mean to you to take ownership of an assignment?

Applicants who speak in terms of deflecting responsibility or waiting for others to act are red flags. Those who describe stepping up, even when uncomfortable, demonstrate ownership.

Resilience Under Pressure

Corrections is not easy. Staff will be yelled at, tested, and challenged daily. Without resilience, they will burn out or withdraw. A burned-out officer quickly begins walking past disorder, not out of malice but out of exhaustion.

Recruiters must identify resilience in applicants. This does not mean only hiring those with military or law enforcement backgrounds. It means looking for those who have overcome adversity, adapted under stress, or demonstrated perseverance. Ask questions such as:

- Tell me about a time you faced significant stress. How did you respond?
- What strategies do you use to stay calm under pressure?
- How do you recover after difficult experiences?

Resilient applicants describe adaptation and perseverance. Fragile applicants describe avoidance or collapse.

Building the Hiring Panel

Recruiting for Broken Windows principles requires more than one administrator scanning résumés. It requires a panel of experienced supervisors and officers who understand what it takes to work in the pods. These panel members recognize the subtle signs such as, a lack of eye contact, vague answers, or overconfidence without substance, that reveal potential problems.

Panels should also be diverse in experience. A sergeant who knows the daily grind of housing units sees qualities an administrator might miss. An administrator who understands policy sees qualities a sergeant might overlook. Together, they evaluate whether an applicant is not just employable but team-ready.

Background Checks and Integrity

Integrity is non-negotiable. Staff who cut corners in their personal lives will cut corners in corrections. Background checks must go beyond criminal records. References should be contacted directly, not just listed on paper. Employment history should be examined for patterns of reliability or inconsistency.

Applicants with histories of dishonesty, irresponsibility, or unreliability should be eliminated. Corrections is too dangerous a profession to gamble on questionable integrity.

The Cost of a Poor Hire

Some administrators resist these standards, arguing that facilities cannot afford to be selective during staffing shortages. The truth is that facilities cannot afford not to be selective. Every poor hire costs more than it fills. Poor hires drain supervisors, frustrate peers, and embolden inmates. They create cracks in discipline that spread faster than they can be repaired.

The cost of one poor hire often equals the cost of multiple good hires because disorder spreads faster than order. One officer who ignores details can undo the work of ten who enforce them. The facility pays the price in fights, contraband, morale, and safety.

Ownership Begins at Hiring

Hiring is the first opportunity to enforce Broken Windows in corrections. It is the first window that can be broken or repaired. Administrators who lower standards to fill vacancies break the window before the applicant ever wears a uniform. Administrators who uphold standards, even when short-staffed, repair the window and communicate that order matters from the beginning.

Ownership begins at hiring. Those who are chosen must demonstrate attention to detail, resilience, and a willingness to own their assignments. Without these qualities, no amount of training or supervision can create consistent enforcement. With them, culture bends toward order before the first shift begins.

Training Staff in Broken Windows Principles

Recruitment determines who enters the facility, but training determines who stays and how they perform. No matter how carefully agencies hire, staff must be trained to see their role not just as enforcing custody but as shaping culture. Broken Windows gives a framework for that training, but it must be more than a lecture. It must be embedded into practice.

From Theory to Practice

New staff are often told to "enforce the rules" but are rarely shown how rules translate into signals. They are given policies, procedures, and manuals but not always the underlying logic of why details matter. When training skips this explanation, officers assume that some rules are cosmetic and can be ignored. They walk past graffiti, noise, or sloppy counts because they do not understand these are not small infractions but cultural signals.

Broken Windows training must begin by making the connection clear. Staff must be taught that every detail communicates ownership or neglect. A door latch not checked is an open invitation. A shirt not tucked is a test of limits. A shower not cleaned is a sign of surrender. Training must emphasize that corrections is not about big gestures but about small consistencies.

Scenario-Based Training

The best way to teach Broken Windows principles is through scenarios. Staff learn not only by hearing but by experiencing. Trainers can create controlled situations that replicate common infractions:

- A pod grows noisy, and an officer must decide whether to intervene.
- An inmate refuses to tuck in his shirt, and the officer must enforce compliance professionally.
- Graffiti appears on a table, and staff must determine how to respond immediately.
- A count is conducted, and one inmate attempts to hide to test whether officers will verify presence.

Each scenario should be followed by debrief. Trainers explain how small details communicate signals, how disorder spreads if tolerated, and how consistency prevents escalation. By living the scenarios, staff internalize the lesson.

Embedding Broken Windows in the Academy

Correctional academies often emphasize defensive tactics, firearms, and control procedures. While these are essential, they should not overshadow the importance of culture management. Broken Windows principles should be woven into every part of the academy.

- During defensive tactics, instructors should explain how consistent enforcement of minor rules reduces the likelihood of major confrontations.
- During communication training, instructors should show how tone, posture, and presence communicate signals inmates interpret instantly.
- During report writing, instructors should emphasize documenting small infractions because they reveal cultural patterns.

By embedding Broken Windows into every topic, staff learn that it is not a separate theory but the foundation of the profession.

The Role of Field Training Officers

After the academy, the most influential period of training occurs in the field. Field Training Officers (FTOs) introduce recruits to the daily realities of housing units. If FTOs are professional and detail-oriented, new staff adopt those habits. If FTOs are careless or cynical, new staff adopt those habits instead.

FTO programs must be deliberate. Agencies should select their most consistent, professional officers to serve as FTOs. They must model Broken Windows enforcement every day, correcting disorder immediately, explaining decisions to recruits, and reinforcing that ownership belongs to staff, not inmates.

Field training should include daily debriefs. FTOs should ask recruits what signals they observed, what infractions they noticed, and how they responded. These conversations reinforce the idea that details matter.

Mentoring Beyond the First Year

Training cannot end with the academy and field period. The first year of correctional service is often the most difficult. New officers face fatigue, inmate manipulation, and the temptation to cut corners. Without mentoring, many lose their initial sharpness and begin tolerating disorder.

Mentoring programs provide continued reinforcement. Pairing newer officers with experienced staff who model Broken Windows principles helps prevent cultural drift. Mentors can answer questions, share strategies, and provide encouragement during difficult shifts. Importantly, mentors must be selected for consistency, not just seniority. A burned-out veteran can do more harm than good.

Reinforcing Through Supervisors

Supervisors are the daily trainers of staff. Every correction, every debrief, and every roll call is a training moment. Supervisors must treat these moments not as discipline but as reinforcement. When an officer overlooks a detail, a supervisor should correct it immediately and explain why it matters. When an officer enforces a detail correctly, supervisors should praise it publicly in roll call.

This constant reinforcement prevents drift. Staff learn that small details are not optional. They are the standard. Supervisors who ignore details teach staff that training ends at the academy. Supervisors who reinforce details daily teach staff that training never ends.

Continuous Professional Development

Agencies should also provide ongoing training sessions for all staff, not just new hires. Broken Windows principles can be revisited annually through workshops, scenario refreshers, and case study reviews. Sharing real incidents from other facilities, anonymized for confidentiality, reinforces that small infractions tolerated always lead to larger problems.

Continuous development prevents complacency. It communicates that professionalism is not a one-time achievement but a daily commitment.

Training for Supervisors

Supervisors require their own training in Broken Windows principles. They must understand that their role is not only to enforce rules but to model them for staff. Training should emphasize:

- How to walk units deliberately.
- How to correct staff and inmates consistently.
- How to back officers publicly and coach privately.
- How to identify cultural drift before it escalates.

Supervisors who lack this training often become sources of inconsistency, sending mixed messages to staff and inmates. Training them to see their role as cultural leaders prevents cracks from forming.

The Cultural Mindset

The ultimate goal of training is to embed a mindset. Staff must leave training with the belief that:

- Details are not small.
- Every action is a signal.
- Ownership begins with them, regardless of rank.
- Consistency creates culture.
- Disorder tolerated becomes disorder multiplied.

When staff internalize this mindset, Broken Windows becomes more than theory. It becomes instinct. Officers see graffiti and respond immediately, not because policy told them to, but because they know it is a cultural signal. Supervisors back officers, not because they were ordered to, but because they know unity is the foundation of order. Administrators walk floors, not because a schedule requires it, but because they know presence is ownership.

Reflections on Training

Training is not about filling notebooks or checking boxes. It is about shaping culture. Corrections professionals must be taught, from their first day to their last, that they are not simply custodians of inmates. They are custodians of culture. The Broken Windows framework provides the map, but training provides the habits.

Recruitment determines who enters the door. Training determines who stays in the fight for order. Without deliberate, consistent training, staff drift, inmates notice, and disorder multiplies. With deliberate, consistent training, staff own the environment, inmates adjust, and culture bends toward order.

Corrections is more about signals than speeches. Training ensures those signals are consistent, deliberate, and professional. Training turns Broken Windows from theory into the daily practice that keeps facilities safe.

Case Study 1: The Rookie Who Changed the Pod

Training is only theory until it is lived in practice. A rookie officer, fresh out of the academy, often finds themselves overwhelmed by the noise, movement, and intensity of a housing pod. Many retreat into caution, relying on veteran staff to handle details. Some cut corners, deciding early that it is easier to overlook small infractions than to confront them. But every so often, a rookie enters the pod and proves that even the newest officer can set culture by owning the details.

The Setting

This case occurred in a county jail in the Southeast that housed roughly 1,100 inmates. The facility used a direct-supervision model, with officers working inside the dayrooms rather than behind glass. The jail had a reputation for being "hard on rookies." New officers were often placed into the busiest pods as a test of their resilience. Many failed.

One pod, in particular, had grown problematic. It held 64 inmates in two tiers. Noise levels were high, graffiti was spreading, and commissary hustles were common. Several rookie officers had rotated through in the months prior, each leaving discouraged. The pod had become a proving ground for staff, and the inmates knew it.

Into this environment walked a rookie officer who had just completed training. She was twenty-three years old, with no prior law enforcement or military experience. Her only work background was in retail. Many staff doubted whether she would last a month.

The First Days

From her first shift, the rookie applied what she had learned in the academy. She walked the pod deliberately, making eye contact, addressing inmates firmly but respectfully, and correcting small infractions immediately. When she saw shirts untucked, she required them to be fixed. When noise rose, she addressed it. When trash accumulated, she ordered it cleaned.

The inmates tested her. They laughed, ignored commands, and mocked her inexperience. At one point, several deliberately refused to tuck their shirts to see if she would back down. She did not. She repeated the command calmly, called for backup when they resisted, and wrote disciplinary reports when defiance continued.

Officers watching from outside expected her to burn out quickly. But the rookie surprised them. She did not raise her voice unnecessarily, but she did not let details slide. She enforced consistently, no matter how small the infraction appeared.

The Resistance

The first week was brutal. Inmates pushed harder, trying to exhaust her. They raised noise during recreation, hoping she would ignore it. They mocked her by carving graffiti onto tables while she was in the pod. They exchanged commissary openly, daring her to intervene.

The rookie refused to yield. She documented every infraction, called for maintenance to remove graffiti, and confiscated traded items. When she ordered quiet, she stood her ground until noise declined. When inmates challenged her authority, she stood firm and called supervisors for reinforcement.

Her persistence created friction. Some inmates grew frustrated, accusing her of being "too strict." Some officers criticized her, suggesting she should "pick her battles." But she refused to change course. She believed her training, that details were signals and that if she surrendered them, she surrendered the pod.

The Shift

After two weeks, the pod began to change. Inmates who had resisted at first began complying. They tucked in shirts without being asked. Noise declined as they recognized that she would never overlook it. Graffiti disappeared as maintenance removed markings and inmates realized new ones would be corrected immediately. Commissary hustles slowed because confiscations became routine.

The rookie had not raised her voice more than necessary. She had not used force. She had not relied on intimidation. She had simply enforced details consistently. The pod adjusted to her consistency.

Other officers noticed the difference. Those who had rotated through the pod before were surprised to see it calmer. Supervisors praised her persistence. Over time, she became known not as the rookie who would fail but as the officer who had changed the pod.

The Lessons

This case demonstrates several truths about Broken Windows in corrections:

1. **Training works when lived.** The rookie applied what she had learned, that small infractions are signals, and the theory proved true
2. **Consistency defeats resistance.** Inmates resisted at first, but when they saw she never wavered, they adjusted.
3. **Presence matters more than experience.** She had no military or law enforcement background, but her presence and consistency outperformed veterans who had tolerated disorder.
4. **Support is essential.** Supervisors who backed her when she enforced details gave her the confidence to remain consistent. Without that backing, her resolve would have crumbled.
5. **One officer can shift culture.** A single rookie, by owning her pod, bent the culture of an entire unit toward order.

Reflection

The rookie who changed the pod demonstrated the essence of Broken Windows in corrections. Details matter. Consistency matters. Presence matters. Inmates test officers constantly, but they adjust quickly to staff who enforce rules without hesitation.

Corrections professionals often underestimate rookies, assuming they must gain years of experience before they can shape culture. This case proves otherwise.

With the right training, mindset, and support, even a brand-new officer can set the tone. The rookie became not just a survivor of the pod but the owner of it because she refused to walk past disorder.

Case Study 2: The Burned-Out Officer

Not all cultural problems come from rookies who do not know what to do. Sometimes they come from experienced officers who once enforced details but over time slip into burnout. Burnout is one of the most dangerous conditions in corrections because it does not appear suddenly. It creeps in quietly, eroding standards shift by shift until disorder multiplies around the officer. This case shows how one burned-out officer nearly surrendered his unit to inmate control and how leadership and mentoring brought him back.

The Setting

This case took place in a state prison housing over 1,800 inmates. The officer at the center of the story was a ten-year veteran. He had once been known as dependable, sharp, and professional. Supervisors trusted him. New officers looked up to him. Inmates respected him.

After a decade of double shifts, mandatory overtime, and the daily grind of inmate testing, his energy began to fade. The signs of burnout appeared gradually. He no longer walked the pod as often. He let noise rise higher before intervening. He stopped checking sanitation as thoroughly. Graffiti spread, but he no longer called for maintenance. Commissary hustles occurred openly in front of him.

Supervisors noticed but at first excused it. After all, he had ten years of service and a record of professionalism. They assumed he was pacing himself. Inmates, however, noticed the change instantly. They tested him more aggressively, realizing his tolerance for disorder had expanded.

The Drift Toward Disorder

The pod grew louder. Inmates began shouting across tiers without correction. Television volumes crept higher. Trash accumulated in corners of the dayroom. Small trades of commissary turned into open hustles.

The officer saw these changes but did little. He rationalized it as "choosing his battles." He told himself that noise was harmless, that trades reduced tension, and that graffiti was inevitable. In reality, he had surrendered details because he no longer had the energy to confront them.

His fellow officers noticed. Some grew frustrated, believing he was leaving them exposed. Others mirrored his behavior, thinking that if a ten-year veteran ignored disorder, perhaps they should too. Inmates recognized the vacuum and claimed ownership. The pod, once orderly, became one of the loudest and least disciplined in the facility.

The Breaking Point

The drift culminated in a violent incident. A commissary debt dispute erupted into a fight involving five inmates. Officers responded, but the burned-out officer hesitated. Instead of moving quickly to intervene, he stood back until backup arrived. By then, one inmate had suffered serious injuries.

The investigation revealed that the fight was not spontaneous. It had been building for weeks. Commissary hustles had grown unchecked, and debts had escalated without staff intervention. Supervisors traced the breakdown to the burned-out officer's tolerance of disorder.

For the first time in his career, his reputation shifted. He was no longer the dependable veteran. He was the officer who had allowed a pod to drift into chaos.

The Intervention

The administration faced a decision. They could discipline the officer harshly or attempt to reset him. They chose the latter. A senior captain met with him privately and addressed the situation directly. He told the officer that burnout was understandable but tolerance of disorder was not. He reminded him of his earlier reputation as a professional who had set the standard for others.

The captain then paired him with a younger officer who had recently demonstrated strong commitment to detail. Together, they worked the pod under close supervision. The younger officer enforced small rules relentlessly. The veteran, at first resentful, gradually began to mirror the energy. With the captain reinforcing both of them, the pod began to reset.

Mentoring reversed the drift. The burned-out officer regained confidence. He began enforcing details again, walking the pod and correcting infractions. His reputation recovered, not fully to its former glory, but enough to restore order and regain respect.

Lessons from the Burned-Out Officer

1. **Burnout erodes standards.** Even experienced staff can drift into tolerance of disorder when fatigue overtakes professionalism.
2. **Tolerance is contagious.** When a respected veteran overlooks details, younger staff often mirror that behavior.
3. **Inmates notice instantly.** Disorder tolerated by staff is claimed by inmates. Burnout is never hidden from the population.
4. **Leadership intervention is essential.** Supervisors must confront burnout directly before it undermines culture.
5. **Mentoring can reset drift.** Pairing a burned-out officer with a detail-oriented peer under strong supervision can restore consistency.

Reflection

Burnout is a hidden danger in corrections. It creeps in quietly, eroding discipline not with defiance but with fatigue. The burned-out officer in this case did not intend to surrender his pod. He simply lost the energy to enforce details. But in corrections, surrender is surrender, regardless of intent.

The lesson is clear. Leaders must watch for signs of burnout and intervene early. Officers must recognize that fatigue cannot excuse tolerance of disorder. Teams must support one another, ensuring that standards are upheld even when individuals struggle.

The Broken Windows Theory teaches that small cracks become collapse. Burnout is one of the first cracks. If ignored, it spreads across shifts and into inmate culture. If addressed, it can be repaired. The difference lies in leadership and mentoring.

Case Study 3: The United Shift

Some of the most powerful corrections stories are not about individuals but about teams. A single officer can influence a pod, a sergeant can reshape a unit, and a captain can reset a division. But when an entire shift commits together, the effect is transformative. Unity communicates strength not only to staff but to inmates, who quickly learn that inconsistency is no longer an option. This case demonstrates how one shift's cohesion reversed a jail's reputation for chaos.

The Setting

The jail was located in the Midwest and housed about 750 inmates. It had three primary shifts, but one, the evening shift, had developed a reputation as the weakest. Inmates viewed it as the shift where rules were relaxed, noise was tolerated, and contraband moved freely. Officers dreaded working it because they knew expectations were inconsistent. Supervisors argued frequently, and officers often felt unsupported.

As a result, disorder multiplied. Noise levels were high. Graffiti spread across multiple pods. Commissary hustles flourished. Inmates openly joked that the evening shift was their "free time." Reports piled up for the day shift to address the following morning. The facility's administration recognized that culture on this shift was undermining the entire jail.

The Turning Point

The change began when a new lieutenant was assigned to oversee the shift. She recognized immediately that the problem was not lack of ability but lack of unity. Officers and sergeants were capable, but they were divided. Some enforced rules, others overlooked them. Some backed staff, others contradicted them. Inmates exploited the divisions, adjusting their behavior depending on which officer or sergeant was on duty.

The lieutenant called a meeting and delivered a simple message: "We succeed together or we fail together. But we will no longer fail separately." She laid out expectations clearly. Every officer, sergeant, and supervisor would enforce rules consistently. Noise would be corrected, commissary trades stopped, sanitation inspected, and counts conducted thoroughly. Disagreements could be discussed privately, but in front of inmates, the shift would be unified.

The First Weeks

The transition was difficult. Officers who had grown accustomed to overlooking details pushed back, arguing that consistency would only create conflict. Inmates tested the new approach aggressively, resisting enforcement and complaining loudly. Several early shifts felt like battles. But the lieutenant remained steady. She backed officers who enforced rules, corrected supervisors who contradicted each other, and reinforced unity at roll call.

Sergeants began supporting officers more openly. Officers began enforcing details more consistently. Over time, the shift moved from divided individuals to a unified team.

The Cultural Shift

The impact on inmates was immediate. They realized that inconsistencies were gone. A command given by one officer would be supported by another. Rules enforced by one sergeant would be enforced by all. Complaints to supervisors no longer produced leniency.

As inmates adjusted, culture shifted. Noise declined because inmates knew it would be corrected regardless of who was on duty. Commissary hustles shrank because officers consistently confiscated unauthorized trades. Graffiti stopped spreading because maintenance was called every time markings appeared. Sanitation improved as inspections became routine.

Inmates no longer viewed the evening shift as "free time." They began referring to it as "tight." The reputation had changed, not because of one officer or one sergeant, but because the entire shift had committed together.

The Ripple Effect

The united shift's impact spread beyond their hours of duty. The day and night shifts, once frustrated by the disorder they inherited, noticed the change. They began modeling similar unity, reinforcing that the jail as a whole was committed to consistency. The administration praised the evening shift publicly, reinforcing that their cohesion was the new standard.

The transformation of one shift reset the culture of the entire facility. What had been known as the weakest period became the strongest, proving that unity among staff is one of the most powerful tools in corrections.

Lessons from the United Shift

1. **Unity eliminates cracks.** Inconsistent enforcement creates cracks inmates exploit. A united team closes those cracks instantly.

2. **Support builds confidence.** Officers who know they will be backed by peers and supervisors enforce rules without hesitation.
3. **Inmates adjust quickly.** Resistance is strongest at first, but once inmates see unity is real, they adapt.
4. **Unity is cultural, not optional.** A facility cannot afford divided shifts. In corrections, division is disorder.
5. **Leadership must model unity.** The lieutenant's insistence on private disagreement and public unity created the foundation for cultural reset.

Reflection

The united shift illustrates that Broken Windows cannot be sustained by individuals alone. It requires collective ownership. A single officer can influence a pod, but an entire shift can influence a jail. When every member enforces details consistently, disorder has nowhere to spread.

Inmates thrive on inconsistency. They exploit it, test it, and multiply it. But when a shift commits together, inmates adjust. They recognize unity as strength. Staff morale rises because officers no longer feel isolated. Culture bends toward order because signals are consistent across every post.

The Broken Windows Theory teaches that small cracks create collapse. Unity prevents cracks from forming in the first place. The evening shift proved that a divided team creates disorder, but a united team creates safety.

Analysis: Teams as Cultural Engines

Corrections is sometimes described as a profession of individuals standing their post. But that image is misleading. No officer stands alone. No sergeant enforces rules without backup. No administrator sustains culture without supervisors carrying the message downward. Corrections is a team profession, and culture is always the product of team behavior.

The case studies in this chapter demonstrate that clearly. A rookie officer enforced details consistently and reset a pod's culture. A burned-out veteran allowed disorder to spread until leadership and mentoring pulled him back. An entire shift committed together and transformed a jail's reputation from chaos to stability.

The common thread is not individuals but teams. The rookie succeeded because supervisors backed her. The veteran recovered because leaders paired him with a consistent partner. The united shift succeeded because officers, sergeants, and supervisors enforced the same standards together.

Broken Windows teaches that small cracks multiply into collapse if left unaddressed. Teams are the sealant that prevents cracks from spreading. When teams commit together, disorder has nowhere to take root. When teams fracture, disorder multiplies quickly.

Why Staff Culture Determines Inmate Culture

Inmate culture is never independent. It is always a mirror of staff culture. Inmates adjust to what they observe from staff. If officers enforce rules consistently, inmates learn that rules are non-negotiable. If officers enforce inconsistently, inmates learn that rules are negotiable.

The rookie's pod proved this. Inmates resisted at first, mocking her commands, but eventually complied because her consistency never wavered. The burned-out veteran's pod proved the opposite. Inmates noticed his tolerance of noise, graffiti, and commissary hustles, and they expanded those cracks into chaos. The united shift proved the principle at scale. Once inmates realized that every officer enforced the same rules, they adjusted to unity.

Staff culture always drives inmate culture. No exceptions.

Consistency Across Shifts

Consistency must extend not only within a shift but across shifts. Inmates are experts at noticing differences between days and nights, weekdays and weekends. If one shift enforces details and another ignores them, inmates adjust to the weakest shift. They resist enforcement during strict shifts and exploit leniency during relaxed ones.

The evening shift in the united shift case had become the weak link. Its inconsistency undermined the work of the day and night shifts. Only when the evening shift unified did the jail stabilize. This illustrates a central principle: culture is only as strong as the weakest shift.

Administrators must demand consistency across all shifts. Supervisors must coordinate regularly, communicating expectations clearly so that staff know rules will be enforced no matter when they are on duty. Without this consistency, Broken Windows cannot hold.

Mentoring as a Cultural Tool

The burned-out officer case demonstrated the importance of mentoring. No staff member remains at peak performance forever. Fatigue, stress, and frustration take their toll. Without intervention, burnout leads to tolerance of disorder.

Mentoring is the antidote. Pairing struggling officers with strong peers under supportive supervision allows habits to be reset. Mentoring communicates that culture is a shared responsibility. It prevents cracks from spreading by addressing them in staff before they spread to inmates.

Agencies must formalize mentoring programs, not only for rookies but for veterans. Culture requires constant renewal. Mentoring provides the structure for that renewal.

Training Teams, Not Just Individuals

Academies often train individuals, but facilities must train teams. Inmates do not face staff one at a time. They face shifts. If only some staff understand Broken Windows principles, inconsistency creeps in. Training must emphasize teamwork:

- □ How officers back each other during enforcement
- □ How sergeants reinforce officers in front of inmates
- □ How supervisors present unity even when they disagree privately
- □ How shifts coordinate across days and nights

When staff are trained to see themselves as a cultural engine rather than isolated individuals, they enforce rules with confidence and consistency.

Tools and Takeaways

This section provides practical strategies to build and sustain teams committed to Broken Windows.

1. **Hire for Culture, Not Just Numbers**
    a. Screen applicants for attention to detail, ownership, and resilience.
    b. Reject applicants who rationalize cutting corners.
    c. Use panels of experienced staff to identify subtle warning signs.
    d. Hiring is the first window. If cracked at the start, it will spread through the team.

2. **Embed Broken Windows in Training**
    a. Use scenarios to show how small infractions escalate.
    b. Reinforce that details are not cosmetic but cultural.
    c. Train FTOs to model consistency every day.
    d. Provide annual refreshers for all staff, not just recruits.
    e. Training must be lived, not just lectured.

3. **Mentor Continuously**
    a. Pair rookies with consistent veterans.
    b. Pair burned-out staff with energetic peers.
    c. Hold regular debriefs to reinforce lessons.
    d. Choose mentors for professionalism, not just seniority.
    e. Mentoring prevents cracks from spreading by repairing them in staff early.

4. **Support Officers Publicly, Coach Privately**
    a. Back officers in front of inmates, even when mistakes are made.
    b. Correct staff privately later to preserve unity.
    c. Never contradict officers in front of inmates.
    d. Public unity builds culture. Private correction preserves professionalism.

5. **Demand Consistency Across Shifts**
    a. Supervisors must coordinate to ensure rules are enforced the same way on every shift.
    b. Administrators must hold all shifts accountable for the same standards.
    c. Inmates must see that time of day does not change enforcement.
    d. Culture is only as strong as the weakest shift.

6. **Treat Burnout as a Cultural Risk**
    a. Monitor staff for signs of fatigue and drift.
    b. Intervene early with mentoring, training, and support.
    c. Do not excuse tolerance of disorder as "choosing battles."
    d. Burnout tolerated is disorder multiplied.

7. **Recognize and Celebrate Unity**
    a. Praise teams that enforce details consistently.
    b. Share success stories in roll call and newsletters.
    c. Use case studies from within the facility to reinforce lessons.
    d. Recognition reinforces commitment.

8. **Remember That Teams Are the Sealant**

Broken Windows cracks will always appear. A rookie will be tested. A veteran will tire. A shift will drift. The difference between collapse and recovery is the team. When teams commit together, cracks are sealed before they spread.

Reflection

Teams are the cultural engines of corrections. Individuals can influence a pod, but only teams can sustain a facility. Broken Windows principles cannot survive in isolation. They require unity, consistency, and ownership across every rank and every shift.

The rookie who enforced details showed that even one officer can shift culture when supported. The burned-out veteran showed that cracks in staff tolerance must be repaired quickly through leadership and mentoring. The united shift showed that when teams commit together, entire facilities can transform.

Corrections is not about heroes. It is about teams. Broken Windows is not about one window. It is about every window, repaired by every staff member, every day. When teams commit to owning the details, inmates adjust, culture stabilizes, and safety follows.

- 5 -

ADDRESSING MINOR INFRACTIONS BEFORE THEY SPREAD

Why Small Infractions Matter

Corrections professionals often face the temptation to let the little things go. Housing units are noisy, inmates push limits constantly, and staff cannot correct every single detail without exhausting themselves. But the Broken Windows Theory teaches that small details are not small. They are signals. A shirt untucked, a lockdown refusal, a loud television, or a commissary trade is not an isolated inconvenience. It is a message.

Inmates send signals through infractions. When they leave cells late after lockdown, they are not simply tired. They are testing whether staff will enforce the rule. When they graffiti a table, they are not simply bored. They are testing whether staff own the environment. When they trade commissary, they are not simply hungry. They are testing whether staff will tolerate an unauthorized economy.

Every ignored infraction communicates tolerance. Tolerance spreads. If one inmate can refuse lockdown without consequence, soon others will test it. If one pod can graffiti walls without correction, soon graffiti will cover the facility. If commissary trades are ignored, gangs will control the economy.

The temptation to overlook small details is understandable. Staff are overworked, tired, and pressured to avoid unnecessary conflict. But ignoring small infractions does not reduce conflict. It multiplies it. What begins as one infraction becomes a pattern, and what begins as a pattern becomes a culture.

Broken Windows in corrections demands that staff treat every infraction as a signal. This does not mean punishing every action harshly. It means correcting every action consistently. Firm, fair, and consistent responses to small infractions prevent escalation. Tolerance invites escalation.

Corrections is a detail profession. The details of inmate behavior, compliance with lockdown, respect for property, and adherence to schedules determine whether order or disorder multiplies. Small infractions matter because they are never small. They are windows. Repaired quickly, they signal order. Left broken, they signal collapse.

The Psychology of Testing

Corrections professionals know instinctively that inmates test limits. What may look to outsiders like casual misbehavior is often deliberate. Small infractions serve as probes. They are not random acts. They are tests of authority, consistency, and control.

Why Inmates Test

Inmates live in compressed societies where every interaction carries meaning. They spend their days under constant supervision, watching staff closely for weaknesses. In this environment, power is currency. Inmates test limits to see where authority resides and how firmly it will be enforced.

Testing is also about survival. Jails and prisons are competitive environments where status matters. An inmate who bends rules without consequence gains standing among peers. An inmate who pressures an officer into backing down demonstrates influence. Even small victories, like refusing lockdown without consequence or walking in the dayroom with a shirt untucked, signal strength.

From the inmate perspective, testing is rational. They are mapping the environment. They want to know which officers are firm, which are hesitant, which supervisors are consistent, and which shifts are weak. Every ignored detail provides information.

Types of Tests

Tests vary in size and strategy, but most fall into predictable categories:

1. **Compliance Tests**
   Refusing or delaying compliance with simple orders, such as lockdown, sanitation, or uniform standards.
   Purpose: to see if the officer will back down or follow through.

2. **Boundary Tests**
   Pushing limits of space, time, or privilege, such as staying out after lockdown, stretching recreation time, or occupying unauthorized areas.
   Purpose: to see whether staff will enforce schedules and boundaries.

3. **Respect Tests**
   Using tone, posture, or language to challenge staff authority without direct violence.
   Purpose: to gauge whether officers will respond firmly and professionally or become flustered.

4. **Unity Tests**
   Multiple inmates engaging in the same minor infraction simultaneously, such as group noise, collective refusal to return trays, or coordinated complaints.
   Purpose: to test whether staff will respond consistently as a team.

5. **Persistence Tests**
   Repeating the same small infraction day after day, such as graffiti, commissary trades, or minor contraband.
   Purpose: to wear down staff and see if tolerance develops.

Each of these tests is designed to answer one question: Do staff own the environment, or do inmates?

Staff Responses as Signals

Every staff response to a test communicates a signal.

- **Firm and Fair Enforcement:** Inmates see that rules are real, authority is consistent, and staff own the environment. Testing slows.
- **Harsh Overreaction:** Inmates see inconsistency and potential weakness. They may exploit the officer's loss of control by provoking further reactions.
- **Tolerance or Hesitation:** Inmates see opportunity. Testing multiplies.

The signal matters more than the infraction itself. A shirt untucked may seem trivial, but when ignored it communicates that staff do not enforce rules consistently. That message spreads faster than the infraction.

How Inmates Share Information

Inmate populations share information quickly. Word spreads through conversations, gestures, and observation. If one officer overlooks a refusal, the entire pod knows within minutes. If one sergeant backs an officer firmly, the news spreads just as fast.

This rapid communication magnifies the importance of staff consistency. A single act of tolerance does not remain isolated. It becomes known, repeated, and exploited. Conversely, a single act of consistent enforcement communicates that standards are firm, and inmates adjust.

The Role of Peer Pressure

Inmates also pressure one another during tests. A single inmate may hesitate to defy an officer, but with peers watching, refusal becomes a chance to gain respect. If staff back down, the inmate gains status. If staff enforce rules consistently, the inmate loses standing.

This peer dynamic explains why small infractions can escalate quickly. What begins as one inmate refusing lockdown can turn into a group refusal if others see opportunity. Staff responses must therefore be immediate and unified.

Why Tests Multiply

Tests multiply because tolerance is contagious. If one inmate gets away with an infraction, others try the same. If one officer tolerates disorder, inmates push harder the next day. The cycle continues until small infractions become cultural norms.

The burned-out officer case from the previous chapter illustrated this. His tolerance of noise, graffiti, and trades multiplied disorder across the pod. Inmates saw cracks and expanded them. Within weeks, the pod was unrecognizable.

The opposite is also true. When staff enforce details consistently, inmates stop testing. Resistance may spike at first, but once inmates see that enforcement is firm, they adjust. Testing slows because boundaries are clear.

Reflections on Testing

Minor infractions are not accidents. They are deliberate tests. Inmates probe for weakness, map authority, and seek opportunities. Staff responses are signals that determine whether testing multiplies or declines.

Corrections is not about ignoring the little things to avoid conflict. It is about enforcing the little things to prevent conflict. The Broken Windows Theory explains why. Every small infraction is a window. Repaired quickly, it signals ownership. Left broken, it signals opportunity.

Staff must learn to see minor infractions not as nuisances but as messages. Each is a test. Each is an opportunity to prove ownership. Each is a chance to send the signal that staff, not inmates, run the facility.

Escalation Pathways

Corrections facilities rarely collapse in a single moment. They collapse over time as small cracks spread into major failures. The Broken Windows Theory teaches that disorder tolerated multiplies. In corrections, that multiplication is accelerated by the compressed environment. One ignored infraction can become ten within hours. Ten tolerated can become cultural collapse within weeks.

Understanding escalation pathways is essential. Staff must recognize that ignoring a small violation does not contain it, it grows. Every infraction left uncorrected takes one step down a pathway that ends in violence, contraband, or escape.

The Pathway from Noise to Violence

Noise is one of the most common infractions in housing units. Officers are often tempted to let it slide, reasoning that loud inmates are better than disruptive ones. Noise is a cultural signal. It communicates that staff are not in control.

When noise is ignored, it becomes normalized. Inmates grow louder, challenging officers to intervene. Staff hesitate, unsure whether to enforce standards after tolerating violations. Eventually, noise emboldens inmates to escalate from verbal defiance to physical defiance. Fights often emerge in noisy pods because chaos provides cover. Officers cannot hear disputes forming, and inmates exploit the environment.

What began as loud talking becomes an atmosphere where violence thrives.

The Pathway from Graffiti to Gang Control

Graffiti is often dismissed as cosmetic. In reality, it is one of the clearest signals of ownership. When inmates mark tables, walls, or doors without consequence, they communicate to peers that the space belongs to them.

When graffiti spreads unchecked, it often becomes linked to gang symbols. Different groups mark territory, claiming specific tables, cells, or areas. Conflicts emerge when one group covers another's graffiti. Officers who once ignored a small drawing on a table now face violent disputes over territory.

The escalation pathway is direct: ignored graffiti → normalization → gang symbolism → territorial disputes → violence.

The Pathway from Commissary Trades to Black Markets

Commissary trades may seem harmless, one inmate swaps chips for soup, another trades cookies for coffee. Officers, overwhelmed with larger responsibilities, sometimes ignore these trades. But when tolerated, trades grow into organized economies.

Inmates with resources stockpile commissary and lend it out for interest. Debts form. Debts lead to intimidation and violence. Gangs step in to control trades, turning commissary into a black market. Contraband, drugs, phones, or weapons often rides the same networks.

The escalation pathway is simple: tolerated trades → black-market economy → gang dominance → violence and contraband.

The Pathway from Lockdown Refusal to Group Defiance

Lockdowns are sacred rituals in corrections. They signal staff control over inmate movement. When one inmate refuses lockdown and staff tolerate it, the signal is devastating. Inmates see that refusal is possible.

The next day, several refuse together. Staff hesitate, uncertain whether enforcement will be supported. Inmates grow bolder. Within weeks, entire pods challenge lockdowns. Group refusals spread quickly, often leading to facility-wide incidents.

What began as one inmate refusing to lock down becomes a riot pathway: tolerated refusal → group defiance → crisis.

The Pathway from Minor Contraband to Escape

Contraband rarely enters a facility as a major threat immediately. It often begins with something small, an extra food item, a pen, or a piece of wire. When tolerated, contraband becomes normalized. Inmates begin hiding more items, testing how much staff will overlook.

Soon, contraband shifts from harmless to dangerous. A pen becomes a weapon. A piece of wire becomes part of a lock-picking tool. A phone hidden in plain sight becomes a hub for criminal communication outside the walls. Escape attempts often trace back to contraband tolerated months earlier.

The escalation pathway is direct: tolerated contraband → organized concealment → weaponization → escape attempt.

Cultural Acceleration of Escalation

What makes corrections unique is the speed of escalation. In neighborhoods, graffiti may spread over weeks. In a housing pod, graffiti can cover every table within days. In neighborhoods, crime may rise over months. In a pod, violence can escalate overnight.

This acceleration is fueled by observation. Inmates see everything. They share information instantly. If one infraction is tolerated, dozens know within minutes. Escalation is contagious.

Why Staff Rationalize Tolerance

Staff often explain tolerance of small infractions as picking battles. They argue that strict enforcement creates unnecessary conflict. In reality, tolerance creates more conflict later. The battle not picked today becomes the riot tomorrow.

Staff rationalize tolerance because they are tired, unsupported, or burned out. Leadership must recognize these rationalizations as red flags. When staff excuse disorder, they are laying the foundation for escalation.

The Role of Leadership in Breaking Pathways

Leaders must break escalation pathways early. This requires:

1. **Clear Standards:** No tolerance for graffiti, sloppy counts, lockdown refusals, or unauthorized trades.

2. **Consistent Enforcement:** Officers backed every time they enforce rules.
3. **Rapid Correction:** Immediate removal of graffiti, confiscation of contraband, and correction of noise.
4. **Visible Leadership:** Supervisors present in pods to reinforce enforcement.

Breaking the pathway early prevents escalation. Waiting until infractions become violence or escape attempts is too late.

Reflections on Escalation

Every major incident begins with a minor infraction tolerated. Fights begin with ignored noise or debts. Gang conflicts begin with graffiti. Black markets begin with commissary trades. Escapes begin with contraband overlooked.

The Broken Windows Theory explains why: disorder tolerated multiplies. In corrections, the multiplication is rapid and severe. Staff must see every infraction as a step on an escalation pathway. The choice is simple: correct it now or face its multiplied form later.

Case Study 1: The Refused Lockdown

Lockdowns are among the most important routines in any correctional facility. They signal staff control over inmate movement, safety, and daily order. When lockdowns fail, the entire chain of discipline can begin to unravel. This case from a county jail in the South illustrates how a single refusal, left unchecked, escalated into group defiance and how restoring control came at significant cost.

The Setting

The jail housed about 1,200 inmates in a mix of dormitory and celled housing. Staff turnover was high, and many new officers were still learning how to manage pods. Lockdowns were scheduled several times a day for counts, meals, and shift changes. Policy required staff to order inmates back into cells, secure doors, and visually confirm compliance.

In one pod, the culture around lockdowns had started to slip. Officers allowed inmates to linger in the dayroom after lockdown was called. A few stragglers would finish card games or conversations before going inside. Supervisors noticed but rarely intervened, rationalizing it as harmless. "As long as they go in eventually," one sergeant explained, "it's not worth making a scene."

That tolerance would soon spread into crisis.

The First Refusal

It began with a single inmate. When lockdown was called one evening, he remained seated at a table, arms folded, ignoring the order. The officer repeated the command, but the inmate stayed put, smirking at peers.

The officer hesitated. He had seen supervisors ignore stragglers before and worried he would not be backed. Rather than escalate, he let the inmate stay out for several extra minutes until the sergeant walked through. By then, the inmate had gone in voluntarily. No report was written.

Inmate observers understood the message immediately: refusal was possible.

The Spread

Within days, several other inmates copied the tactic. They lingered in the dayroom when lockdown was called, watching to see whether staff would enforce it. Some delayed for seconds, others for minutes. Officers, uncertain of support, hesitated to intervene. Supervisors continued to tolerate it.

The behavior spread until a dozen inmates routinely delayed going into cells. Staff grew frustrated but felt powerless. "If we press the issue," one officer later explained, "we're the ones who get yelled at for overreacting."

Inmates now recognized that staff hesitated. They pushed further.

The Group Defiance

Two weeks later, the pod reached a breaking point. During evening lockdown, nearly twenty inmates refused simultaneously. They sat at tables, crossed arms, and ignored commands. The officer on duty radioed for assistance, but backup arrived slowly. By the time supervisors entered, the group was openly mocking staff.

The supervisors, realizing how far tolerance had gone, demanded compliance. Inmates resisted verbally, some shouting and refusing to move. Staff eventually had to call in a response team. The standoff ended without serious injuries, but the pod was shaken. What had started as a single refusal had escalated into group defiance.

The Investigation

The administration reviewed incident reports and quickly identified the pattern. The first refusal had not been corrected. The officer on duty had hesitated because he believed supervisors would not back him. The supervisors themselves had tolerated lingering for weeks. The culture had shifted from strict enforcement to casual tolerance, and inmates had seized the opportunity.

One captain summarized it bluntly in the review meeting: "We broke our own window. They saw the crack and climbed through it."

The Reset

The jail moved quickly to reset culture. Policy was re-emphasized: every lockdown order had to be enforced immediately. Supervisors were required to be present during lockdowns for the next month. Officers were instructed to write reports on any inmate who delayed, even briefly. Maintenance repainted pod doors to remove graffiti that had multiplied alongside the refusals, signaling a full reset of order.

At first, inmates resisted. Several tested enforcement by refusing again. This time, staff responded immediately, documenting every refusal and applying discipline consistently. Within two weeks, the culture shifted. Inmates began going into cells promptly because they saw staff unity and enforcement had returned.

The pod stabilized, but only after significant strain.

Lessons from the Refused Lockdown

1. **Lockdowns are sacred.** They symbolize staff authority over movement. Any tolerance undermines control.
2. **Hesitation multiplies.** The first officer's hesitation, combined with supervisor tolerance, created a crack that spread instantly.
3. **Group behavior begins with individuals.** One inmate's defiance multiplied into twenty. Small refusals always escalate.
4. **Staff backing is essential.** Officers who doubt support will hesitate, and hesitation is always exploited.
5. **Resets are costly.** It took weeks of strict enforcement and added supervision to repair what one refusal started.

Reflection

This case proves that no infraction is too small to matter. A single inmate refusing lockdown may appear minor, but the signal it sends is profound. If tolerated, it invites others to test. Tests multiply until they become crises.

Corrections professionals must remember that every order enforced or ignored communicates who runs the facility. Lockdowns are not schedules. They are signals. Each one proves whether staff own the environment or inmates do. The refused lockdown began as a crack. Left uncorrected, it became a fracture that nearly broke a pod. Only deliberate enforcement repaired it.

Case Study 2: The Unauthorized Commissary Economy

Commissary is intended to give inmates small comforts—snacks, hygiene items, writing supplies, and other goods that make daily life more manageable. However, when commissary shifts from privilege to currency, it becomes far more dangerous. Left unchecked, trades and debts can evolve into organized black markets. This case from a large Midwestern jail shows how a few overlooked commissary exchanges escalated into gang-controlled commerce, threatening both staff safety and inmate stability.

The Setting

The jail held about 2,300 inmates, divided across multiple housing units. Commissary was delivered twice a week, with inmates ordering from a catalog of food, hygiene products, and stationery items. Policy clearly prohibited trading, selling, or bartering commissary items, but enforcement was inconsistent.

In one unit, staff had grown accustomed to overlooking small trades. An officer might see an inmate swap a soup for a bag of chips and shrug. A sergeant might notice inmates exchanging cookies for coffee but decide it wasn't worth the paperwork. The prevailing culture was that "as long as they're quiet, let them be."

That tolerance planted the seeds of a black-market economy.

The Growth of Trades

At first, trades were small and limited to snacks. Inmates swapped to satisfy cravings or personal preferences. But quickly, patterns formed. A handful of inmates with large commissary accounts, often funded by family, began using their resources strategically. They lent items to others with the expectation of repayment plus "interest."

An inmate might borrow a soup and owe two back the following week. Another might receive a bag of coffee and owe a future favor. These debts created hierarchy. Inmates with commissary power became creditors. Inmates with little commissary became debtors.

Staff observed but did not intervene. The trades were not loud or violent, and as long as the pod remained relatively calm, officers let them continue.

The Emergence of Control

Within weeks, commissary trades were no longer casual. They had become organized. Inmates with resources pooled together, creating small networks. These networks soon fell under gang influence. Gang leaders recognized that controlling commissary meant controlling power.

Debts began to carry consequences. Inmates who failed to repay faced intimidation or violence. Workouts, "body shots," and thefts increased. Inmates without commissary were pressured to smuggle items, clean cells, or act as lookouts in exchange for borrowed goods.

The pod was no longer controlled by staff authority. It was increasingly controlled by commissary creditors.

The Warning Signs

Officers began noticing tension. Inmates whispered during commissary distribution, groups formed around tables, and fights erupted more frequently.

Graffiti linked to gang symbols appeared on dayroom tables. Contraband began flowing more freely, with reports of tobacco, drugs, and even cell phones entering the unit.

Still, enforcement of commissary rules remained inconsistent. Officers rationalized that fights and contraband were "separate issues" from commissary. In reality, commissary had become the foundation of those issues.

The Breaking Point

The crisis came during a Sunday lockdown. Two inmates fought violently in the dayroom, one stabbed with a sharpened plastic utensil. The cause was traced back to commissary debt. One inmate owed several soups to a gang-affiliated creditor and had failed to repay. The fight was staged as punishment.

The incident forced a full investigation. When staff searched cells, they discovered commissary stockpiles worth hundreds of dollars in inmate currency. Some inmates had dozens of soups, bags of coffee, and snacks stacked like inventory. Ledgers detailing debts and repayment schedules were found hidden in books and letters.

It was no longer an informal trade network. It was a structured economy, with interest rates, enforcers, and consequences. Inmates admitted that gangs controlled who could borrow, how much interest was charged, and how debts were collected.

The Response

The administration realized that their tolerance of small trades had created a crisis. They moved quickly to shut down the commissary economy. Policies were reinforced. Officers were required to confiscate any items traded openly. Debts discovered during interviews were documented and addressed. Commissary orders were monitored more closely, with patterns of large purchases flagged for review.

The facility also increased searches, breaking up stockpiles and redistributing confiscated items back into the system. Gang leaders identified as controlling commissary trades were placed into segregation, and intelligence officers worked to dismantle networks.

Importantly, supervisors emphasized consistent enforcement at the line level. Officers were reminded that even a small swap, a soup for a cookie, was a signal. Every trade overlooked was a crack that could grow into a black-market economy.

The Recovery

The reset was difficult. Inmates resisted, hiding trades more carefully. Officers initially struggled to adjust, frustrated by the paperwork involved in enforcing minor commissary violations. But with persistence, the culture began to shift.

Inmates realized that trades would be confiscated, debts would be tracked, and commissary could no longer be used as unchecked currency. Fights over debts declined. Contraband networks slowed. While commissary trading never disappeared entirely, it returned to the margins rather than dominating pod culture.

The jail regained control not through force but through consistent enforcement of small details.

Lessons from the Commissary Economy

1. **Trades are not harmless.** What begins as casual swapping quickly becomes currency, hierarchy, and exploitation.
2. **Debts create violence.** Commissary debts always lead to intimidation or fighting. Tolerating trades tolerates violence.
3. **Gangs follow money.** Once trades multiply, gangs inevitably step in to control the economy.
4. **Tolerance is complicity.** Officers who overlook trades, even small ones, feed the growth of black markets.

5. **Reset requires persistence.** Breaking a commissary economy requires consistent enforcement and cultural reset.

Reflection

The commissary economy demonstrates the compounding effect of ignored details. Officers thought they were avoiding conflict by overlooking small trades. In reality, they were planting the seeds of violence. Inmates understood immediately that commissary could be used to build power. They organized, exploited, and expanded until staff no longer controlled the pod.

The Broken Windows Theory explains why. Each trade overlooked was a broken window. Each debt unaddressed was another crack. Left unchecked, the cracks connected into collapse. Only when staff reclaimed ownership by correcting every small violation did order return.

Commissary is not simply food and hygiene items. It is potential currency. And currency in inmate hands without staff control always becomes power. Staff must understand that every trade is a signal, and every signal ignored is a window surrendered.

Case Study 3: The Contraband Phone

Contraband is one of the most dangerous forces inside correctional facilities. It undermines staff authority, fuels inmate power, and links the inside world to the outside. Among all types of contraband, cell phones are especially destructive. They provide unmonitored communication, access to criminal networks, and the ability to coordinate violence or escape. This case from a state prison in the South illustrates how small lapses in supervision allowed a phone to circulate unchecked, ultimately leading to an organized escape attempt.

The Setting

The prison held more than 2,000 inmates across multiple housing units. Staffing shortages were chronic, and officers were stretched thin. Contraband control relied on routine searches, inmate tips, and occasional shakedowns. While staff were vigilant about weapons and drugs, cell phones were often viewed as "hard to find" and at times treated as lower priority.

In one medium-security unit, inmates had begun hiding a contraband phone. At first, the phone was shared quietly among a small group. They used it for calls to family and girlfriends, conversations that avoided monitored facility lines. Officers suspected something was wrong when they noticed inmates whispering about "outside calls," but no searches uncovered the device.

Because no immediate problems surfaced, staff attention drifted elsewhere. That drift proved costly.

The Growth of the Network

Over several weeks, the phone's use expanded. What began as a few personal calls turned into organized communication with outside contacts. The inmates began coordinating contraband deliveries, arranging money transfers, and sharing facility intelligence. The phone was passed between inmates like currency, with time on the device traded for commissary items or favors.

Staff noticed hints: inmates lingering in corners, covering cameras with shirts, or gathering in unusual groups. But those behaviors were explained away. Officers told themselves that if the phone were real, it would have caused problems by now.

The tolerance of small suspicious behaviors, unexplained gatherings, brief camera obstructions, and whispered references created the environment where the contraband phone thrived.

The Escalation

Within two months, the phone had become the hub of an organized network. Outside contacts used it to coordinate contraband drops near the facility. Inmates arranged for staff manipulation and even attempted to blackmail a correctional officer through information gathered online.

The most dangerous development was escape planning. Inmates used the phone to coordinate with outside accomplices about transportation, timing, and tools. Maps of the facility were drawn, escape routes discussed, and supplies arranged. All of it happened through a device that staff suspected but never found.

The phone had moved from a convenience to a weapon.

The Discovery

The crisis came when intelligence officers intercepted a tip from an outside law enforcement agency. A vehicle had been stopped near the facility, and inside were wire cutters, civilian clothes, and cash. The driver admitted he was waiting for instructions from inmates inside.

The facility launched a full-scale shakedown. After hours of searching, officers discovered the contraband phone hidden inside a false panel in a cell vent. Records revealed hundreds of calls and text messages over several weeks. The phone had been used not only for contraband but for escape planning.

The escape was stopped, but only narrowly. The investigation concluded that the failure was not simply the phone but the tolerance of signals. Officers had noticed camera obstructions, strange gatherings, and whispered references but had dismissed them as minor. Each ignored signal was a broken window. Together, they created an opening for organized escape.

The Reset

The prison responded aggressively. Contraband sweeps were intensified. Staff were retrained to treat small suspicious behaviors as serious signals, not nuisances. Supervisors emphasized that phones were not "just communication devices" but threats to safety.

The administration also reinforced consistent enforcement. Officers were told explicitly that camera obstruction, unusual inmate gatherings, and unexplained behavior would no longer be tolerated. Every signal would be addressed. The reset shifted culture, reducing opportunities for phones to circulate undetected.

Lessons from the Contraband Phone

1. **Phones are not privileges.** A contraband phone is as dangerous as a weapon. It connects inmates to unmonitored criminal networks.
2. **Minor lapses create openings.** Camera obstruction, strange gatherings, and whispered conversations are signals that must be corrected immediately.
3. **Tolerance multiplies danger.** Staff rationalization, "it's just suspicious behavior," allowed the phone to thrive.
4. **Intelligence depends on detail.** Every ignored detail weakens security. Every enforced detail strengthens it.
5. **Reset requires unity.** Staff must treat all contraband, especially phones, as urgent. Inmates must see consistency across all posts.

Reflection

The contraband phone case demonstrates that escapes and major crises rarely appear suddenly. They grow out of tolerated details. Officers saw signals, unusual gatherings, covered cameras, whispers, but ignored them. Each ignored detail was a broken window. Inmates interpreted those windows as permission. The result was an organized escape plan.

Corrections professionals must understand that contraband control is not about occasional shakedowns alone. It is about daily ownership of details. Every suspicious act is a signal. Every signal ignored is an opening. Phones do not appear in a vacuum. They thrive in cultures where small lapses are tolerated.

The lesson is clear. Staff must treat every detail as significant. The difference between control and collapse is never one dramatic moment. It is dozens of small signals ignored until collapse occurs. Broken Windows reminds us that those signals are the windows. Repaired, they communicate order. Ignored, they invite chaos.

Analysis: The Compounding Effect of Neglected Details

The case studies in this chapter reveal a consistent truth: small infractions are never small. Each is a signal, and signals multiply. A single inmate refusing lockdown communicated that refusal was possible, and within weeks, twenty inmates defied staff together. A few ignored commissary trades grew into a black market controlled by gangs, with violence as enforcement. A contraband phone, tolerated because signals were overlooked, evolved into a hub for organized crime and an escape attempt.

The Broken Windows Theory explains why this happens. Disorder tolerated becomes disorder multiplied. In corrections, that multiplication is faster and more severe because inmates live in compressed environments, sharing information instantly. What takes months to escalate in a neighborhood can escalate in days inside a pod.

The lesson is clear. Corrections professionals must stop seeing small infractions as nuisances and start seeing them as messages. Each ignored detail communicates tolerance. Each enforced detail communicates ownership. The choices staff make daily—enforce or tolerate—determine whether order or disorder multiplies.

Why Early Intervention Shapes Expectations

Inmate behavior is shaped by expectations. When staff correct minor violations immediately, inmates adjust. They learn that staff own the environment and that rules are non-negotiable. Resistance may be strong at first, but it declines when inmates realize consistency is real.

When staff ignore minor violations, inmates adjust differently. They learn that rules are flexible, that some officers can be pressured, and that boundaries are negotiable. Resistance increases, not decreases.

Early intervention matters because it sets expectations. Once expectations shift toward tolerance, recovery is difficult and costly.

The Cultural Cost of Hesitation

Hesitation is one of the most dangerous signals staff can send. When officers hesitate to enforce rules, inmates interpret it as weakness. When supervisors hesitate to back officers, staff lose confidence. Every hesitation is magnified because inmates observe carefully.

The refused lockdown began with hesitation. The officer, unsure of supervisor support, let an inmate linger. That hesitation multiplied into group defiance. The contraband phone thrived because staff hesitated to investigate unusual behavior. Hesitation is always read as tolerance.

Corrections professionals must recognize that hesitation is not neutrality. It is a broken window.

How Inmates Multiply Disorder

Inmates are not passive recipients of tolerance. They actively multiply disorder when they see opportunity:

- One ignored refusal becomes group defiance because inmates encourage each other.
- One ignored commissary trade becomes a gang-controlled economy because inmates organize around profit.
- One ignored suspicious act becomes an escape plan because inmates use small openings to build networks.

Staff may see minor infractions as isolated. Inmates see them as invitations.

Balancing Firmness and Fairness

Firm enforcement of details does not mean harshness. It means consistency. Inmates respect officers who are firm but fair. They resist officers who are harsh or arbitrary. The key is balance:

- **Firmness:** Every infraction is corrected. Rules are enforced consistently.
- **Fairness:** Enforcement is professional, not personal. Discipline is applied evenly, without favoritism or bias.

Firmness without fairness creates resentment and rebellion. Fairness without firmness creates tolerance and disorder. Both must exist together.

Supervisors as Multipliers

Supervisors are the amplifiers of culture. When they back officers who enforce rules, confidence grows and enforcement multiplies. When they undermine officers or tolerate disorder, hesitation spreads and tolerance multiplies.

Supervisors must recognize that their role is not only to enforce rules but to set the example for how rules are enforced. They are the link between policy and practice. Every decision they make sends a message not only to inmates but to staff.

Tools and Takeaways

1. Treat Every Infraction as a Signal

- ☐ Lockdown refusals, commissary trades, graffiti, and contraband are not small issues.
- ☐ Each communicates whether staff own the environment or inmates do.
- ☐ Correct every infraction consistently to send the message of ownership.

2. Enforce Lockdowns Relentlessly

- ☐ Require immediate compliance. Do not tolerate delays.
- ☐ Supervisors must be present during lockdowns regularly.
- ☐ Discipline even minor refusals to prevent group defiance.

Lockdowns are sacred. They are non-negotiable.

3. Control Commissary Trades Early

- ☐ Confiscate traded items immediately.
- ☐ Track patterns of large purchases and unusual stockpiles.
- ☐ Educate staff that trades are not harmless but the foundation of black markets.

Every soup or cookie swapped without correction is a step toward gang control.

4. Treat Suspicious Behavior as Contraband Signals

- ☐ Camera obstruction, unusual gatherings, and whispered references are red flags.
- ☐ Search proactively when signals appear.
- ☐ Reinforce that contraband phones are as dangerous as weapons.

Suspicious behavior tolerated is contraband multiplied.

5. Back Officers Consistently

- ☐ Supervisors must support officers who enforce details, even if inmates complain.
- ☐ Corrections can be addressed privately later, but public support is essential.
- ☐ Inmates watch unity among staff as closely as enforcement.

Hesitation destroys confidence. Unity builds it.

6. Balance Firmness with Fairness

- ☐ Be consistent, not harsh.
- ☐ Apply rules evenly across all inmates.
- ☐ Avoid favoritism, which communicates that enforcement is negotiable.

Firm and fair enforcement creates respect.

7. Train Staff to See Escalation Pathways

- ☐ Use case studies to show how ignored infractions grow into crises.
- ☐ Reinforce that the "battle not picked today" becomes tomorrow's riot.
- ☐ Teach staff that every infraction is part of a larger pattern.

Awareness prevents tolerance.

8. Reset Culture Quickly When Cracks Appear

- ☐ Do not wait for collapse to intervene.
- ☐ Reinforce policy immediately when drift is noticed.
- ☐ Use presence, consistency, and discipline to send a reset signal.

Cracks widen fast. Repairs must be faster.

Reflection

The case studies in this chapter prove that minor infractions are never minor. They are the seeds of collapse or the seeds of order, depending on how staff respond. The Broken Windows Theory teaches that small cracks spread into larger failures. In corrections, those cracks spread with alarming speed.

Staff must learn to see each infraction as a window. Enforced quickly, it communicates ownership. Ignored, it invites escalation. The refused lockdown became group defiance. The commissary trade became a black market. The contraband phone became an escape plan.

The difference between safety and crisis was never the size of the infraction. It was the staff response. Corrections is not about tolerating disorder in the name of peace. It is about enforcing details in the name of order. Ownership belongs to staff. Every day, in every pod, the choice remains the same: repair the window, or watch it break.

- 6 -

INCENTIVIZING COMPLIANCE AND ORDERLY CONDUCT

Corrections is built on standards. Doors must be secure, counts must be accurate, movement must be controlled, and housing units must remain clean and orderly. These are the foundations of custody—and the foundations of culture. A jail communicates what it values not through slogans or mission statements, but through the daily details that staff enforce or ignore.

The Broken Windows Theory explains why small details matter. If a broken window is left unrepaired, people conclude that nobody cares and disorder spreads. The same logic applies inside a cell block. A towel stuffed in a window, graffiti scratched into a table, or trash left in the dayroom are not isolated annoyances. They are messages. If ignored, they signal that order is optional. When staff pass by disorder without addressing it, they quietly tell inmates that details do not matter.

Discipline Alone Cannot Carry Culture

Discipline is the traditional answer to disorder. Officers write reports, supervisors assign sanctions, and administrators enforce penalties. Discipline is necessary. It makes clear that disorder has a cost. But discipline alone cannot carry a facility. If the only time staff act is when rules are broken, inmates learn that misbehavior is the quickest way to get noticed. The strongest signal they hear is that disruption brings attention, while compliance is invisible.

Incentives balance this equation. They communicate that order is not taken for granted. When compliance is tied directly to access, inmates learn that staff not only punish disorder but also reinforce stability. Incentives are not handouts or extras. They are the structure that locks privileges behind compliance. Televisions, telephones, tablets, and commissary are part of general population, but they are never unconditional. They remain tied to order.

How Incentives Shape Daily Life

This distinction is not abstract. Consider the routine of a housing unit. Inmates finish meals and leave trays on tables. Officers can either ignore the mess or demand it be cleaned immediately. If ignored, the message is that sanitation does not matter. If enforced and followed by continued access to privileges, the message is that sanitation is the condition of normal life. One path multiplies disorder. The other multiplies order.

The psychology behind this is straightforward. People repeat what is noticed. If staff notice only disorder, inmates will repeat disorder. If staff notice compliance and tie it to privileges, inmates will repeat compliance. Even small signals carry weight in a compressed environment like a jail. Inmates have limited choices, so minor privileges matter. The ability to watch television, use a phone, access a tablet, or purchase commissary items is enough to influence daily behavior when those privileges are tied to order.

Conditional Access vs. Entitlement

Staff often resist this idea. Many officers argue that inmates should comply because it is the rule, not because privileges are tied to it. They believe incentives amount to rewarding people for doing what they should already be doing. On the surface, that argument feels logical. In practice, it misses the point. The privileges already exist in general population. The question is not whether inmates should have them. The question is whether access remains unconditional, or whether it is always tied to compliance.

Unconditional access erodes authority. If inmates keep televisions and phones regardless of whether they meet sanitation standards, follow counts, or comply with lockdowns, then privileges become entitlements. Staff may still discipline inmates after the fact, but the daily message is that privileges are permanent. Conditional access reinforces authority. Inmates learn that disorder closes access, and compliance restores it. Privileges are not entitlements—they are cultural reinforcers.

Broken Windows and Cultural Signals

The Broken Windows Theory makes this clear. On the street, a broken window left unrepaired tells the community that disorder is tolerated. A piece of graffiti left untouched tells gangs that territory is theirs. Trash piling up tells everyone that nobody is paying attention. In jail, the same signals exist. If a dirty shower is ignored, it tells inmates that staff do not care. If a towel remains stuffed in a window, it tells inmates that staff missed it or decided it was not worth enforcing. When these details go unchecked, inmates adjust. They push further, testing how much disorder is tolerated.

Now apply incentives. Imagine a housing unit where every shift begins with a sanitation inspection. If the unit passes, televisions, phones, tablets, and commissary remain available. If it fails, privileges pause until order is restored. The message is constant and clear: compliance keeps access, disorder closes it. The signal is as powerful as fixing a broken window on the street the moment it cracks. It tells everyone that order matters.

Clarity Protects Staff

Officers may see this as adding another task, but in practice it reduces conflict. Instead of arguing about whether a shower is "clean enough" or whether trash is "really a problem," staff have a simple structure. The inspection determines compliance. If the unit fails, privileges pause. When the unit complies, privileges return. No arguments, no bargaining, no room for inconsistency. The process speaks louder than words.

This clarity is also a protection for staff. Inmates are experts at spotting inconsistency. They notice when one officer enforces a rule and another ignores it. They share information instantly across units. Inconsistent enforcement becomes leverage, and leverage becomes manipulation. A structured incentive system removes this leverage by applying the same outcome every time. It protects staff from being placed in the role of negotiator and keeps authority in the policy, not the individual.

Incentives vs. Bribes

The greatest danger is when incentives collapse into bribes. A bribe is offered reactively, usually in desperation to stop a disturbance. A lieutenant promises extra commissary if a pod locks down, or extra phone time if inmates quiet down. The signal is disastrous. It communicates that disruption has value. Inmates learn that misbehavior is currency, and soon every unit begins testing how much it can buy. A single bribe can undo months of discipline.

Incentives are the opposite. They are proactive, built into the daily rhythm of the facility. They are tied to compliance already in place, not to disorder in progress. They require no negotiation, no promises, no improvisation. They do not reward inmates for doing the minimum. They reinforce the idea that privileges exist only when the environment remains orderly. The difference between incentives and bribes is the difference between reinforcing authority and surrendering it.

Cleaning and Collective Responsibility

Cleaning provides the clearest example. Some facilities assign housemen to manage sanitation. On the surface, this seems efficient. Floors are mopped, tables are wiped, showers are scrubbed. Inspections are passed. But the cultural signal is wrong. Inmates learn that sanitation is someone else's job. General population treats its environment as disposable. Responsibility is outsourced, and with it goes ownership.

Sanitation must be collective. Each inmate must clean his cell, and each unit must maintain its common areas. Officers must inspect every shift, and privileges must remain conditional on those inspections. When staff enforce this structure, the environment communicates ownership. Inmates learn that they cannot live in disorder and still keep access. They pressure each other to maintain compliance because they do not want to lose privileges as a group. Peer pressure bends toward order.

Culture Is Built Daily

This is not about making jail easy. It is about making jail consistent. Inmates will test staff every day, in small and large ways. They want to know if rules can be bent, if details can be ignored, if disorder can be tolerated. Staff responses to these tests shape culture. Discipline tells inmates that disorder has consequences. Incentives tell inmates that compliance has value. Together they create a balanced system where order is not just enforced but sustained.

The introduction of incentives into daily operations is not a sign of weakness. It is a recognition of how culture forms. A jail without incentives relies entirely on discipline, and over time that reliance breeds cynicism. A jail that confuses incentives with bribes undermines itself, teaching inmates that disruption has value. The correct approach is structured, consistent, and measurable. Privileges remain locked behind compliance, and no negotiation can open the gate.

Case Studies Preview

This chapter explores how facilities succeed or fail depending on how they handle this balance. The following case studies show three paths:

1. The cultural collapse that follows a single concession.
2. How reliance on housemen corrodes responsibility and spreads disorder.
3. How vague standards fuel conflict instead of reducing it.

Together, they prove that incentives are not optional extras. They are essential cultural tools. But like any tool, they must be wielded with precision.

Case Study 1: The Riot That Paid

Echo pod had a reputation. It was not the most violent unit, but it was loud, slow to comply, and consistently a step behind expectations. Trash collected in the corners of the dayroom, graffiti appeared on the walls, and lockdown orders were met with complaints and delay. Officers described Echo as "manageable but frustrating," a pod that never caused a crisis but always flirted with one.

The culture was predictable. Officers gave orders. Inmates responded late, or only after being told twice. Small infractions went unchecked because staff were busy escorting medical runs, processing commissary, and logging count sheets. When officers cleaned up trash themselves, Echo learned the lesson: if they waited long enough, someone else would do it for them.

The Standoff

One Tuesday night, the 2100 lockdown order went out. Half the cells shut their doors. The rest remained open. Inmates stood in the doorways, pounding on the metal and shouting that they would not comply.

The control officer called the sergeant, who arrived and repeated the order. The noise grew louder. Some inmates shouted that they wanted "something in return" before they would lock down. Others laughed and told officers they had no reason to comply.

The lieutenant arrived within minutes. She knew she had two choices. She could order extractions and prepare for reports, video review, and possible injuries. Or she could look for a quick resolution. She chose the second. Over the intercom she told Echo that if they locked down immediately, the pod would receive an extra hour of television the next night and additional commissary items on Thursday.

The effect was instant. Within five minutes, the doors closed. Staff were relieved. The lieutenant believed she had resolved the problem without force. But the signal had already been sent.

The Spread

By morning, word of Echo's deal spread across the jail. Inmates in Bravo pod asked if they could also get extra television "for being good." When the officer said no, they pointed out that Echo had refused lockdown and still received privileges.

Two weeks later, Bravo staged its own refusal. They demanded that phones remain on late into the night. After hours of noise, a captain approved the request to restore calm. Bravo got what it wanted.

Within a month, three different units had refused lockdowns. None turned into riots. None produced serious injuries. But all ended in negotiation. Inmates learned that disruption had value. Staff learned that enforcement was not consistent. The jail's culture shifted.

The Cultural Collapse

The real damage was not in the noise or the late lockdowns. The damage was in the signal. Echo had taught the population that privileges could be earned through disruption. Bravo proved it again.

Officers who had enforced rules consistently began to question why. Why write reports if leadership would give the same inmates television the next day? Why correct details if defiance earned commissary? The system had reversed itself. Disorder had become the path to reward.

Inmates adapted quickly. When commissary delivery was late, they joked about refusing lockdown. When shower time was shortened by a maintenance issue, they discussed "making noise until we get something back." Defiance became a bargaining chip.

The Reset

Eventually the administration recognized the damage. A new directive was issued: no privilege would ever be promised or granted in response to misbehavior. If a unit failed to comply with sanitation, counts, or lockdown orders, televisions, telephones, tablets, and commissary access would pause until compliance was restored.

The next time Echo tested lockdown, the extraction team was staged. Doors were secured one by one. A few inmates received disciplinary reports. Privileges were paused until the unit passed inspection and complied with orders. There were no concessions.

The resistance faded. Inmates saw that the rules had changed. Disorder brought only consequences. Compliance restored privileges, nothing more.

Lessons Learned

The riot that paid left scars. It showed how quickly a single sentence can reshape an entire facility. When staff offered privileges to end a disturbance, inmates learned that misbehavior carried value. Other units copied the lesson, and authority collapsed.

The fix required a hard reset. Concessions were eliminated. Privileges were tied only to compliance. Staff were told to enforce standards consistently, even when it meant confrontation. Inmates saw that culture had shifted back toward stability.

The case of Echo remains a lesson across corrections: never buy peace with privileges. Once disorder becomes a currency, the entire jail begins to trade in it.

Case Study 2: The Houseman Trap

At first glance, Riverside County Jail looked orderly. Floors shined, tables were clear, and the showers had the smell of bleach instead of mildew. Inspectors noted the cleanliness, and supervisors praised the staff. To anyone walking through, sanitation seemed to be a strength.

The truth was less stable. The facility relied on housemen—two or three inmate workers assigned to each housing unit responsible for sweeping, mopping, scrubbing showers, and wiping tables. Staff leaned on them heavily. When a unit inspection was scheduled, housemen knew to scrub every corner. When trash piled up, officers called the houseman to clean it. For a time, this arrangement seemed to work.

But order built on a few shoulders is fragile.

Outsourced Responsibility

General population inmates quickly adopted a simple attitude: *"That is the houseman's job."* Cups and wrappers were left on tables. Toilets in cells went unscrubbed. Showers grew filthy within hours of heavy use. Inmates treated sanitation as someone else's duty because, in their minds, it was.

Housemen grew resentful. They were responsible for cleaning up after dozens of men who ignored the standards themselves. Some demanded favors or commissary from peers in exchange for cleaning. Others embraced the role as a way to gain influence. Both dynamics created division inside the pod.

Worse still, the responsibility gap showed in the environment. Showers that were scrubbed at 0900 smelled of mildew by evening. Trash cans overflowed at night because housemen were not scheduled to work again until morning. Sanitation became episodic rather than constant.

The Outbreak

The consequences surfaced during a flu outbreak. In a two-week span, sick call requests for fever, stomach illness, and headaches tripled. Two housing units had to be placed on modified movement. Medical staff searched for the source, expecting a spoiled meal or water issue. What they found instead was neglect in sanitation.

Cell toilets were ringed with stains that had clearly built up over time. Dayroom floors had sticky patches where drinks had spilled and never been mopped. Trash was left behind after meals. The housemen worked hard, but they were outnumbered and overwhelmed. The population had abdicated responsibility, and the result was illness.

The outbreak showed the flaw in the system. Outsourcing sanitation meant the jail looked clean during inspections but was failing in daily maintenance. Housemen could not carry the load for an entire unit.

The Reset

Administration ended the practice. A new policy was introduced: every inmate is responsible for his own cell, and the unit is collectively responsible for common areas.

Housemen were reassigned to handle non-routine jobs such as biohazard cleanups, maintenance spills, and heavy scrubbing after incidents. But the daily sweeping, mopping, and wiping down of tables was returned to the population.

Sanitation checks were conducted every shift. If a unit failed, televisions, telephones, tablets, and commissary access were paused until standards were restored. The message was clear: compliance meant privileges stayed. Noncompliance meant privileges paused.

Resistance and Adjustment

At first, inmates resisted. Many said they would not clean, claiming it was "trustee work." Some refused altogether. But when phones and tablets were shut off after failed inspections, attitudes changed.

Peer pressure became the deciding factor. Inmates who dragged their feet were pressured by others who wanted privileges back. Showers were scrubbed, floors swept, and tables wiped down not because staff demanded it alone, but because inmates knew their own access was on the line.

Within weeks, the system became routine. Inmates cleaned daily. Privileges remained open as long as compliance was verified.

Long-Term Impact

The change in sanitation standards had ripple effects. Showers stayed cleaner through the evening. Trash was removed quickly. Noise levels dropped in units where privileges were steady. Medical staff reported a decline in sick call volume tied to stomach illness.

The resentment toward housemen disappeared. No longer seen as janitors for the unit, they focused on specialized cleaning tasks and no longer carried the burden of daily sanitation. General population inmates recognized that cleanliness was their own responsibility, not someone else's.

Lessons Learned

Riverside showed how dangerous it is to outsource responsibility. Housemen created the illusion of order, but the culture underneath was hollow. When only a few owned sanitation, the rest neglected it. Illness spread, resentment grew, and staff authority weakened.

The fix was simple but firm: return responsibility to everyone. Tie access to televisions, telephones, tablets, and commissary to compliance with sanitation standards. Make inspections daily and enforce the consequences immediately. Order improved not because housemen cleaned harder, but because the population had no choice but to comply.

Reflection

The houseman trap proved that order cannot be carried by a few. When inmates are allowed to treat compliance as someone else's duty, they stop owning their environment. The jail becomes reactive instead of stable.

Sanitation is not cosmetic. It is cultural. A clean unit communicates ownership, discipline, and pride. A dirty unit communicates neglect, indifference, and weakness. The lesson is clear: compliance must be collective. Responsibility cannot be outsourced.

Case Study 3: The Quiet Hours Failure

Fairview City Jail held over 1,200 inmates across multiple pods and dormitories. Like many large facilities, its biggest cultural challenge was noise. Dayrooms echoed with overlapping voices, televisions blared over shouting matches, and inmates slammed doors to get staff attention. Officers often had to raise their own voices to issue basic orders.

Noise itself did not pose a direct security threat, but it undermined the environment. Officers finished shifts exhausted and struggled to be heard. Tensions rose among inmates irritated by the volume. Complaints from nearby pods came daily. Leadership believed change was necessary and decided to test a program they hoped would bring relief.

The Program

The initiative was called "Quiet Hours." Leadership instructed that between 1900 and 2100, housing units were to keep volume at what they called "acceptable levels." Units that complied would receive an additional hour of television and expanded access to commissary.

On paper, the plan looked promising. Televisions and commissary were privileges inmates valued, and leadership believed tying them to calmer evenings would lower tensions and make units more manageable. But the design was flawed from the start.

The Problem with "Acceptable"

The program's weakness was in its wording. "Acceptable noise" was never defined. Officers were left to interpret the standard however they chose. Some allowed talking and laughter as long as it did not spiral into chaos. Others expected near silence.

By the second night, differences in interpretation caused problems. One pod earned extended television even though the volume was high. Another pod was denied privileges despite being quieter. Inmates noticed immediately.

The inconsistency bred resentment. Units accused staff of playing favorites and argued over what "acceptable" meant. Officers faced constant disputes defending standards that had never been clearly written.

Manipulation and Gamesmanship

Inmates adapted quickly. Some learned which officers were lenient and raised their volume during those shifts. Others intentionally grew louder when stricter officers were on duty to ensure privileges would be denied and blame would fall on staff.

A few inmates cut deals. They promised officers that the pod would stay quieter if they were guaranteed television time, even if the unit failed to meet the program's intent. Others argued for commissary privileges because they had "tried hard," not because they were truly compliant. The structured program collapsed into bargaining.

Division Among Staff

Uneven enforcement fractured staff. Some officers rewarded pods freely to avoid confrontation. Others withheld privileges and insisted on stricter standards. Supervisors struggled to support staff because there was no clear policy to reference. Inmates exploited the cracks, playing lenient officers against strict ones and sowing division between shifts.

The original goal had been to reduce tension. Instead, tension multiplied.

Escalation

The program raised noise rather than lowering it. Inmates shouted across dayrooms that they had "earned" privileges. Others threatened to riot if television time was denied.

The breaking point came when two pods clashed. One had been rewarded despite being loud. Another quieter pod had been denied. Inmates from both units encountered each other in the recreation yard and fought over claims of favoritism. Several were injured.

Even inmates not directly involved lost trust. They argued the program was a scam designed to create division. The jail had aimed to calm evenings but instead sparked violence and distrust.

The Reset

Administration canceled Quiet Hours. A facility-wide announcement clarified that privileges would no longer be tied to vague standards. Televisions, phones, tablets, and commissary would remain available only when measurable compliance was verified.

The new approach was simple. Was the unit clean? Were counts correct? Did the pod meet lockdown time? These facts could be checked, not interpreted.

Once the change was made, disputes declined almost immediately. Officers reported fewer conflicts at night. Inmates understood the rules because they were no longer tied to opinion. If sanitation failed, privileges paused. If compliance returned, privileges reopened.

The Cultural Damage

The real damage from Quiet Hours was not just the noise or the fight between pods. It was the message the program sent. Inmates saw that staff could not agree on standards. They saw that privileges could be negotiated. They saw that compliance was flexible.

Once that perception set in, it took months to reverse. Supervisors retrained officers, reinforced clear rules, and emphasized that incentives must always be tied to measurable compliance. Every shift was instructed to apply the same standard so inmates could not pit one officer against another.

The lesson was costly. What began as a well-intentioned idea ended up creating division, resentment, and violence.

Lessons Learned

The Fairview case proved that vague standards destroy credibility. Incentives cannot rest on words like "acceptable" or "reasonable." They must be tied to clear, visible facts. Was the unit clean? Did the count clear? Did lockdown occur on time? These are measurable conditions.

The failure also showed how quickly inconsistency spreads. Once inmates saw that officers disagreed, they exploited the differences. Staff lost credibility not because they failed to enforce, but because the standard had no meaning.

Finally, Fairview showed that when programs collapse into bargaining, inmates gain leverage. A privilege becomes a chip to trade. Staff authority erodes, and culture bends toward manipulation.

Reflection

Quiet Hours was born from good intentions but collapsed under poor design. It replaced order with confusion, consistency with favoritism, and structure with bargaining. It stands as proof that vague incentives are worse than none at all.

The lesson is clear. Incentives must be tied to measurable compliance. They must be enforced consistently across shifts. Standards must never be left open to interpretation. When standards are clear, privileges reinforce authority. When standards are vague, privileges undermine it.

Analysis

The three case studies show how incentives can either reinforce order or unravel it depending on how they are applied.

- **The Riot That Paid** proved that concessions during a disturbance destroy authority. Once inmates learned that refusing lockdown earned extra privileges, the culture shifted overnight. That single decision turned disorder into a bargaining chip, leaving staff to chase compliance instead of setting the terms of it.

- **The Houseman Trap** demonstrated that order cannot be outsourced. By placing responsibility for sanitation on a few inmate workers, the jail signaled that standards belonged to someone else. The rest of the population neglected their own spaces, illness spread, and resentment grew. When responsibility was returned to every inmate, compliance became collective, and culture improved.

- **The Quiet Hours Failure** revealed the danger of vague standards. Incentives tied to "acceptable noise" collapsed because staff could not enforce what had never been clearly defined. Inmates exploited the ambiguity, favoritism became an accusation, and tensions escalated into violence. Once again, the message was clear: incentives only work when tied to facts that are visible and measurable.

Across all three examples, the lesson is the same: incentives are not gifts and they are not bribes. They are tools that reinforce compliance when built into the daily structure of the jail. Privileges like televisions, telephones, tablets, and commissary cannot be unconditional. They must be tied directly to compliance with sanitation, counts, lockdowns, and schedules.

When staff enforce details firmly and consistently, and when compliance is required for privileges to remain, inmates stop looking for ways to manipulate the system. Disorder loses its value. Compliance becomes the only path forward.

Tools and Takeaways

1. **Never negotiate.** Do not offer privileges during a disturbance. Once a privilege is traded for peace, disorder becomes currency.
2. **Tie access to compliance.** Televisions, telephones, tablets, and commissary remain available only when sanitation, counts, and lockdown standards are met.
3. **Inspect every shift.** Sanitation and compliance must be checked consistently. Failures pause privileges until compliance is restored.
4. **Keep standards measurable.** Tie outcomes to facts that can be verified, not opinions that vary by shift.
5. **Be consistent.** Apply the same rules across all housing units and shifts. Inmates exploit differences instantly.
6. **Act immediately.** If a unit fails inspection, pause privileges right away. Delays weaken credibility.
7. **Require collective ownership.** Every inmate cleans his cell, and the unit is responsible for common areas. No one cleans for the group.
8. **Use peer pressure.** Make it clear that privileges depend on the group meeting standards. Inmates will pressure each other to comply.
9. **Train staff.** Officers must know the difference between incentives and bribes and be able to explain it clearly.
10. **Document outcomes.** Record pauses and restorations of privileges. Documentation protects staff and reinforces fairness.

Reflection

Incentives in corrections are not extras—they are part of the cultural framework that determines whether order holds or falls apart. Misused, they weaken authority, create bargaining chips, and spread disorder. Used correctly, they reinforce staff control, align peer pressure with compliance, and make order the norm.

The balance is simple: discipline corrects disorder; incentives reinforce compliance. Together they create respect. When staff notice everything, correct failures immediately, and keep privileges tied to compliance, culture bends toward stability and authority remains in the hands of those who must hold it.

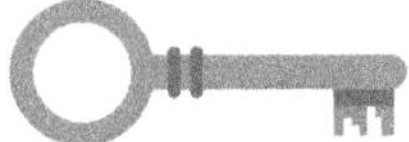

- 7 -

CLEANLINESS AS THE FIRST LINE OF ORDER

Why Cleanliness Matters

Every correctional facility tells a story the moment someone walks inside. Visitors, staff, and inmates alike can read the culture of a jail or prison in seconds by looking at the floors, the walls, and the air itself. Is the unit clean, or filthy? Are showers maintained, or do they reek of mildew? Are walls freshly painted, or covered in graffiti? Each detail communicates a message.

Cleanliness is not cosmetic. It is cultural. A clean jail communicates staff ownership, professionalism, and safety. A dirty jail communicates neglect, weakness, and disorder. Inmates are experts at interpreting these signals—they know instantly whether staff care enough to maintain order.

The Broken Windows Theory explains why this matters. Just as a broken window left unrepaired invites more broken windows, a filthy shower left unattended invites more filth and disorder. Graffiti multiplies. Broken fixtures become symbols of indifference. In corrections, these signals spread faster than in neighborhoods because inmates live in compressed environments where every detail is noticed and shared.

Cleanliness is directly tied to safety. Dirty environments breed disease, pests, and resentment. Neglected facilities provide cover for contraband, from hidden drugs to improvised weapons. Inmates who see staff tolerating filth conclude that other rules are negotiable as well. Disorder in the environment invites disorder in behavior.

The opposite is true. Clean environments communicate staff control. When inmates see graffiti removed immediately, floors polished daily, and showers sanitized regularly, they understand staff ownership. Cleanliness becomes a daily demonstration of order.

Corrections professionals must treat sanitation as strategy, not chore. It is not about aesthetics—it is about culture. Cleanliness is one of the most powerful tools for enforcing Broken Windows principles because the environment itself becomes the window: repaired, it signals order; ignored, it signals collapse.

The Link Between Physical Disorder and Behavioral Disorder

One of the most important insights of the Broken Windows Theory is that environments shape behavior. Disorder in the physical environment sends signals that rules do not matter and authority is weak. People respond to those signals, and disorder multiplies. In corrections, the connection between physical disorder and behavioral disorder is immediate and unmistakable.

The Environment as a Teacher

Inmates learn about a facility's culture not through handbooks, but through their surroundings:

- Graffiti-covered walls signal that property damage is tolerated.
- Dirty showers signal that sanitation is optional.

- Broken fixtures signal that maintenance and security are not priorities.
- Cluttered dayrooms signal that disorder is the norm.

When inmates see disorder, they act accordingly. They assume if staff do not care about walls or showers, they will not care about rules. The environment teaches behavior.

Disorder as Permission

Physical disorder is not neutral—it is permission. Each ignored detail is read as a signal of tolerance:

- A piece of graffiti ignored today becomes ten tomorrow.
- A broken window left unrepaired becomes a hiding place for contraband.
- Trash left in corners breeds vermin and resentment.
- Dirty showers provide reasons to challenge lockdowns.

Once that signal is sent, inmates begin asserting ownership themselves: marking territory, hiding contraband, and resisting staff direction.

The Pathway to Violence

Disorder in the environment often leads directly to violence:

- **Graffiti → Gang Conflict:** Symbols escalate into claims of territory, provoking fights.
- **Dirty Showers → Hostility:** Neglected conditions generate anger redirected at staff or peers.
- **Clutter → Contraband:** Disorder provides cover for hidden contraband, fueling debt, intimidation, and eventual violence.

Physical disorder is never cosmetic. It is cultural. Cultural disorder breeds violence.

Staff Stress and the Environment

Physical disorder affects staff as much as inmates. Dirty, graffiti-covered environments wear down morale. Officers working in filth feel unsupported and begin tolerating disorder themselves. Disorder in the environment becomes disorder in staff performance.

A staff member walking into a clean, orderly pod feels empowered. A staff member walking into a filthy, chaotic pod feels defeated before the shift begins. The environment is a silent partner, shaping morale as powerfully as policy.

Why Inmates Exploit Disorder

Inmates exploit disorder because it benefits them. Graffiti provides cover for communication. Broken vents hide contraband. Dirty dayrooms justify resisting staff orders. Disorder is opportunity. When staff ignore it, inmates use it to manipulate, creating footholds that grow into control.

Disorder Spreads Faster in Corrections

In neighborhoods, physical disorder may take weeks or months to spread. In corrections, it spreads in hours. Inmates live in constant contact, sharing information instantly. A single ignored graffiti mark is seen by dozens of eyes within minutes. A single ignored broken fixture is tested by dozens of hands within hours.

The speed of spread makes vigilance essential. Staff cannot afford to "let small things go." In corrections, small things become large things before the next shift begins.

Cleanliness as Prevention

The connection between physical and behavioral disorder makes cleanliness a tool for prevention. A clean, orderly environment removes opportunities for exploitation, communicates staff control, and reduces violence before it begins.

- Graffiti painted over immediately stops marking behavior.
- Showers scrubbed daily prevent resistance to sanitation orders.
- Clutter removed eliminates easy hiding places for contraband.

Cleanliness cuts off escalation pathways before they form.

Reflection on Disorder

The link between physical disorder and behavioral disorder is direct. Dirty facilities breed dirty behavior. Neglected environments breed neglected rules. Every broken fixture, every piece of graffiti, and every pile of trash communicates a message. The message is either staff ownership or staff indifference.

The Broken Windows Theory reminds us that every environment sends signals. In corrections, those signals are magnified by compression. Physical disorder is never cosmetic. It is always cultural, and culture determines safety.

Ownership of the Environment

A jail or prison is an ecosystem. Its condition communicates ownership: staff or inmates. There is no middle ground.

Ownership is about more than cleaning floors or painting walls. It is the daily message that staff set standards and enforce them. Inmates may assist, but they must never control it. True ownership rests with staff.

Why Staff Must Own Sanitation

Relying solely on inmate labor sends the wrong message. When standards rise or fall based on inmate motivation, the environment communicates inmate ownership. Graffiti left until inmates decide to clean erodes authority. Broken fixtures unrepaired because inmates delay reporting reduces staff control.

Sanitation cannot be optional or left to inmates alone. Staff must set standards, supervise work, and inspect results. Inmates can do the labor, but staff claim ownership.

The Role of Inspections

Inspections demonstrate ownership clearly:

1. **Consistency:** Daily, not occasional. Inmates must always see staff notice.
2. **Thoroughness:** Cover every detail—showers, vents, trash, tables, doors, ceilings.
3. **Follow-Through:** Correct violations immediately.

Inspections without follow-through signal that staff see disorder but do not care—worse than no inspection at all.

Inmate Work Programs Done Right

Inmate labor is valuable but must reinforce staff ownership:

- **Structured Assignments:** Specific duties with accountability communicate order.
- **Supervised Labor:** Officers or supervisors inspect all work.
- **Visible Standards:** Cleaning supplies, schedules, and checklists reinforce non-negotiable standards.

- **Recognition Without Concession:** Reward effort without favoritism.

Properly structured, inmate labor reinforces staff ownership instead of replacing it.

Respect, Not Resentment

Some officers assume inmates do not care about cleanliness, but this is often mistaken. Many inmates value order because it reduces pests, disease, and conflict. Resistance arises when standards are enforced inconsistently, not when they are applied fairly. When inmates observe staff enforcing sanitation daily, they respect the consistency. When clean pods earn recognition or privileges, peers pressure each other to comply. Respect comes not from tolerance but from clarity.

The Danger of Inmate-Controlled Sanitation

Trustees or porters who control cleaning independently communicate inmate ownership:

- Access to supplies becomes bargaining tools.
- Schedules are adjusted for allies.
- Contraband is hidden during cleaning shifts.
- Staff presence declines.

This is dangerous. When inmates own sanitation, staff lose credibility. Staff must claim ownership.

Supervisors and Ownership

Supervisors are the guardians of ownership. Officers may oversee daily cleaning, but supervisors ensure standards are maintained across all shifts. Their presence in housing units signals that cleanliness is not optional.

When supervisors walk pods regularly, addressing graffiti, trash, or broken fixtures, they send a clear message: staff notice everything. When supervisors ignore sanitation, they signal that standards do not matter. Inmates pick up on that signal immediately.

Supervisors who model ownership cultivate officers who enforce it. Supervisors who tolerate disorder produce officers who overlook it.

Ownership as Culture

Ownership must be internalized at all staff levels. Cleanliness is operational, not cosmetic. Inmates must see:

- Graffiti painted over immediately.
- Broken fixtures repaired quickly.
- Trash never left to accumulate.

Ownership is about daily signals, not perfection. Every day, staff must send the signal: this is our facility, and we own it.

Reflection on Ownership

The environment belongs to staff or inmates. There is no in-between. Ownership is communicated through details: clean floors, painted walls, working doors, scrubbed showers.

Inmates respect facilities owned by staff and exploit those owned by disorder. The Broken Windows Theory reminds us that every detail is a window: repaired quickly, it signals control; left broken, it signals opportunity.

Ownership is culture. Corrections professionals must claim it, enforce it, and live it daily.

Case Study 1: The Filthy Showers

Showers are among the most revealing spaces in a correctional facility. They are used daily, shared by dozens or hundreds of inmates, and difficult to maintain without constant attention. A well-kept shower communicates that staff own the environment and that sanitation is non-negotiable. A filthy shower communicates neglect, weakness, and tolerance of disorder.

This case from a large county jail in the Southeast shows how staff neglect in maintaining showers led to cultural breakdown, health hazards, and a crisis that required an expensive reset.

The Setting

The jail held more than 2,000 inmates across multiple housing pods. Each pod had two communal shower areas with tiled walls, concrete floors, and metal partitions. Maintenance staff were responsible for periodic deep cleaning, but daily upkeep was left to inmate workers. Officers were expected to check showers during rounds, but enforcement varied widely across shifts.

Over time, standards slipped. Inmates showered unsupervised. Cleaning schedules were irregular. Maintenance requests for broken drains and cracked tiles were delayed due to budget constraints. Slowly, showers became breeding grounds for mildew, graffiti, and trash.

Early Signs of Neglect

The first signals were cosmetic: dark stains on grout, lingering odors, and graffiti carved into partitions. Officers noticed but rarely acted. Inmates began complaining about unsanitary conditions, but complaints were dismissed as routine grumbling.

Soon, neglect became more serious. Trash clogged drains, leaving standing water on floors. Mold spread along walls. Water pressure declined due to unrepaired fixtures. Officers walked past these issues daily, assuming maintenance would eventually address them. Inmates, seeing indifference, stopped caring as well.

By this stage, showers had become disorder zones. Inmates lingered for hours, gambling, smoking contraband, and hiding items in broken tile gaps. Staff presence dwindled because officers dreaded entering the space.

The Escalation

Disorder in the showers quickly spread to behavior. Inmates interpreted staff tolerance of filth as tolerance of defiance. Smoking became routine. Graffiti escalated from crude drawings to gang symbols marking territory. Broken tiles were used to hide contraband, from tobacco to makeshift weapons.

Conflicts emerged as gangs claimed specific stalls as "theirs." Fights broke out when others challenged those claims. Staff, overwhelmed, began avoiding the area altogether. The showers, once a routine part of daily life, became a no-go zone for officers.

The final escalation was health-related. Several inmates developed skin infections linked to unsanitary conditions. A medical review concluded that poor sanitation contributed to the spread. Lawsuits were filed by families alleging neglect. The facility was forced to confront what had long been ignored.

The Crisis

The tipping point came when a major fight broke out inside one of the shower areas. Two gangs clashed over territory, using sharpened pieces of broken tile as weapons. Several inmates were injured, and staff had to deploy chemical agents to restore control. Media attention and public outrage followed when photos of the filthy showers surfaced.

The administration realized that the facility had lost not only control of the showers but also of the signals they communicated. Inmates saw filth as permission for misconduct. Staff saw filth as reason to disengage. Ownership had been abandoned, and the environment had collapsed into chaos.

The Reset

The reset was costly and difficult. Leadership closed the showers for two weeks while contractors replaced tiles, repaired drains, and repainted surfaces. Inmate workers, under close supervision, scrubbed every surface and disinfected every stall. Officers were retrained to check showers daily and enforce strict cleaning schedules.

Supervisors were ordered to inspect showers personally and document conditions each shift. Graffiti had to be removed within 24 hours. Broken fixtures had to be reported immediately and prioritized for repair.

At first, inmates resisted, mocking the sudden emphasis on cleanliness. But when staff enforced standards consistently and repaired damage promptly, behavior shifted. Graffiti declined. Contraband incidents dropped. Fights over shower territory ceased. Inmates began treating showers as functional spaces again.

Lessons from the Filthy Showers

1. **Sanitation is not optional.** Dirty showers are not cosmetic issues—they are signals of neglect that invite disorder.
2. **Delays communicate tolerance.** Maintenance problems left unaddressed become cultural problems.
3. **Filth provides cover.** Dirty environments give inmates opportunities to hide contraband and engage in misconduct.
4. **Health and safety are inseparable.** Unsanitary conditions invite lawsuits, medical issues, and public criticism.

5. **Resets are expensive.** Neglect that could have been prevented with daily attention required costly overhauls.

Reflection

The case of the filthy showers demonstrates the direct link between physical disorder and behavioral disorder. Staff thought they were saving time by tolerating filth and delaying repairs. In reality, they were creating a cultural and operational crisis.

The Broken Windows Theory explains why. Each piece of graffiti left in place, each drain left clogged, each mold patch ignored was a broken window. Together, they signaled that staff no longer owned the environment. Inmates seized ownership, and the result was chaos.

The lesson is simple. Cleanliness is not cosmetic. It is control. Corrections professionals must treat showers, floors, walls, and fixtures as operational priorities. Every detail communicates ownership. Every ignored detail communicates surrender.

Case Study 2: The Painted Reset

Sometimes the most powerful tool for resetting culture in a correctional facility is not a new policy or a disciplinary crackdown but a brush, a bucket of paint, and a mop. Cleanliness and physical renewal communicate ownership more clearly than any memo or speech. This case from a regional detention center in the Northeast shows how a full repainting and sanitation overhaul became a turning point for a housing pod drowning in disorder.

The Setting

The detention center housed 1,100 inmates across multiple pods. Pod C had long been a problem area. Designed for 80 inmates, it was usually filled to 100 or more. Sanitation had deteriorated badly over the years. Walls were covered in graffiti, paint was peeling, and the air smelled of mildew. Tables bore carvings and burns from cigarettes smuggled years earlier. Showers leaked constantly, and drains were clogged.

Staff avoided spending time in Pod C. Officers performed rounds quickly, avoiding eye contact. Supervisors rarely walked the unit. Inmates, recognizing the neglect, seized control of the space. They claimed tables, spread graffiti, and hid contraband in peeling wall paint and broken furniture.

The pod's physical condition became a symbol of staff surrender. Disorder was visible, and it bred more disorder.

The Breaking Point

The crisis came after a series of fights linked to gang disputes over graffiti-covered walls. Rival groups had been competing to mark their territory. When one group painted over another's symbols, violence followed. Officers reported that inmates openly mocked staff for failing to control the pod.

The administration realized that discipline alone could not fix the problem. Inmates had been sanctioned repeatedly, but sanctions had little effect because the environment itself communicated tolerance of disorder. Something more dramatic was needed.

The Reset Plan

The warden ordered a full reset of Pod C. Walls would be repainted, furniture replaced, showers repaired, and floors polished. Graffiti would be erased entirely. The goal was not just cosmetic improvement but cultural transformation.

The project was explained to both staff and inmates. Inmates were told that the reset marked a new standard: from that point forward, graffiti, filth, and neglect would not be tolerated. Staff were told that the environment would only stay clean if they enforced sanitation daily and corrected graffiti immediately. Supervisors were directed to walk Pod C personally each shift.

The message was clear: staff were reclaiming ownership of the environment.

The Transformation

The reset took two weeks. Contractors repaired fixtures, painted walls, and restored showers. Inmate work crews, supervised closely, scrubbed every surface. When the pod reopened, it looked like a different facility. Bright paint covered every wall. Floors shone. Tables were clean. The air smelled fresh.

The change was dramatic not just physically but psychologically. Inmates, accustomed to filth and neglect, walked into a pod that communicated staff ownership. Officers, previously demoralized, now walked the pod with confidence. Supervisors began making rounds consistently, pointing out even the smallest marks or pieces of trash.

The physical reset set the stage for a cultural reset.

Resistance and Enforcement

At first, some inmates resisted. Within days, graffiti appeared on a bathroom wall. In the past, staff might have overlooked it. This time, supervisors ordered immediate repainting. The responsible inmate was identified, disciplined, and reassigned to a less privileged housing unit.

Other inmates tested the new order by carving initials into a table. The same response followed: immediate correction, discipline, and repair. Inmates quickly realized the difference. Staff were serious, and graffiti would no longer be tolerated.

As enforcement proved consistent, resistance faded. Inmates began policing each other, pressuring peers not to ruin the pod for everyone. Graffiti declined sharply, and fights linked to territory disputes disappeared.

Cultural Impact

The Painted Reset transformed Pod C's culture. Inmates no longer saw the pod as theirs to deface. They saw it as staff-owned space. Sanitation improved dramatically. Trash was removed daily, showers were maintained, and walls stayed clean.

Staff morale rose as well. Officers no longer dreaded Pod C. They took pride in walking a clean, orderly unit. Supervisors used Pod C as an example, bringing visitors to show how a unit could be transformed through ownership of the environment.

The pod that had once been a symbol of disorder became a model of order.

Lessons from the Painted Reset

1. **Physical renewal is cultural renewal.** Repainting and sanitation overhaul reset more than walls—they reset expectations.
2. **Immediate correction is essential.** Every mark, every piece of graffiti, every broken fixture must be repaired immediately. Delay communicates tolerance.
3. **Staff must enforce the reset.** A clean environment collapses quickly if staff slip back into tolerance.
4. **Supervisors set the tone.** Their presence communicates seriousness. Their absence communicates surrender.
5. **Order multiplies.** Cleanliness reduced graffiti, which reduced fights, which improved morale. One reset transformed an entire culture.

Reflection

The Painted Reset shows how physical environments shape behavior. Pod C had collapsed because filth and graffiti communicated tolerance of disorder. Inmates claimed ownership, and staff retreated. The reset reclaimed ownership for staff.

The Broken Windows Theory explains the success. Each repainting was a repaired window. Each cleaned shower was a sealed crack. Each polished floor was a message that staff owned the pod. Inmates responded by adjusting behavior. Disorder no longer paid.

The lesson is clear. Sometimes the most powerful correctional strategy is not force or punishment but paint, soap, and consistency. Cleanliness is control, and control is culture.

Case Study 3: The Inmate-Run Sanitation Team

Sanitation programs are often viewed as chores to be managed, but when structured properly, they become cultural drivers. Cleanliness not only keeps facilities safe and healthy but also communicates staff ownership and inmate accountability. This case from a state correctional institution in the Midwest demonstrates how a carefully structured inmate-run sanitation team, overseen closely by staff, transformed housing unit culture, reduced contraband opportunities, and reinforced Broken Windows principles.

The Setting

The prison housed just over 1,600 inmates. The facility faced chronic sanitation problems: trash piled in corners, showers stained with mold, graffiti spreading across dayroom walls. Staff cleaned occasionally, but without consistent inmate involvement, conditions deteriorated quickly. Officers were frustrated, and supervisors struggled to enforce standards across so many housing units.

Leadership recognized that sanitation could not be sustained through staff effort alone. Inmate labor was essential, but inmate labor without structure led to indifference, shortcuts, and manipulation. A new deputy warden proposed creating a formal Sanitation Team in each housing unit, a group of inmates assigned to clean daily under staff supervision.

Program Design

The program began with clear guidelines:

- **Selection:** Sanitation team members were screened carefully. Only inmates with clean disciplinary records for at least six months were eligible. Gang-affiliated inmates were excluded to prevent manipulation.
- **Structure:** Each team consisted of four to six inmates assigned to specific tasks (showers, floors, tables, and trash removal). Duties rotated weekly.
- **Supervision:** Officers supervised cleaning daily and signed off on checklists. Supervisors inspected weekly.
- **Accountability:** Sanitation team inmates who failed to perform were removed from the team and lost privileges.
- **Privileges:** Team members earned small but valued rewards such as extra commissary items, additional recreation time, or preferred work assignments.

The message was clear: sanitation was no longer optional, and ownership rested with staff. Inmates could participate, but only under close supervision.

Early Challenges

At first, some inmates mocked the program. They called sanitation team members "janitors" and accused them of working for staff. Others predicted the program would collapse like past efforts.

Sanitation team members themselves tested the limits. Some attempted to cut corners, skipping tasks when officers were distracted. Others tried to use their positions to gain status, offering to "protect" peers from cleanup duties in exchange for favors.

Staff responded quickly. Supervisors reinforced that the program was not voluntary charity but mandatory order. Inmates who mocked or interfered were disciplined. Sanitation team members who cut corners were removed immediately and replaced. Officers learned to inspect closely and to hold inmates accountable for every detail.

Consistency broke down resistance. Within weeks, inmates realized the program was serious.

The Transformation

As the sanitation teams stabilized, housing units began to transform. Showers were scrubbed daily. Graffiti was painted over immediately. Trash was removed before it piled up. Dayrooms became orderly.

The visible difference had ripple effects. With fewer hiding places, contraband incidents declined. Inmates who once used trash piles or broken tiles to conceal items lost those opportunities. The environment no longer provided cover for disorder.

Behavior improved as well. Clean environments reduced tension. Inmates who once argued over filthy showers or cluttered tables had fewer reasons for conflict. Officers noticed that noise levels declined and units became calmer.

Most importantly, inmates began to respect the program. Even those not on sanitation teams acknowledged that clean pods were easier to live in. Peer pressure emerged, with inmates urging team members to perform their duties properly so privileges were not lost.

Staff Morale

The program improved staff morale dramatically. Officers reported pride in walking into clean, orderly pods. Supervisors noticed fewer sanitation-related complaints. Staff who had once dreaded inspections began using them as opportunities to showcase progress.

Officers also appreciated that sanitation teams reduced their burden. Instead of constantly correcting filth, they could focus on security tasks. The program reinforced that staff controlled the environment, but inmates were expected to contribute under supervision.

Long-Term Impact

After one year, the program showed measurable results:

- Sanitation scores in inspections rose by more than 60 percent.
- Contraband incidents related to hidden items declined by 35 percent.
- Inmate grievances about showers and cleanliness dropped sharply.
- Staff sick days related to exposure to mold or unsanitary conditions decreased.

The program also built a pool of inmate workers who took pride in their assignments. Some sanitation team members later transitioned into vocational programs or facility maintenance roles, carrying forward the discipline learned.

Lessons from the Sanitation Team

1. **Structure is essential.** Inmate labor must be organized, supervised, and documented.
2. **Selection matters.** Limiting team membership to inmates with clean records prevented gang manipulation.
3. **Privileges motivate compliance.** Small but consistent rewards kept inmates engaged.
4. **Supervision is the key.** Staff presence ensured the program reinforced authority rather than undermined it.
5. **Ripple effects multiply.** Cleanliness reduced contraband, lowered tension, and improved staff morale.

Reflection

The Sanitation Team program proved that inmate labor, when structured and supervised, can reinforce Broken Windows principles rather than undermine them. Disorder had once spread unchecked through graffiti, trash, and filth. The program reversed that trend by sending daily signals that cleanliness was enforced, valued, and rewarded.

The environment shifted from inmate-owned disorder to staff-owned order. Inmates adjusted behavior, contraband declined, and staff morale improved. Cleanliness was no longer a chore. It was a culture.

The lesson is clear. Sanitation is not about cosmetics. It is about control. Inmate labor can assist, but staff must set the standard, supervise the work, and enforce consistency. When they do, the environment itself becomes a tool of order.

Analysis: Sanitation as Strategy, Not Chore

The three case studies in this chapter—the filthy showers, the painted reset, and the inmate-run sanitation team—all point to the same conclusion: sanitation is not cosmetic. It is operational. It is cultural. It is strategic.

For too long, correctional facilities have treated cleanliness as a chore to be delegated, postponed, or ignored. Showers were cleaned "when time allowed." Graffiti was painted over "when maintenance could get to it." Trash was removed "when inmate workers remembered." These small lapses created enormous cultural consequences.

The Broken Windows Theory explains why. Physical disorder is not neutral. It sends signals. Each dirty shower, each graffiti mark, each pile of trash communicates tolerance. Tolerance multiplies into disorder. Disorder multiplies into violence, contraband, and staff disengagement.

Cleanliness is not about appearances. It is about signals. Every scrubbed floor, every painted wall, every repaired fixture communicates staff ownership. Staff ownership builds credibility. Credibility builds compliance. Compliance builds culture.

Why Sanitation Is Security

- **Filth breeds cover for contraband.** Dirty showers hide weapons. Piles of trash conceal drugs. Cluttered dayrooms create blind spots.
- **Graffiti breeds violence.** Symbols on walls mark territory. Rival groups fight over space. Violence erupts not because of drawings, but because of the signals those drawings communicate.
- **Neglect breeds rebellion.** Inmates who see staff tolerate filth assume other rules are negotiable. They test lockdowns, counts, and orders with the same attitude.

Clean facilities, by contrast, choke off these pathways. Graffiti removed immediately prevents gang signaling. Trash removed daily eliminates hiding places. Scrubbed showers reduce health complaints and the resentment that comes with neglect.

Cleanliness is security because it communicates that staff see everything, care about everything, and enforce everything.

The Psychology of Clean Environments

The environment shapes not only inmate behavior but also staff behavior.

- **For inmates:** Clean environments reduce excuses for defiance. Inmates resist less when they know sanitation standards are real and enforced. Cleanliness reduces resentment and increases peer pressure to maintain order.
- **For staff:** Clean environments build pride. Officers entering a spotless pod feel empowered. They see that their presence makes a difference. Dirty environments breed cynicism and disengagement. Officers stop correcting small things because they feel leadership does not care.

The psychology of order is powerful. People rise or fall to the level of their environment. Cleanliness sets the level higher for everyone.

Leadership and Sanitation

Leaders determine whether sanitation is treated as strategy or as chore.

- Leaders who prioritize sanitation, inspecting daily, demanding reports, and correcting lapses, create cultures of order.
- Leaders who tolerate filth, ignoring graffiti, delaying repairs, and leaving sanitation to inmates, create cultures of neglect.

The difference is visible in minutes. A leader walking through a pod with sharp eyes and high standards communicates ownership. A leader walking past filth communicates surrender. Inmates and staff alike adjust accordingly.

Why Resets Are Costly

The filthy showers and painted reset case studies show that neglect always ends in costly resets. When sanitation is ignored, conditions collapse. To repair collapse, facilities must spend thousands on contractors, materials, and manpower. Staff must invest weeks or months in resetting culture.

The truth is simple: small daily effort prevents massive future expense. Scrubbing showers daily costs little. Replacing tile after years of neglect costs tens of thousands. Painting over graffiti immediately costs a few minutes. Repainting an entire pod after years of tolerance costs weeks of labor and credibility.

Facilities either pay for cleanliness daily or pay for collapse later.

Inmate Labor as Cultural Tool

The inmate-run sanitation team demonstrates that inmate labor can reinforce order when supervised properly. Inmates are not just laborers; they are cultural participants. When they see that staff demand and supervise cleanliness, they internalize the message that order is valuable.

Inmate labor fails when staff surrender ownership. It succeeds when staff claim ownership. Supervisors who inspect closely, correct quickly, and reward compliance properly turn inmate labor into cultural reinforcement. Inmates learn that standards are non-negotiable because staff presence makes them non-negotiable.

The Broken Windows Connection

Broken Windows applies directly to sanitation because the environment is the window.

- A graffiti mark painted over is a window repaired.
- A trash pile removed is a window repaired.
- A shower scrubbed daily is a window repaired.

Each repaired window communicates staff control. Each ignored window communicates surrender.

The connection between physical disorder and behavioral disorder is not abstract. It is daily, visible, and immediate. Cleanliness is the most obvious Broken Windows tool in corrections.

The Standard of Excellence

The best facilities understand that sanitation is not about looking good for visitors. It is about living good for staff and inmates. Excellence in sanitation is the foundation for excellence in security.

- ☐ Clean facilities reduce contraband.
- ☐ Clean facilities reduce violence.
- ☐ Clean facilities improve morale.
- ☐ Clean facilities save money in lawsuits and repairs.

Excellence is not perfection. It is consistency. The standard must be simple: no graffiti, no filth, no tolerance. Every shift, every officer, every supervisor must enforce it.

Reflection

Sanitation is not a chore. It is strategy. Cleanliness is not cosmetic. It is cultural. The Broken Windows Theory shows that small details shape safety, and in corrections, cleanliness is the clearest of those details.

Every floor swept, every wall painted, every shower scrubbed is more than a task. It is a message. The message is ownership. Staff own the facility. Disorder does not.

When corrections professionals treat sanitation as strategy, they transform culture. They prevent violence, reduce contraband, and improve morale. Most importantly, they communicate daily that the jail or prison belongs to staff, not to disorder.

Tools and Takeaways

The case studies and analysis in this chapter have shown that sanitation is not cosmetic. It is strategy. Cleanliness is one of the strongest daily signals staff can send to inmates, fellow officers, leadership, and the public. A clean jail communicates ownership, control, and care. A dirty jail communicates tolerance, neglect, and weakness.

To sustain culture, staff need practical tools. The following framework offers concrete steps that correctional leaders, supervisors, and officers can apply immediately.

1. **Make Sanitation Non-Negotiable**
   Write clear policies that classify sanitation as an operational priority equal to counts and security checks.
   Communicate that graffiti, trash, and filth are not minor issues but security risks.
   Include sanitation in every daily briefing so staff understand its importance.
2. **Daily Inspections by Officers**
   Require officers to check sanitation during every round.
   Instruct them to note graffiti, trash, broken fixtures, and odors.
   Provide logbooks for documenting observations, even minor ones.
3. **Weekly Inspections by Supervisors**
   Supervisors must walk every housing unit at least once per week.
   Their inspections should be thorough and documented with checklists.
   Any graffiti, damage, or filth must be corrected within 24 hours.
4. **Immediate Correction of Graffiti**
   Provide paint supplies on-site in each unit for quick removal.
   Train staff to photograph graffiti for intelligence purposes before removing it.
   Enforce discipline against inmates who mark property, but never delay cleanup for the sake of investigation.
5. **Repair Fixtures Quickly**
   Treat broken doors, showers, or vents as operational priorities.
   Create a "fast track" for maintenance requests related to sanitation and security.
   Document repair times and hold facilities accountable for delays.

6. **Structure Inmate Labor**
   Assign sanitation tasks daily with rotating schedules.
   Post duty rosters publicly to communicate expectations.
   Inspect all inmate labor and provide feedback immediately.
7. **Use Incentives Wisely**
   Reward pods that maintain sanitation consistently with small privileges.
   Publicize inspection scores so inmates see that compliance matters.
   Tie incentives to clear benchmarks, not vague standards.
8. **Document and Display Results**
   Keep sanitation inspection logs posted in housing units.
   Share progress with staff and inmates to reinforce accountability.
   Recognize staff teams that maintain high standards.
9. **Train Staff on Sanitation as Strategy**
   Include sanitation principles in academy and in-service training.
   Teach officers how physical disorder leads to contraband, violence, and cultural collapse.
10. **Lead by Example**
    Administrators must walk the facility regularly and point out sanitation issues.
    Leaders should never walk past graffiti, trash, or filth without correction.

Sample Daily Sanitation Checklist

Housing Unit Level

- ☐ Floors swept and mopped
- ☐ Tables wiped and graffiti-free
- ☐ Trash removed from corners and under bunks
- ☐ Showers scrubbed, drains clear, no mold visible
- ☐ Toilets and sinks clean and operational
- ☐ Vents free of dust and obstructions
- ☐ Doors and locks inspected for damage

Common Areas

- ☐ Hallways clear of debris
- ☐ Lighting functional
- ☐ No graffiti on walls
- ☐ Emergency exits accessible and clean

Outdoor Areas

- ☐ Yards free of litter
- ☐ Perimeter fences inspected for tampering or hidden contraband

Every officer should walk with this checklist mentally, if not physically. Every supervisor should audit it weekly.

Reflection

Sanitation is one of the clearest expressions of Broken Windows in corrections. Dirty showers, graffiti-covered walls, and broken fixtures are not nuisances. They are broken windows. They communicate tolerance, invite misconduct, and multiply disorder.

The three case studies prove the point. The filthy showers collapsed into chaos because staff tolerated filth. The painted reset transformed culture because staff reclaimed ownership through renewal. The inmate-run sanitation team succeeded because staff structured and supervised labor rather than surrendering it.

The lesson is clear. Sanitation is not cosmetic. It is strategic. Every mop stroke, every coat of paint, every inspection communicates ownership. Staff own the environment, or inmates do. There is no middle ground.

Corrections professionals must embrace sanitation as operational strategy.

When they do, they prevent contraband, reduce violence, and improve morale. Most importantly, they send the daily message that the jail or prison belongs to staff, not to disorder.

Broken Windows teaches us that every detail is a signal. Sanitation is the clearest signal of all.

- 8 -

MAINTENANCE, DESIGN, AND VISIBILITY

Why Design Matters

Every correctional officer knows that some housing units "run themselves" while others feel like constant battles. The difference is often not staff effort but facility design. The architecture of a jail or prison is more than walls and doors. It is a daily environment that shapes behavior, communicates authority, and influences culture.

Design matters because space itself sends signals. A well-lit pod with clear sightlines communicates that staff see everything. Inmates adjust behavior because they know disorder will be noticed. A cluttered, shadowed pod with blind spots communicates that staff cannot see and therefore cannot enforce. Inmates adjust by exploiting gaps.

The Broken Windows Theory explains why design is critical. Every detail of a space either communicates order or disorder. Broken furniture, flickering lights, and obstructed sightlines are broken windows. They signal neglect and invite misbehavior. Fresh paint, working fixtures, and clear visibility are repaired windows. They signal ownership and deter misconduct.

Historically, many correctional facilities were built for containment, not control. Thick walls and barred cells confined inmates but created blind spots, dark corridors, and opportunities for hidden disorder. Modern correctional design recognizes that containment alone is not enough. Control requires visibility, accessibility, and staff ownership of space.

When space supports staff, order multiplies. When space undermines staff, disorder multiplies. This chapter explores how facility design communicates authority, influences behavior, and either strengthens or weakens Broken Windows corrections.

Environmental Design and Behavior

Correctional facilities are more than containers for people. They are environments that teach behavior. Just as a broken window in a neighborhood communicates neglect and invites crime, poor design in a jail or prison communicates weakness and invites disorder.

Inmates are hyper-observant. They notice every detail of their surroundings and quickly learn what can be exploited. Staff, too, are influenced by the spaces they occupy. Facilities that support their work make order sustainable. Facilities that hinder their work breed frustration and burnout.

Layout as a Signal

The layout of a housing unit communicates authority before staff ever give an order.

- **Open layouts** with clear sightlines communicate staff presence. Inmates know they are seen, even when officers are not standing over them.

- **Cluttered layouts** with blind spots communicate opportunity. Inmates know they can act without being observed.

For example, a dayroom with corners blocked by partitions or poorly placed furniture becomes a natural gathering place for misconduct. Inmates use those spaces for gambling, contraband exchange, or intimidation. Officers know the risks but often avoid constant patrols because the design itself makes observation difficult. The layout, not laziness, undermines control.

By contrast, a well-designed dayroom with central officer stations and unobstructed views communicates ownership. Inmates learn that staff see everything. Misconduct decreases not because officers yell louder but because design itself deters it.

Visibility as Deterrence

Visibility is the foundation of environmental control. Inmates act differently when they know they are being watched. Even the possibility of observation changes behavior.

- **Direct visibility** occurs when officers can see inmates with their own eyes.
- **Indirect visibility** occurs when cameras or mirrors expand coverage.

Both forms matter. Inmates constantly test blind spots. A housing unit where showers are hidden from officer view will quickly become a hotspot for contraband or assaults. A hallway with unmonitored corners will become a staging area for fights.

The lesson is simple: what staff cannot see, they cannot control. Every blind spot is a broken window waiting to be shattered.

Lighting as Ownership

Lighting is one of the most overlooked signals of ownership. Bright, functional lighting communicates staff presence and care. Flickering bulbs, dark corners, or dim hallways communicate neglect.

Inmates interpret poor lighting as opportunity. Assaults and contraband exchanges spike in dark spaces. Officers dread patrolling them, reinforcing inmate control.

Conversely, upgraded lighting transforms culture. Bright spaces reduce misconduct, increase staff confidence, and improve morale. Clean, well-lit environments communicate professionalism to visitors, staff, and inmates alike. Light is more than visibility. It is authority.

Noise and Acoustics

Sound is another environmental factor that shapes behavior. Housing units with poor acoustics amplify noise, making it difficult for staff to communicate orders or hear disturbances. Inmates exploit loud environments by masking misconduct.

Well-designed units reduce noise through materials and layout, allowing staff to project authority clearly. Quiet environments also lower stress for both staff and inmates. Noise is not just an annoyance. It is a cultural signal. Constant shouting communicates chaos. Controlled sound communicates order.

Maintenance and Order

Design does not end at construction. Maintenance determines whether design communicates strength or weakness over time.

- **Working locks and doors** communicate control. Broken locks communicate opportunity.

- **Fresh paint and clean walls** communicate ownership. Graffiti communicates surrender.
- **Functional plumbing** communicates professionalism. Leaks and odors communicate neglect.

Every maintenance issue left unaddressed is a broken window. Inmates notice instantly. If a shower leaks for weeks, they assume rules are negotiable. If graffiti stays on walls, they assume staff have given up. Maintenance is not a background task. It is daily reinforcement of authority.

How Inmates Exploit Poor Design

Inmates do not miss opportunities. They exploit poor design in predictable ways:

- Blind spots become contraband exchange zones.
- Dark corners become assault staging areas.
- Cluttered layouts become gang-controlled spaces.
- Broken fixtures become hiding places or weapons.

When design creates opportunities, inmates fill them. When design denies opportunities, inmates adjust. The environment does not eliminate misconduct, but it shapes its likelihood.

How Staff Respond to Poor Design

Staff also respond to their environment. When design supports them, they engage. When design hinders them, they retreat.

- Officers in open, visible units patrol confidently.
- Officers in cluttered, blind units cut corners to avoid danger.
- Supervisors in well-maintained pods conduct inspections proudly.
- Supervisors in filthy, broken pods avoid walking the floor.

The result is predictable. Poor design leads to staff disengagement, which inmates interpret as weakness. Good design leads to staff engagement, which inmates interpret as strength.

The Multiplier Effect of Environment

The environment multiplies whatever culture exists. In a well-maintained, well-designed unit, staff presence multiplies authority. In a poorly designed, neglected unit, staff presence multiplies frustration.

For example, an officer enforcing rules in a clean, well-lit pod is supported by the environment. Inmates resist less because disorder is absent. The same officer enforcing rules in a dirty, dim pod is undermined by the environment. Inmates resist more because disorder is already the norm.

The environment is not neutral. It is either staff's ally or staff's enemy.

Reflections on Environment

Environmental design is one of the most powerful but least discussed tools in corrections. Layout, visibility, lighting, noise, and maintenance are not cosmetic. They are operational. They shape inmate behavior, influence staff performance, and determine culture.

The Broken Windows Theory explains why. Every blind spot, every dark corner, every broken fixture is a broken window. It communicates neglect and invites disorder. Every clear sightline, every bright light, every repaired fixture is a repaired window. It communicates ownership and deters misconduct.

Correctional leaders must recognize that design is strategy. Facilities built for containment alone collapse into disorder. Facilities built for visibility, clarity, and staff ownership sustain control.

Design as Staff Support

Correctional facilities are not just environments for inmates. They are workplaces for staff. Every hallway, every housing pod, and every control station either supports staff or undermines them. Design can make enforcement easier, safer, and more sustainable. Poor design can make even the best staff feel ineffective.

The Broken Windows Theory reminds us that details shape culture. This applies as much to staff as to inmates. A well-designed space communicates professionalism and authority, boosting staff morale. A poorly designed space communicates neglect and frustration, draining morale. If facilities are built or maintained without considering staff needs, culture collapses from within.

Why Design Matters for Staff

Staff spend twelve or more hours inside housing units. They feel the weight of every blind spot, flickering light, and broken fixture. Poorly designed facilities create constant stress. Officers feel vulnerable in blind spots, dread entering dark corners, and burn out faster because the environment itself undermines their authority.

By contrast, well-designed facilities make officers feel confident. Clear sightlines, bright lighting, and open layouts allow effective supervision without constant confrontation. Staff feel safer and more professional. Their authority is reinforced not only by policy but by the space around them.

Visibility as Staff Protection

Visibility does not only deter inmates; it protects officers.

- When officers can see the entire pod, they can anticipate problems before they escalate.
- When supervisors can see staff, they can provide backup quickly.

- When cameras provide full coverage, staff have documentation to support enforcement.

Blind spots endanger staff. Officers forced to walk into areas they cannot see risk ambushes. Assaults on staff often occur in poorly designed areas where inmates know observation is impossible. Staff remember those experiences and adjust by avoiding the space altogether. That avoidance communicates weakness, reinforcing inmate control.

Visibility is not only inmate management. It is staff safety.

Lighting and Morale

Lighting affects staff as powerfully as inmates. Dim units sap energy and make officers feel unsupported. Bright units boost morale and reduce stress.

Staff working in poorly lit pods often report feeling "forgotten" by leadership. They see the neglect of their workspace as a sign that their safety is not valued. This resentment seeps into enforcement. Officers become more likely to cut corners, avoid rounds, or disengage from inmates.

Upgraded lighting communicates care. Officers feel safer entering showers or dayrooms when they know they can see clearly. Morale improves because the environment supports them.

Noise and Stress

Poor acoustics increase stress for staff. Units where voices echo constantly create fatigue. Officers struggle to give clear commands and cannot hear threats or fights until it is too late.

Noise is not just an inconvenience; it is a safety issue. Loud, chaotic pods cause exhaustion, reducing vigilance. Quieter pods with good acoustics allow officers to communicate with authority and detect problems early.

Design that reduces noise is design that reduces stress.

Maintenance and Professional Pride

Officers draw pride from the condition of their work environment. Clean, functional spaces reinforce professionalism and respect. Dirty, broken spaces send the opposite message.

An officer walking into a pod with polished floors, freshly painted walls, and working fixtures feels pride in the facility and is more likely to enforce rules with confidence. An officer entering a pod with graffiti, leaks, and broken doors feels defeated before the shift begins. They are more likely to let things slide, believing leadership does not care.

Maintenance is not just about inmates. It is about staff pride.

Staff as Owners of Space

Design must reinforce that staff own the space. Officer stations should be central, visible, and slightly elevated for authority. Corridors should allow safe movement without blind corners. Break areas should allow staff to decompress safely.

When officers feel they own the space, they project confidence. When they feel the space owns them, they withdraw. Ownership of space is cultural, and design either reinforces or undermines it.

Supervisor Presence and Design

Supervisors are also influenced by design. If offices are tucked away far from housing pods, supervisors appear disconnected. If units are designed so supervisors can walk them easily, presence becomes normal.

Design should make it easy for supervisors to be seen. Their visibility reinforces staff authority and inmate compliance. Facilities that isolate supervisors from housing units create gaps in accountability.

The Multiplier Effect

Design multiplies whatever culture exists. In a clean, well-designed facility, staff enforcement is amplified. Officers feel supported, inmates comply more readily, and supervisors reinforce standards. In a neglected, poorly designed facility, staff enforcement is undermined. Officers feel unsafe, inmates exploit weakness, and supervisors disengage.

The same staff member can feel effective in one unit and defeated in another, depending solely on design.

Reflection on Staff Support

Design is not neutral. It either supports staff or undermines them. Every blind spot, broken fixture, and dim light drains staff confidence. Every clear sightline, fresh coat of paint, and bright light builds it.

The Broken Windows Theory applies to staff as much as to inmates. Disorder in the environment communicates neglect to officers, just as it communicates weakness to inmates. Order communicates professionalism to officers, just as it communicates authority to inmates.

Correctional leaders must see design as staff support. Facilities that invest in layout, visibility, lighting, noise control, and maintenance invest directly in staff morale and safety. Officers cannot project authority if the environment strips it from them. Design is strategy, and strategy determines culture.

Case Study 1: The Blind Spot Pod

Blind spots are among the most dangerous design flaws in a correctional facility. When officers cannot see an area, inmates quickly learn to exploit it. What begins as minor misconduct can escalate into contraband trafficking, intimidation, and violence. This case from a large metropolitan jail in the Midwest shows how unaddressed blind spots nearly cost staff authority over an entire housing unit.

The Setting

The jail housed nearly 2,500 inmates across multiple pods. Pod F was designed in the late 1970s, when correctional architecture emphasized containment over visibility. Cells were stacked around a central dayroom, and the officer station sat near the entrance with limited sightlines. Corners of the dayroom and the rear tiers of cells were invisible to staff unless they walked the floor.

Officers complained from day one. They could not see inmates gathering in far corners or monitor activity on upper tiers without climbing stairs. Cameras installed in the 1990s were broken or poorly angled. Inmates quickly learned where they could act without being seen.

Early Signs of Trouble

Initially, the blind spots were used for small acts of defiance. Inmates gathered in corners to gamble or trade commissary items. Officers occasionally intervened but could not monitor constantly.

Within months, contraband flowed through the pod. Tobacco, drugs, and makeshift weapons were exchanged in hidden corners. Inmates knew officers would not notice unless they happened to walk the floor at the right moment. Graffiti also spread in these blind spots. Walls and tables bore markings that went uncorrected for days. Each mark sent a clear message: these spaces belonged to inmates.

Escalation into Violence

Disorder escalated quickly. Rival gangs used blind spots to plan assaults. Weaker inmates were cornered out of officer view, and extortion schemes flourished.

The worst incident involved two inmates ambushing a rival in a blind corner. Armed with sharpened metal, they stabbed the victim repeatedly. Officers were alerted only when other inmates shouted. The attackers fled to their cells, and the victim survived, but the message was clear: the blind spot had become a battlefield.

Afterward, officers reported feeling unsafe and avoided walking the floor. Inmates noticed the fear and grew bolder. Pod F teetered on the edge of collapse.

Administrative Response

The administration launched an investigation. Video confirmed daily exploitation of blind spots. Cameras that could have covered the areas were broken, and officers admitted they rarely patrolled dangerous corners.

Rebuilding the pod was costly, but doing nothing meant continued violence. Leadership approved a redesign.

The Redesign

The redesign focused on eliminating blind spots and reinforcing staff ownership:

- **Camera upgrades:** Digital cameras were installed in every corner with overlapping fields of vision.
- **Mirror placement:** Convex mirrors covered areas cameras could not fully see.
- **Officer station relocation:** The control booth moved to a central location with improved sightlines.

- **Furniture reconfiguration:** Tables and chairs were bolted down, preventing hidden gathering spots.
- **Tier adjustments:** Upper-tier barriers were replaced with see-through fencing, allowing officers to observe activity from below.

During the three-month construction, inmates were rotated to other pods. Officers were trained on using new surveillance tools and instructed to enforce sanitation and order with zero tolerance for graffiti or loitering.

The Transformation

When Pod F reopened, the difference was dramatic. Inmates quickly realized their hiding places were gone. Officers could now see every corner from the control booth or on camera. Mirrors eliminated remaining gaps. Surveillance felt constant even when staff were not physically present.

Inmates initially tested the system, but groups were immediately dispersed. Graffiti appeared once and was painted over within hours. Contraband exchanges dropped sharply, and violence declined. Gangs lost private staging areas, and inmates adjusted behavior accordingly.

Staff Confidence Restored

Staff morale improved. Officers felt safer, more professional, and in control. Supervisors reported increased presence on the floor, as officers trusted the design to protect them. Visitors noted Pod F's orderliness compared to other units, reinforcing that design is more than cosmetic; it shapes culture.

Lessons from the Blind Spot Pod

- **Design communicates authority:** Blind spots signal weakness, clear sightlines signal control.
- **Inmates exploit gaps instantly:** Every blind spot can become a site for misconduct, contraband, or violence.
- **Staff respond to design:** Poor design drains morale; good design builds confidence.
- **Technology matters:** Cameras and mirrors correct flaws only when maintained and monitored.
- **Redesign is worth the cost:** Eliminating blind spots is far cheaper than paying for violence, lawsuits, or lost credibility.

Reflection

The Blind Spot Pod shows that poor design is not neutral. It actively undermines order. Inmates interpret blind spots as invitations, and staff interpret them as threats. Disorder multiplies because the environment communicates weakness.

The Broken Windows Theory explains the turnaround. Every blind spot eliminated was a repaired window. Every new camera, mirror, and sightline signaled ownership. Inmates adjusted behavior not because rules changed but because the environment changed.

The lesson is clear: design is strategy. Facilities must prioritize visibility in every pod, hallway, and cell. What staff cannot see, they cannot control. What staff can see, they can own.

Case Study 2: The Lighting Upgrade

Lighting is one of the simplest yet most powerful environmental signals in a correctional facility. Inmates and staff alike interpret the quality of lighting as a sign of ownership, safety, and professionalism. Bright, functional lighting communicates that staff control the space. Dim, flickering, or broken lights communicate neglect and create opportunities for misconduct.

This case from a medium-sized jail in the South illustrates how a facility plagued by dim, failing lights transformed its culture by investing in a comprehensive lighting upgrade.

The Setting

The jail housed around 1,200 inmates in pods and dormitory-style units. For years, staff had complained about the poor lighting throughout the facility. In many housing units, bulbs were dim or completely out. Flickering lights were common. Shadows lingered in corners and hallways. Outdoor recreation yards had inadequate floodlights, creating risks during evening recreation periods.

Officers reported feeling unsafe in poorly lit areas, particularly in dorms where rows of bunks created long shadowed aisles. Inmates exploited those shadows for contraband exchanges, assaults, and intimidation. Supervisors documented repeated incidents but lacked funds for large-scale repairs. The culture in these units reflected the neglect: graffiti spread, sanitation declined, and tension increased.

Early Signs of Trouble

The first problems linked to poor lighting were subtle but consistent. Officers missed contraband hidden in dark corners. Inmates staged fights in shadowed areas where visibility was limited. Complaints about safety grew louder, but leadership initially dismissed lighting as a maintenance issue rather than a cultural one.

The turning point came when an officer was assaulted during rounds in a dimly lit dorm. The officer did not see two inmates waiting for him in a shadowed aisle. They struck him from behind, and by the time backup arrived, he had suffered serious injuries. The incident prompted a full review of lighting conditions across the jail.

The Upgrade Plan

The review revealed what staff already knew: lighting was failing throughout the facility. Leadership approved a comprehensive upgrade to high-efficiency LED lighting. The project included:

- **Housing pods:** Installation of bright, evenly distributed lights that eliminated shadows in corners and around bunks.
- **Dayrooms:** Upgraded overhead lighting combined with targeted fixtures for officer stations.
- **Hallways and corridors:** Uniform lighting to eliminate dark stretches where contraband could be passed or assaults staged.
- **Outdoor yards:** Floodlights positioned to ensure full coverage during evening hours.
- **Emergency backup:** Redundant systems to ensure lights remained functional during power outages.

Contractors completed the project over six months, unit by unit. Staff and inmates alike noticed the difference immediately.

The Transformation

The lighting upgrade had a dramatic effect. Areas that once felt dangerous became easier to supervise. Inmates who once gathered in dark corners found their hiding places gone. Contraband incidents dropped sharply because staff could see exchanges happening in real time.

The atmosphere of the facility shifted as well. Cleanliness improved because dirt and graffiti were now visible. Inmates realized that disorder could no longer hide in shadows. Officers walked units with more confidence, projecting authority more consistently.

The impact on outdoor recreation was especially notable. Evening recreation, once tense and chaotic, became safer. Floodlights illuminated every corner of the yard. Inmates reported fewer fights, and officers said they felt more secure supervising larger groups.

Staff Morale

Perhaps the most powerful impact was on staff morale. Officers described feeling "seen" by leadership for the first time in years. The lighting upgrade communicated that their safety mattered. Walking into brightly lit pods gave them confidence. They no longer dreaded dark rounds or shadowed dorms.

Supervisors noticed that officers were more engaged. Instead of rushing rounds to avoid danger, staff slowed down and interacted more with inmates. The change in body language was obvious: officers walked taller, spoke with more confidence, and enforced rules consistently.

Inmate Behavior

Inmates adjusted quickly to the new reality. They recognized that staff could now see everything. Attempts to pass contraband or stage fights were detected immediately. Peer pressure increased as inmates realized misconduct risked sanctions that were now unavoidable.

Interestingly, some inmates reported feeling safer themselves. Fewer assaults occurred in dark corners, and intimidation declined. The brighter environment reduced tension. Even inmates who once mocked the project admitted that better lighting improved daily life.

Long-Term Impact

One year after the upgrade, the facility reported measurable improvements:

- Assaults on staff declined by 30 percent.
- Contraband incidents decreased by 25 percent.
- Graffiti reports fell by nearly half.

- Staff sick leave related to stress and fatigue declined significantly.
- Energy costs also dropped because the new LED lights were more efficient.

The project, once considered a costly luxury, paid for itself in both savings and improved safety.

Lessons from the Lighting Upgrade

- **Lighting is ownership:** Bright lights communicate that staff control the space. Dim lights communicate neglect.
- **Shadows are opportunity:** Inmates exploit every dark corner for misconduct. Eliminating shadows eliminates opportunities.
- **Staff confidence rises with visibility:** Officers enforce rules more consistently when they feel safe.
- **Inmates adjust to being seen:** Misconduct declines when inmates know they cannot hide.
- **Investment pays dividends:** Lighting upgrades reduce violence, contraband, and energy costs.

Reflection

The Lighting Upgrade demonstrates how something as simple as illumination can transform culture. The jail had tolerated dim, broken lights for years, assuming they were a minor maintenance issue. In reality, they were broken windows. They communicated neglect, fueled misconduct, and endangered staff.

By upgrading lighting, the facility repaired those windows. Each bright bulb was a message of ownership. Each floodlight was a signal of authority. The culture shifted not because policies changed, but because the environment changed.

The lesson is clear: lighting is not cosmetic. It is control. Corrections professionals must treat lighting as an operational priority. When staff and inmates can see clearly, order follows.

Case Study 3: The Open Dayroom Model

Housing design determines how staff and inmates interact. In some facilities, layouts separate officers from inmates, limit visibility, and create an "us versus them" atmosphere. In others, design encourages constant surveillance and interaction, reducing tension and misconduct.

This case from a newly constructed regional correctional facility in the West demonstrates how the open dayroom model became a cultural anchor, reinforcing Broken Windows principles and making order sustainable.

The Setting

The facility opened in 2015 and was designed to house 900 inmates. Unlike older linear jails with stacked tiers and hidden corners, this facility adopted an open dayroom model. Cells lined the perimeter of each housing unit, with a large open space in the center for tables, phones, and programming.

The officer station sat inside the unit at ground level, slightly elevated but open, with 360-degree visibility across the pod. Sightlines were unobstructed. Lighting was bright, and mirrors were placed to eliminate minor blind spots.

The philosophy behind the design was simple: constant visibility and staff presence deter misconduct.

Early Implementation

From the start, leadership emphasized that the open dayroom model was not cosmetic but strategic. Officers were trained to remain present in the unit rather than withdraw into control rooms. Their authority would come from visibility, consistency, and ownership of the environment.

Inmates were told the same: order was expected, and every detail would be enforced. Graffiti, trash, or disorder would be corrected immediately. The open layout meant nothing could be hidden.

Some staff resisted the approach, fearing increased exposure to inmates. They were used to the separation of secure booths. Supervisors reinforced that visibility was safety. Officers were reminded that the design worked in their favor. They could see everything, and inmates knew it.

Early Resistance

At first, some inmates tested the environment. Small groups loitered near tables, carved initials, and left trash behind. Others challenged officers verbally, hoping to intimidate them into retreating to their stations.

The tests failed. Officers enforced sanitation and order daily. Graffiti was painted over within hours. Trash was removed immediately. Minor defiance was met with consistent correction. Officers stayed present, walked the floor, made eye contact, and reinforced authority.

Because the design eliminated hiding places, inmates quickly realized their actions were visible at all times. Defiance brought swift consequences, while compliance earned privileges. Resistance faded within weeks.

The Cultural Shift

Within six months, the open dayroom model was producing results:

- **Infractions declined:** Constant surveillance allowed contraband exchanges and fights to be detected and interrupted early.
- **Sanitation improved:** Inmates cleaned up after themselves consistently because officers could see violations immediately.
- **Staff–inmate interactions normalized:** Officers engaged with inmates directly. Small conversations reduced tension and humanized relationships without sacrificing authority.

- **Staff morale rose:** Officers felt supported by the design and no longer dreaded blind spots or shadowed corners.

The pod began running smoothly. Staff projected confidence, and inmates adjusted behavior to match.

Long-Term Impact

Over five years, data confirmed the cultural transformation:

- Disciplinary reports in open dayroom pods were 40 percent lower than in older linear pods.
- Assaults on staff dropped by nearly half.
- Contraband incidents declined because inmates had fewer opportunities to conceal items.
- Staff sick leave related to stress decreased, and turnover slowed.

Officers reported feeling safer and more professional. Inmates reported fewer grievances about unfair treatment because enforcement was consistent and visible.

The open dayroom model reinforced Broken Windows principles daily. Disorder was corrected immediately because disorder could not hide. Order became the cultural norm because both staff and design reinforced it.

Lessons from the Open Dayroom Model

1. **Visibility is prevention:** Open layouts eliminate hiding places and make misconduct riskier.
2. **Staff presence is authority:** Officers inside the pod project confidence and control.
3. **Immediate correction matters:** Graffiti, trash, and defiance were handled swiftly, preventing escalation.
4. **Design and culture must align:** Layout alone is not enough. Staff training and consistency sustain order.

5. **Long-term dividends are real:** Reduced infractions, improved morale, and safer environments saved time, money, and credibility.

Reflection

The Open Dayroom Model demonstrates that design itself can enforce Broken Windows principles. By eliminating blind spots and placing staff at the center of the unit, the facility created a culture where order was visible, consistent, and sustainable.

The lesson is clear: architecture is not neutral. Facilities built for visibility and staff presence create cultures of compliance. Facilities built for containment alone create cultures of defiance.

Broken Windows teaches us that every detail communicates ownership. In open dayrooms, the message was unmistakable: staff owned the space, and inmates adjusted accordingly.

Analysis: Design as Silent Enforcement

The three case studies in this chapter—the Blind Spot Pod, the Lighting Upgrade, and the Open Dayroom Model—demonstrate a single truth: design is not neutral. Every wall, window, and light either strengthens staff ownership or undermines it. Architecture itself can act as silent enforcement of Broken Windows principles, shaping daily behavior without a single command.

Design as Daily Communication

Inmates constantly read their environment for signals. Blind spots signal opportunity. Dim lighting signals neglect. Layouts that isolate officers signal weakness.

By contrast, eliminating blind spots signals that misconduct will be seen. Bright, consistent lighting signals that staff care and control the environment. Open layouts that place officers at the center signal that staff own the space.

Design speaks even when staff are silent. It communicates authority, order, or neglect. Broken Windows teaches that disorder multiplies when ignored. Poor design is disorder written into the walls. Good design is order made visible.

Design as Staff Support

Design does not only send signals to inmates. It also communicates to staff. Officers working in poorly designed pods interpret neglect as indifference to their safety. Morale collapses, and enforcement weakens. Officers in well-designed pods interpret visibility and lighting as leadership investing in their authority. Morale rises, and enforcement strengthens.

The case studies illustrate this clearly:

- In the Blind Spot Pod, officers withdrew because they felt unsafe. Their absence communicated surrender, and inmates filled the void.
- In the Lighting Upgrade, officers re-engaged because they felt protected. Their renewed presence shifted culture.
- In the Open Dayroom Model, officers projected confidence because design placed them at the center. Authority became natural.

Design either undermines staff or multiplies their authority.

Design as Inmate Control

Design also shapes how inmates regulate each other. In poorly designed pods, gangs exploit blind spots and shadows to assert dominance. Peer pressure reinforces disorder. In well-designed pods, inmates pressure each other to comply because misconduct is visible and invites swift consequences.

The Open Dayroom Model proved this. When inmates realized staff could see everything, they stopped tolerating graffiti and trash from peers. Cleanliness became a shared expectation because the environment provided no cover for defiance.

Design makes culture contagious. Poor design spreads disorder. Good design spreads compliance.

Why Architecture Is Enforcement

Correctional leaders sometimes think of enforcement only in terms of staff presence and policy. Architecture enforces as well:

- **Walls enforce:** Open walls enforce visibility. Opaque barriers enforce blind spots.
- **Lighting enforces:** Bright lights enforce surveillance. Dim lights enforce opportunity.
- **Layout enforces:** Central officer stations enforce staff presence. Isolated stations enforce staff withdrawal.

Every architectural choice either supports or undermines Broken Windows enforcement. Facilities designed for order enforce order silently, every minute of every day. Facilities designed poorly enforce disorder silently, every minute of every day.

The Cost of Neglect

Neglected design is as dangerous as neglected sanitation. The Blind Spot Pod nearly collapsed because blind spots allowed assaults to be staged. The cost of redesign was far greater than designing for visibility in the first place.

The Lighting Upgrade showed that years of broken lights led to assaults, contraband, and staff fear. The cost of upgrading was significant but far less than the lawsuits, injuries, and turnover caused by poor lighting.

Neglect in design is neglect in culture. Both are costly in terms of finances, credibility, and safety.

The Multiplier Effect

Design multiplies the culture that exists. A clean, well-designed pod makes good staff great. A dirty, poorly designed pod can make even great staff ineffective. The same officer enforcing rules in two different pods can have entirely different outcomes, not because of skill but because of design.

Broken Windows reminds us that details multiply disorder when ignored. In corrections, design multiplies culture. It either multiplies order or multiplies chaos.

Redesign as Cultural Reset

The Painted Reset in the previous chapter showed how sanitation overhaul transformed culture. The same principle applies to design. Redesigning a pod with cameras, mirrors, lighting, and open layouts does more than fix infrastructure. It resets culture.

When inmates see that blind spots are gone, they adjust behavior. When officers see shadows eliminated, they re-engage. Redesign sends a clear message: the facility belongs to staff again.

The Long-Term View

Correctional leaders must think beyond daily operations. Design decisions last decades. A poorly designed jail built in the 1970s still undermines staff today. A well-designed jail built in the 2010s still supports staff today.

Every choice—camera placement, officer station location, lighting system—becomes permanent culture. Leaders must view design not as construction but as strategy.

Reflection on Silent Enforcement

Architecture enforces culture silently. Blind spots enforce weakness. Bright lights enforce presence. Open layouts enforce ownership.

The Broken Windows Theory explains why. Every physical detail is a window. Left broken, it communicates neglect and invites defiance. Repaired, it communicates order and deters misconduct.

Design is not neutral. It is either a daily ally of staff or a daily ally of inmates. Correctional leaders must choose. Facilities built for containment collapse into disorder. Facilities built for visibility, lighting, and staff ownership sustain order for decades.

The lesson is clear: design is strategy, and strategy is enforcement.

Tools and Takeaways

Design is not decoration. It is control. The three case studies show that architecture either enforces order or enforces disorder. Leaders must treat design with the same seriousness as staffing and policy.

Key Recommendations

1. **Conduct Visibility Audits**
   a. Walk every housing unit and identify blind spots.
   b. Document where inmates congregate or misconduct occurs.
   c. Use cameras or mirrors to fill gaps but never rely on technology alone.

   Principle: What staff cannot see, they cannot control.

2. **Upgrade and Maintain Lighting**
    a. Replace dim or broken lights immediately.
    b. Standardize brightness across all areas.
    c. Inspect monthly and document outages until repaired.
    d. Use LED fixtures for efficiency.

    Principle: Light is ownership. Shadows are opportunity.

3. **Position Officer Stations Strategically**
    a. Place stations inside housing units with 360-degree visibility.
    b. Avoid isolation behind glass or in corners.
    c. Slightly elevate stations for presence but not disconnection.

    Principle: Staff must own the space physically, not symbolically.

4. **Design for Sanitation and Maintenance**
    a. Use durable, easy-to-clean surfaces.
    b. Avoid surfaces that absorb graffiti or trap dirt.
    c. Build in maintenance access for fast repairs.
    d. Require daily inspections.

    Principle: Clean design communicates control. Neglect communicates surrender.

5. **Reduce Noise with Smart Materials**
    a. Use wall and ceiling materials that absorb sound.
    b. Test acoustics before occupancy.
    c. Eliminate echo chambers.

    Principle: Noise is culture. Quiet communicates control.

6. **Keep Layouts Simple and Open**
   a. Avoid cluttered corners, dead-end hallways, and poor visibility tiers.
   b. Arrange furniture to keep sightlines clear from officer stations.
   c. Reconfigure older pods where possible. Remove or bolt down obstructive furnishing.

   Principle: Open layouts enforce presence. Cluttered layouts enforce weakness.

7. **Use Cameras Wisely**
   a. Cameras supplement but do not replace staff presence.
   b. Ensure overlapping coverage with no blind spots.
   c. Train staff to monitor actively, not relying on post incident recordings.

   Principle: Cameras are tools, not substitutes.

8. **Incorporate Natural Light**
   a. Windows or skylights reduce stress and improve visibility.
   b. Avoid dark, cave-like environments.

   Principle: Light communicates care.

9. **Plan for Flexibility**
   a. Build adaptable spaces for changing populations and security needs.
   b. Keep infrastructure accessible for upgrades: technology, lighting, and visibility.

   Principle: Design must adapt to sustain ownership.

10. Train Staff to Read Design as Signals

a. Teach officers how blind spots, poor lighting, or clutter communicate weakness.
b. Train supervisors to identify environmental signals.
c. Include design principles in academy and in-service training.

Principle: Design is strategy, not backdrop.

Sample Design Evaluation Checklist

Visibility

- ☐ Are there blind spots in units, hallways, or yards?
- ☐ Can officers see all activity from their stations?
- ☐ Are mirrors or cameras positioned to cover gaps?

Lighting

- ☐ Are bulbs functional and bright enough?
- ☐ Are shadows eliminated in corners and behind furniture?
- ☐ Are outdoor areas fully lit for evening activity?

Officer Stations

- ☐ Are stations centrally positioned with 360-degree visibility?
- ☐ Are they elevated enough to project authority but not disconnected?
- ☐ Do they allow staff to engage directly with inmates?

Sanitation and Maintenance

- ☐ Are surfaces durable and easy to clean?
- ☐ Is graffiti removed quickly?
- ☐ Are broken fixtures repaired promptly?

Noise and Acoustics

- ☐ Can officers be heard clearly across the unit?
- ☐ Are materials chosen to reduce echoes and shouting?

Layout

- ☐ Are hallways and pods free of clutter?
- ☐ Is furniture arranged to maintain sightlines?
- ☐ Are inmate gathering areas visible from officer stations?

Technology

- ☐ Are cameras functional with overlapping coverage?
- ☐ Are staff trained to use surveillance actively?

Culture

- ☐ Does design communicate staff ownership or inmate opportunity?
- ☐ Do officers feel safe and supported?
- ☐ Do inmates recognize that misconduct will be noticed immediately?

Reflection

Design is silent enforcement. It either strengthens order or multiplies disorder. Blind spots, dim lights, and poor layouts are not just inconveniences—they are broken windows.

The three case studies prove the point. The Blind Spot Pod collapsed into violence because inmates exploited invisible corners. The Lighting Upgrade transformed culture because shadows disappeared. The Open Dayroom Model reduced infractions because visibility made misconduct impossible to hide.

Correctional leaders cannot afford to treat design as background. Architecture is strategy. Every wall, light, and station communicates ownership. Every blind spot, shadow, or broken fixture communicates surrender.

Broken Windows reminds us that details determine culture. In corrections, design is one of the most powerful details. Facilities built for containment alone will collapse. Facilities built for visibility, cleanliness, and staff presence will sustain order for generations.

- 9 -

PROACTIVE SECURITY AS PREVENTION

Why Security is Prevention, Not Reaction

Every corrections professional knows the old saying: an ounce of prevention is worth a pound of cure. Nowhere is this truer than in jail and prison security. Escapes, riots, and assaults rarely erupt from nowhere. They almost always trace back to ignored details—a broken door latch, a skipped round, a sloppy count, a perimeter fence unrepaired.

The Broken Windows Theory explains why. Small cracks in order communicate that rules are optional. In corrections, those cracks appear in security practices. When inmates see that staff tolerate weak doors, mishandled keys, or inconsistent rounds, they interpret those signals as permission to test boundaries. Each small lapse multiplies into larger risks.

The public often imagines corrections as reactive: alarms sounding, tactical teams rushing, officers restoring control. True security, however, is quiet. It is the daily prevention of breaches. When doors are locked, counts are precise, rounds are consistent, and contraband is intercepted early, crises never materialize.

Prevention is not glamorous, but it is lifesaving. The best security systems are invisible because nothing happens. Inside the walls, staff know that nothing happening is the result of everything being done right.

Broken Windows reframes security as ownership of details. Every locked door, every completed round, every checked key communicates that staff own the facility. Every skipped detail communicates that inmates have room to maneuver.

The Chain of Security

Security in a correctional facility is like a chain. Each link—doors, locks, keys, counts, rounds, and searches—must be strong. A chain is only as strong as its weakest link. Inmates know this better than anyone. They test the chain daily, probing for weaknesses, and once they find one, they exploit it.

The Broken Windows Theory explains why this matters. Each neglected detail sends a signal. A lock not repaired is not just a maintenance issue—it is a message that staff do not own that link. A skipped round is not laziness—it is a signal that staff presence is optional. Small cracks in security, like broken windows in a community, multiply into larger breaches when ignored.

Doors and Locks

Doors and locks are the foundation of physical security. They separate housing areas, control inmate movement, and protect staff. Yet many facilities treat broken locks as minor inconveniences rather than critical failures.

Every broken lock is a broken window. Inmates notice instantly. A failing cell door lock will be tested. A sticking sally port door will be pushed. A door that can be propped open will be exploited. A facility can have the best staff in the world, but if doors and locks fail, order collapses.

Locks must be inspected daily. Every malfunction must be treated as a priority. Inmates will never ignore a broken lock. Staff cannot either.

Keys

Key control is one of the most underestimated elements of jail and prison security. Keys are the literal authority of staff. When key boxes are left unsecured, sign-out procedures ignored, or spare keys unaccounted for, the chain weakens.

Inmates notice sloppy key practices. They see when boxes hang open, when officers fumble, when staff grow careless. Keys in the wrong hands are catastrophic. History is full of escapes and riots that began with a single key.

Broken Windows explains why key lapses are dangerous. Every unlocked key box is a broken window. It signals to inmates that staff are careless with the very tools of control. That signal multiplies risk.

Counts

Counts are not paperwork—they are the backbone of security. Every inmate must be accounted for, visually confirmed, and logged accurately. Complacency creeps in when staff rush counts, mark inmates as present without confirmation, or treat discrepancies as minor paperwork errors.

Inmates notice sloppy counts. They test hiding places, slip away during movement, or exploit gaps. A careless count is an invitation to escape.

Broken Windows applies here as well. A poorly conducted count sends the signal that details do not matter. If staff ignore this fundamental duty, inmates assume other rules can be ignored too.

Rounds

Rounds are staff presence made visible. Officers walking units communicate ownership. Their eyes on inmates deter misconduct. Skipped, rushed, or falsified rounds send a clear signal: staff are absent, rules are optional, and disorder can flourish.

Consistent rounds communicate control. They prevent escalation by catching problems early and reinforce to inmates that staff are watching at all times.

Searches

Searches close gaps that inmates exploit. Cells, common areas, and even staff must be searched consistently. Contraband thrives when searches are inconsistent. Inmates test staff by hiding small items first. If missed, they escalate to larger contraband.

Each missed contraband item is a broken window. It tells inmates staff are not thorough and rules can be bent. Over time, small oversights compound into weapons, drugs, and phones, fueling violence and undermining safety.

Regular, thorough searches done consistently and professionally communicate ownership. They prevent disorder from spreading.

How the Links Work Together

The chain of security is only as strong as its weakest link. A facility can have excellent key control but sloppy counts. It can enforce strong rounds but ignore broken locks. Inmates do not need every link to fail—they only need one.

Consider the progression: a broken lock left unrepaired allows an inmate to slip out of a cell. A sloppy count fails to notice it. A skipped round gives time to prepare an escape. Weak key practices open another door. One weakness multiplies, and the chain breaks.

Broken Windows teaches that small signals matter. Each broken lock, sloppy count, or skipped round is not isolated—it is a signal. Inmates read those signals, connect the dots, and exploit them.

Staff Ownership of the Chain

Ownership must begin at the lowest level. Officers must treat every lock, key, round, and count as critical. Supervisors must enforce standards daily. Administrators must hold the system accountable.

When staff treat details as optional, inmates do too. When staff own the chain, inmates respect it. The difference between control and collapse lies in how staff treat each link.

Reflection on the Chain

Security in corrections is not a single wall or a tactical team. It is a chain of details. Doors, locks, keys, counts, rounds, and searches form the links. One weak link breaks the entire chain.

The Broken Windows Theory explains why. Every neglected detail is a broken window. It communicates weakness, invites testing, and multiplies disorder. Every enforced detail is a repaired window. It communicates ownership, deters testing, and multiplies order.

Correctional leaders must ensure the chain never weakens. Staff must own each link daily. Only then can facilities sustain true security: quiet, consistent, and preventive.

Case Study 1: The Broken Key Box

Key control is one of the least glamorous but most critical aspects of jail and prison security. Officers handle keys every day, often without thinking. Yet keys are authority in physical form: whoever controls them controls the facility. When keys are mishandled, misplaced, or neglected, security can collapse.

This case from a large county detention center in the South shows how a seemingly small issue—a broken key box—nearly led to a full escape, and how staff ownership of details prevented disaster.

The Setting

The detention center housed over 2,000 inmates. Like many older facilities, it relied heavily on manual keys for doors, sally ports, and secure storage areas. Some pods had electronic systems, but most of the jail depended on physical keys.

Key control procedures were clear:

- All keys must be stored in locked boxes when not in use.
- Keys must be signed out at the start of a shift and returned immediately afterward.
- Supervisors must verify inventories daily.

On paper, the system was airtight. In practice, years of wear and complacency had eroded standards.

Early Signs of Neglect

One key box in Housing Unit D had a broken lock. Officers discovered they could open it without a key by jiggling the handle. Instead of reporting it, staff began treating the flaw as a convenience. Supervisors, aware of the issue, delayed repair because maintenance was backlogged.

The broken key box became a tolerated detail. Officers joked about it, and inmates noticed the box hanging open and staff skipping proper sign-outs. The message was clear: keys—the foundation of authority—were treated casually.

Inmate Awareness

Inmates notice everything. They observed officers accessing keys without signing them out, heard jokes about the broken lock, and saw the box left unsecured. For inmates, this was not harmless—it was opportunity.

A group of inmates planned a simple operation: distract officers during shift change, slip into the office, grab the keys from the unsecured box, and move into restricted areas, eventually reaching the sally port.

The Incident

The attempt occurred on a Friday evening. During shift change, two inmates staged an argument in the dayroom. While officers responded, another inmate entered the office. He found the key box open and grabbed a ring of keys, running for the janitorial closet.

He was intercepted because one officer, skeptical of the staged fight, turned back early. The keys were recovered, and the escape attempt failed.

Investigation revealed how close the facility had come to disaster: the inmate had selected the correct key ring. A few more seconds' delay could have allowed access to restricted areas and a potential breach of the sally port.

Administrative Response

The near-escape shook the administration. A small detail—a broken key box lock—had nearly escalated into catastrophe. The review identified several failures:

- **Broken equipment tolerated:** The box had been left unrepaired for weeks.
- **Procedures ignored:** Officers were not signing out keys consistently.
- **Supervisors disengaged:** Daily verifications were pencil-whipped rather than enforced.

- **Inmate observation underestimated:** Staff forgot that inmates always watch, always learn, and always test.

The administration responded with urgency. The key box was replaced within 24 hours, and every other box in the facility was inspected. Key control policies were rewritten with stricter accountability measures, including electronic tracking systems in high-security areas.

Officers were retrained to treat key control as sacred, and supervisors were held personally accountable for any lapses.

Cultural Reset

The incident became a teaching moment. Leadership emphasized that keys are not routine tools—they are symbols of authority. Sloppy attitudes toward keys equate to sloppy attitudes toward security.

Staff became meticulous in signing out keys, supervisors began personally inspecting boxes, and maintenance prioritized repairs linked to security equipment. The culture shifted: what staff once treated as convenience, inmates recognized as opportunity.

Lessons from the Broken Key Box

1. **Keys are authority.** Whoever controls them controls the facility. Mishandling them is catastrophic.
2. **Broken equipment is not harmless.** A broken lock is a broken window—it communicates neglect and invites testing.
3. **Inmates see everything.** What staff laugh off, inmates analyze for opportunity.
4. **Supervisors must verify.** Paperwork is meaningless without real inspection.
5. **Culture is the true safeguard.** Procedures only work when staff believe in their importance.

Reflection

The Broken Key Box demonstrates how small lapses create enormous risks. A single broken lock nearly allowed inmates to access restricted areas and attempt an escape. The detail seemed minor, but it was a signal of neglect that inmates seized upon.

Broken Windows explains the danger. Every casual use of the broken box reinforced the message that security details were negotiable. That signal multiplied into a near escape.

The lesson is clear: key control is sacred. Every lock, every inventory, every signature must be enforced. When staff treat keys casually, inmates treat security casually. When staff treat keys as sacred, inmates respect the chain of control.

Case Study 2: The Ignored Perimeter Fence

Perimeter security is the outer wall of trust between a correctional facility and the community. Citizens assume that fences, walls, and gates are solid, monitored, and enforced. When they are not, the consequences ripple far beyond the jail yard. Small weaknesses are not just gaps—they are signals to inmates, staff, and outsiders that the facility is vulnerable.

This case from a state correctional institution in the Midwest illustrates how an ignored tear in a perimeter fence led to months of contraband smuggling and nearly enabled a group of inmates to escape.

The Setting

The prison housed 1,800 inmates on a sprawling campus surrounded by two layers of chain-link fencing topped with razor wire. Between the inner and outer fences lay a sterile zone, a cleared strip designed for visibility and deterrence.

The system had functioned for years, but like any infrastructure, it required constant maintenance. Weather, vegetation, and inmate testing created wear that demanded timely repair.

In early spring, staff discovered a small tear in the outer fence behind an industrial workshop. A fallen tree limb had bent several sections, leaving a gap large enough to reach through. The repair was logged, but staffing shortages and competing priorities delayed action. Weeks passed. The gap remained.

Early Signals

Staff initially treated the gap as minor. The inner fence was intact, so escape seemed unlikely. Supervisors assumed maintenance would address it eventually.

Inmates noticed immediately. From the workshop yard, they saw that the area was rarely inspected. Notes were passed through the gap, and soon packages of tobacco and cell phones appeared near the fence for retrieval during work assignments. The gap had become a contraband pipeline.

Escalation

Over two months, contraband smuggling escalated. What began with tobacco expanded to drugs and weapons. Street gangs coordinated with incarcerated members to drop packages near the damaged section at night.

Inmates used workshop tools to widen the gap gradually, testing limits and waiting for intervention. None came. The signal was clear: staff tolerated a broken perimeter. Inmates interpreted it as permission to push further.

The Escape Plot

By summer, a group of inmates began planning an escape. They studied guard shifts and discovered patrols were inconsistent; some shifts skipped the far corner entirely.

Their plan: slip through the outer fence during a shift change, enter the sterile zone, and cut the inner fence using smuggled tools. The gap had started as a minor tear—a broken window—and grown into a door of opportunity.

The Discovery

The plot was discovered by chance. An officer conducting an unusually thorough evening round noticed suspicious movement near the fence. Backup arrived, and staff intercepted inmates retrieving contraband. Searches uncovered maps of the yard and hidden wire cutters in the workshop.

Investigation revealed how close the prison had come to a major breach. Without that officer's vigilance, the escape might have occurred within days.

Administrative Response

The administration acted urgently:

- The damaged fence was repaired within 48 hours.
- Additional razor wire was added.
- Perimeter patrols were restructured for consistent coverage.
- Cameras were installed to monitor the previously blind zone.

Leadership recognized the problem was cultural as well as structural. Staff had tolerated the broken fence because the inner fence remained intact. In reality, the minor gap communicated weakness, which multiplied into contraband pipelines and an escape plan.

Training was reissued to emphasize that the perimeter is sacred. No damage, however small, could ever be ignored.

Cultural Reset

The incident changed staff attitudes. Officers began daily inspections with renewed seriousness. Supervisors personally checked reports. Maintenance crews were directed to prioritize perimeter issues above all other non-emergency repairs.

The fence itself became a teaching symbol. What appeared to be a small tear had nearly compromised the entire institution. Every detail mattered.

Lessons from the Ignored Perimeter Fence

1. **The perimeter is sacred.** Any weakness undermines public trust and staff credibility.
2. **Small damage multiplies.** A bent section of fence became a contraband pipeline and then an escape plan.
3. **Inmates test constantly.** What staff ignore, inmates exploit.
4. **Staff presence is prevention.** Consistent patrols detect and deter exploitation early.
5. **Culture matters.** Tolerating a broken fence communicates tolerance of disorder; repairing it immediately communicates ownership.

Reflection

The Ignored Perimeter Fence demonstrates how a single neglected detail can unravel an entire security system. What staff dismissed as minor became a signal of weakness that inmates exploited for contraband smuggling and escape planning.

Broken Windows explains the danger: each day the fence went unrepaired communicated neglect. Each package passed through multiplied disorder. Each day without patrols reinforced inmate ownership.

The lesson is clear: security begins with prevention. Perimeter integrity is non-negotiable. Small gaps are never small—they are broken windows on the outer wall of public trust. Correctional professionals must treat them as immediate priorities, not delayed maintenance.

Case Study 3: The Sloppy Round

Rounds are one of the simplest and most powerful security tools in corrections. Walking a housing unit, checking cells, observing inmates, and documenting presence sends the clearest message: staff are here, watching, and in control. Done properly, rounds prevent violence, detect contraband, and reinforce order. Done poorly, they communicate the opposite.

This case from a large urban jail in the Northeast demonstrates how sloppy rounds, tolerated for months, eroded staff authority, encouraged inmate misconduct, and nearly ended in tragedy.

The Setting

The jail housed over 2,800 inmates in multiple pods and dormitory units. Policy required officers to conduct rounds in each housing unit every 30 minutes. Rounds were to include:

- Visual confirmation of inmate presence and condition
- Inspection of doors and windows
- Notation in electronic logbooks

Supervisors were tasked with verifying documentation and conducting random spot checks.

On paper, the policy was strict. In practice, enforcement was lax. Staffing shortages, officer complacency, and supervisor disengagement led to a culture where rounds were rushed or skipped. Officers grew accustomed to "badge tapping" log stations without actually walking the unit. Inmates, as always, noticed.

Early Signals

The first signs of sloppiness were subtle:

- Inmates remained out of place during lockdown without correction.
- Showers stayed occupied beyond scheduled times.
- Contraband appeared more frequently.

Officers, pressed for time, began cutting corners. Instead of inspecting each cell, they glanced quickly down tiers and assumed compliance. Instead of walking the entire dorm, they checked only front rows of bunks. Supervisors, overwhelmed with paperwork, signed off without verifying.

Each skipped step was a broken window. Inmates read the signals clearly: rounds were optional, staff presence was negotiable, and details were unenforced.

Escalation

Once inmates realized staff were not truly watching, misconduct multiplied. Gambling, tattooing, and contraband exchanges flourished in areas officers ignored. Fights were staged in back rows of bunks where officers never ventured.

One group of inmates discovered that utility closets were never checked during rounds. They began storing makeshift weapons there. Another coordinated distractions during rounds to facilitate contraband exchanges.

Sloppy rounds communicated weakness. Inmates filled the void with their own order.

The Breaking Point

One night during third shift, an officer conducted a round in Dormitory B. Instead of walking the entire dorm, he checked only the first two rows, tapped the log station, and returned to his desk.

Unbeknownst to him, two inmates in the back row were assaulting another with a padlock in a sock. The victim was beaten unconscious. Other inmates stayed silent, knowing staff were not watching.

The officer discovered the victim an hour later, alerted by another inmate. The injuries were severe, including a fractured skull. The victim survived, but the incident shocked the facility.

Administrative Response

The investigation confirmed what many had already suspected: sloppy rounds had become the norm. Officers admitted they regularly skipped or rushed rounds, and supervisors acknowledged they rarely verified log accuracy. Electronic records revealed consistent gaps where rounds were entirely missed.

The administration acted decisively:

- Officers involved were disciplined.
- Supervisors were held accountable.
- Training was reissued emphasizing rounds as mandatory, not optional.
- Leadership reinforced that rounds are the backbone of inmate safety and staff authority.

New safeguards were introduced:

- Supervisors conducted surprise checks to verify rounds in person.
- Body-worn cameras confirmed rounds were completed properly.
- A culture campaign reminded staff: "Rounds Save Lives."

Cultural Reset

The campaign worked. Officers understood that rounds were active prevention, not busywork. Walking units consistently deterred misconduct, reassured compliant inmates, and reinforced authority.

Supervisors prioritized enforcement, treating gaps as serious violations rather than paperwork issues. Inmates noticed. With staff walking units consistently, gambling and fights declined, contraband exchanges decreased, and the message became clear: staff presence was back, and rules mattered.

Lessons from the Sloppy Round

1. **Rounds are presence.** Skipped rounds are skipped ownership. Inmates read absence as permission.
2. **Details matter.** Every cell, bunk, and closet must be checked. A glance is not a round.
3. **Supervisors are key.** Paperwork alone is meaningless. Verification through personal presence is essential.
4. **Culture determines compliance.** Consistent rounds reinforce authority; sloppy rounds undermine it.
5. **Rounds prevent tragedy.** The assault in Dormitory B could have been stopped or prevented with proper rounds.

Reflection

The Sloppy Round demonstrates how neglecting small details can have catastrophic consequences. Rounds are simple, requiring no special equipment—only staff presence and vigilance. Yet complacency and disengagement allowed inmates to fill the void with their own order.

Broken Windows explains the outcome: each skipped round was a broken window, communicating that staff presence was optional. Inmates multiplied disorder until tragedy struck.

The lesson is clear: rounds are sacred. They must be thorough, consistent, and owned. Officers cannot cut corners, supervisors cannot pencil-whip logs, and administrators cannot tolerate lapses. Staff presence is prevention. Without it, order collapses.

Analysis: Security as Daily Ownership

The three case studies in this chapter—the Broken Key Box, the Ignored Perimeter Fence, and the Sloppy Round—point to a single truth: security is not reaction, it is ownership.

Movies and media often portray corrections as a profession defined by emergencies: alarms ringing, tactical teams rushing, riots being quelled. Professionals inside know better. Real security is not measured by how a facility reacts to chaos, but by how consistently it prevents chaos from happening at all.

The Broken Windows Theory explains why prevention matters. Each small lapse, such as a mishandled key, a torn fence, or a skipped round, is a broken window. It signals to inmates that rules are negotiable, that order is fragile, and that opportunities exist. Each lapse multiplies into greater disorder. Conversely, each enforced detail, such as a locked key box, a repaired fence, or a completed round, is a repaired window. It signals staff ownership and deters misconduct.

Security as a Daily Habit

Security is not a single act but a series of disciplined habits. Locks must be checked, keys inventoried, rounds walked, and counts verified. These habits are simple but require consistency. Once discipline weakens, habits break, and inmates exploit the gaps.

- The Broken Key Box showed what happens when a broken lock becomes convenience. Inmates nearly escaped.
- The Ignored Perimeter Fence showed what happens when delays are tolerated. Neglect became a contraband pipeline and an escape plan.

- The Sloppy Round showed what happens when staff presence is optional. An inmate was nearly killed under staff watch.

Security fails not in dramatic moments but in daily ones. Habits determine outcomes.

Staff Presence as Security

Presence is the foundation of security. Walking units, observing inmates, and correcting details deter misconduct. Presence is not limited to rounds.

- A sergeant checking doors communicates ownership.
- A lieutenant inspecting fences communicates vigilance.
- An officer correcting a uniform violation communicates attention to detail.

Presence tells inmates, "Staff own this place." Absence tells them, "You can."

Inmate Perception of Security

Inmates interpret security lapses immediately. They notice when keys are mishandled, fences sag, or rounds are skipped. They exploit patterns ruthlessly.

Inmates also respect vigilance. They notice when officers check locks, when supervisors inspect units, and when contraband is seized. Consistent enforcement deters testing. When staff enforce details daily, risk outweighs reward and compliance becomes rational.

Broken Windows reinforces this logic. Each lapse signals opportunity. Each correction signals authority.

Supervisors as Culture Keepers

Supervisors determine whether security is culture or paperwork. Policies mean nothing if supervisors overlook lapses or pencil-whip logs. Culture changes only when supervisors enforce standards personally.

In the Sloppy Round case, supervisors failed to verify rounds. In the Broken Key Box, they tolerated unrepaired equipment. In the Ignored Perimeter Fence, inspections were delayed. In each case, the absence of supervisory ownership allowed collapse.

Supervisors must model vigilance. Their presence on the floor, insistence on correction, and refusal to walk past disorder sets the tone.

Security as Ownership at Every Level

Ownership cannot be reserved for administrators. It must begin at the lowest level. The officer walking a round owns security. The maintenance worker repairing a fence owns security. The sergeant verifying keys owns security.

When ownership begins at the bottom, culture is sustained. When staff believe security is "someone else's job," culture collapses. The Broken Windows framework reinforces this point: every officer owns every window. Every small detail is their responsibility. Waiting for leadership to enforce details is waiting for collapse.

Why Reaction Is Not Enough

Facilities often pride themselves on tactical response, measuring readiness by how quickly teams can gear up and storm a unit. While emergency response is necessary, it is not sufficient. By the time teams are activated, order is already broken.

Reaction measures recovery; prevention builds culture. The case studies prove this. No tactical team could have prevented the Broken Key Box from being exploited if the inmate had seconds more. No emergency plan could have restored order if the perimeter fence had been breached. No riot gear could undo the damage caused by sloppy rounds.

True security is invisible to the public because nothing happens. That invisibility is the product of daily ownership.

The Cost of Neglect

Neglecting security details carries enormous costs. An escape can shatter public trust, trigger lawsuits, and end careers. A single assault caused by sloppy rounds can cost millions in liability and morale. Contraband pipelines can fuel gang activity for years.

By contrast, enforcing security details costs little. Replacing a key box lock is inexpensive. Repairing a fence section is simple. Walking rounds takes only minutes. The choice is not between cost and savings; it is between paying small costs daily or massive costs after collapse.

Security as Culture

Ultimately, security is culture. A facility where officers treat keys, doors, rounds, and counts as sacred creates a culture of vigilance. A facility where staff treat details casually fosters neglect. Inmates adapt accordingly.

Broken Windows is a cultural theory applied to security. Every enforced detail builds culture. Every ignored detail erodes it. Staff either project ownership or invite inmates to claim it.

Reflection on Daily Ownership

The Broken Key Box, the Ignored Perimeter Fence, and the Sloppy Round all point to the same lesson: security is not a special event. It is not sirens and tactical teams. It is not crisis response. Security is the quiet, consistent ownership of details by every staff member, every day.

Broken Windows shows why. Each neglected detail is a broken window. Each enforced detail is a repaired window. In corrections, security is measured not by how staff respond to alarms but by how few alarms ever need to sound.

The lesson is simple but profound: security is prevention, not reaction. Prevention is ownership, not paperwork. Ownership begins at the lowest level and rises to the highest. When staff own details, inmates respect authority. When staff neglect details, inmates seize it.

Correctional leaders must embed this truth into culture: security is daily ownership.

Tools and Takeaways

Security is prevention, not reaction. The Broken Windows Theory shows that details matter because every lapse communicates weakness, and every enforced detail communicates ownership. Security collapses when staff tolerate small cracks. Security thrives when staff close those cracks quickly and consistently.

Practical tools for correctional leaders, supervisors, and line staff can embed proactive security into culture, making vigilance a daily habit rather than a reaction after the fact:

1. **Treat Every Detail as Sacred**
   a. Keys, locks, doors, counts, rounds, and searches are not paperwork. They are the foundation of safety.
   b. Staff must treat these details as sacred obligations, not optional tasks.
   c. Supervisors must enforce that no lapse is too small to correct.

   Principle: What staff treat as sacred, inmates treat as unbreakable.

2. **Daily Security Inspections**
    a. Officers must check doors, locks, and key boxes every shift.
    b. Supervisors must verify reports through physical inspection, not just paperwork.
    c. Any broken or malfunctioning item must be reported and repaired immediately.

    Principle: Prevention begins with inspection.

3. **Key Control Protocols**
    a. Keys must be secured in locked boxes when not in use, signed out, tracked, and inventoried daily.
    b. Spare keys must be logged and inspected regularly.
    c. Broken locks must be repaired within 24 hours. No exceptions.

    Principle: Keys are authority. Authority cannot be mishandled.

4. **Perimeter Integrity**
    a. Inspect the perimeter daily.
    b. Repair any damage immediately.
    c. Patrols must be consistent, documented, and verified by supervisors.
    d. Cameras and lighting should support, not replace, human presence.

    Principle: The perimeter is sacred. Cracks in the outer wall are cracks in public trust.

5. **Rounds as Ownership**
    a. Conduct full visual checks of every cell, bunk, and utility space.
    b. Supervisors must verify logs through surprise inspections.
    c. Skipped rounds are serious violations, not minor issues.

    Principle: Presence is prevention. Absence is permission.

6. **Searches as Culture**
   a. Conduct searches consistently and thoroughly.
   b. Correct every contraband find immediately.
   c. Supervisors must review reports and verify techniques personally.
   d. Proper staff training on the results of contraband.

   Principle: Every missed item multiplies. Every seized item deters.

7. **Supervisor Accountability**
   a. Supervisors must verify details personally. Paperwork cannot substitute for presence.
   b. Random checks must be documented and reviewed by administration.
   c. Supervisors model the vigilance they demand.

   Principle: Culture follows supervisors.

8. **Empower Staff at the Lowest Level**
   a. Officers must be empowered to report and correct lapses immediately.
   b. Line staff suggestions should be encouraged and acted upon.
   c. Ownership begins at the lowest level.

   Principle: Security is owned from the bottom up.

9. **Document and Display Security Wins**
   a. Share statistics on contraband seizures, repairs, and completed rounds.
   b. Recognize officers and teams who enforce details consistently.
   c. Use visual reminders to reinforce security as culture.

   Principle: Visibility reinforces vigilance.

10. Train Constantly

a. Include security basics in every academy class and annual training cycle.
b. Use anonymized case studies to show consequences of lapses.

Principle: Training sustains culture.

Sample Daily Security Checklist

- ☐ *Keys and Locks:* Locked and secured key boxes, keys signed out and logged, functional locks.
- ☐ *Doors and Perimeter:* Secured cell doors, pod doors, sally ports; inspected perimeter; intact fence lines.
- ☐ *Counts and Rounds:* Completed counts with visual confirmation; rounds every 30 minutes; supervisor verification.
- ☐ *Searches and Contraband:* Random searches conducted; contraband removed; utility and common areas checked.
- ☐ *Culture and Presence:* Officers visible and engaged; supervisors walk units daily; lapses corrected immediately.

Reflection

Security is not reactive; it is proactive. It is the daily ownership of small details that prevents chaos. The Broken Key Box showed how mishandled keys nearly caused an escape. The Ignored Perimeter Fence showed how a small tear became a contraband pipeline. The Sloppy Round showed how skipped presence nearly cost a life.

Broken Windows explains why. Each neglected detail is a broken window. Each enforced detail is a repaired window. Security is measured not by alarms but by how few alarms are ever needed.

Correctional leaders must instill this truth: security is daily ownership. Every officer owns every detail. Every supervisor owns every standard. Every administrator owns every culture. When ownership is shared, prevention is constant.

The public does not see prevention; they see safety. They assume order is natural. Inside, staff know better. Order is not natural; it is built, detail by detail, round by round, count by count. When staff own details, facilities run smoothly. When staff neglect details, facilities collapse.

The lesson is simple but absolute: proactive security is prevention, and prevention is ownership.

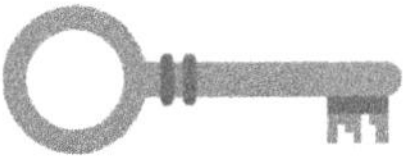

- 10 -

TECHNOLOGY AS A PARTNER, NOT A CRUTCH

Technology as Support, Not Substitute

In the modern correctional environment, technology is everywhere. Cameras line walls and ceilings. Radios connect staff across sprawling compounds. Electronic rounds systems track officer presence. Sensors monitor doors, fences, and movement. Newer facilities are built with technology woven into every corner, while older facilities scramble to retrofit systems into outdated layouts.

Technology is a powerful ally. It extends staff presence, multiplies observation, and provides documentation that reinforces accountability. When used well, it embodies Broken Windows principles. A working camera repaired immediately sends the message that staff control every corner. A functioning radio system sends the message that staff support is always a call away. An electronic key tracker that never fails sends the message that authority is guarded and precise.

But technology is also a broken window if neglected. A camera left broken for months is no different than graffiti left unpainted—it tells inmates that staff cannot see. A dead radio zone is the equivalent of a dark hallway—it tells inmates staff cannot reach each other. A key-tracking system ignored or bypassed tells inmates that procedures are a façade. Technology is not neutral. Like the environment itself, it communicates ownership or neglect.

Too often, administrators fall into the myth that technology can replace staff presence. They believe cameras can substitute for rounds or sensors can substitute for inspections. That belief is dangerous. Technology cannot prevent disorder on its own. It can only extend staff presence. Cameras record, but they cannot intervene. Radios transmit, but they cannot act. Systems track, but they cannot correct.

The Broken Windows Theory makes this distinction clear. Technology that is repaired quickly, used consistently, and enforced daily is a repaired window. Technology that is neglected or relied on as a substitute is a broken window. It communicates that staff are absent and that order is fragile.

The lesson is simple: technology is support, not substitute. Facilities thrive when staff and tools work together. Facilities collapse when tools replace staff or when tools are neglected.

Technology as Signals of Ownership

Technology in corrections is more than equipment—it is communication. Every working camera, every clear radio call, every accurate round log, and every functioning key tracker sends a message that staff own the facility. Every broken device, every static-filled dead zone, every bypassed system sends the opposite message: staff are absent, rules are flexible, and opportunity exists.

The Broken Windows Theory reminds us that details matter because details send signals. Technology is no different. Tools either reinforce culture or undermine it. Their presence and functionality are visible to inmates and staff alike. A broken device tolerated is no different than broken glass ignored on a city street—it tells everyone watching that ownership has slipped.

Cameras

Cameras are perhaps the most visible form of technology in corrections. They extend staff presence into every corner, capture misconduct, and provide documentation that reinforces accountability. When functional and monitored, they deter misconduct. Inmates think twice before acting under the unblinking eye of surveillance.

But cameras are only effective when they are credible. A broken or misaligned camera communicates neglect. Inmates quickly learn which cameras are inoperative, and those blind spots become zones of misconduct. A single broken camera tolerated for weeks is a broken window—it signals to inmates that surveillance is not taken seriously.

Maintenance is critical. Cameras must be repaired within hours, not weeks. Staff must treat every outage as urgent. Supervisors must verify that monitoring is active, not symbolic. Technology loses its deterrent power the moment it loses credibility.

Signal of ownership: A repaired camera tells inmates staff see everything.
Signal of neglect: A broken camera tells inmates staff are blind.

Radios

Radios are lifelines. They connect staff across units, respond to emergencies, and provide instant backup. A clear, functioning radio system communicates strength and presence. Staff know they are not alone. Inmates know that staff can summon help instantly.

But radios also fail. Dead zones in basements or hallways create vulnerabilities. Static-filled transmissions frustrate staff. Batteries that fail mid-shift undermine confidence. Inmates notice when radios falter. They know where staff cannot call for help—and they exploit those weaknesses, staging misconduct where response will be delayed.

Radios are not optional. They are staff survival. They must be tested daily, batteries checked every shift, and dead zones documented and corrected. A dead zone tolerated for months is a broken window—it tells inmates staff are isolated.

Signal of ownership: A clear call answered immediately shows staff are united.
Signal of neglect: A call lost in static shows staff are vulnerable.

Electronic Rounds Systems

Many facilities now use electronic systems to track rounds. Officers tap devices or scan barcodes as they walk units. When used properly, these systems document presence and reassure supervisors.

But inmates quickly learn whether the system reflects real rounds or just paperwork. If officers tap without walking, if supervisors accept gaps, if logs are falsified—the system loses credibility. A round recorded without presence is a broken window. It signals to inmates that staff are absent and to staff that dishonesty is tolerated.

Electronic rounds systems must be enforced with integrity. Supervisors must verify physically, not just electronically. Logs must be matched with body-worn cameras or in-person checks. The system must reflect reality, not ritual.

Signal of ownership: A round walked thoroughly reinforces authority.
Signal of neglect: A round tapped without presence reinforces inmate control.

Key Tracking Systems

Electronic key control systems track when keys are removed and returned. They enforce accountability by logging every transaction. When functional, they transform culture. Staff know they are accountable, and inmates know keys are secure.

But when systems are bypassed, their credibility collapses. If spare keys are hidden in drawers, if supervisors ignore discrepancies, or if broken readers go unrepaired, the system becomes a façade. Inmates notice sloppiness and interpret it as opportunity.

Key tracking systems must be treated as sacred. Every discrepancy must be investigated. Every broken reader must be repaired immediately. The system is only as strong as the culture enforcing it.

Signal of ownership: A functioning tracker shows staff guard authority carefully.
Signal of neglect: A bypassed system shows authority is negotiable.

Other Tools

Beyond the core systems, correctional facilities employ dozens of other technologies—body-worn cameras, door sensors, metal detectors, mail scanners, and more. Each tool communicates ownership or neglect depending on how it is used.

- **Body-worn cameras** deter misconduct when activated consistently. When staff fail to turn them on, they communicate neglect.
- **Door sensors** reinforce security when alarms are responded to immediately. When alarms are ignored, they communicate tolerance for disorder.
- **Metal detectors** reinforce contraband control when enforced without exception. When staff wave inmates through casually, they communicate weakness.
- **Mail scanners** deter smuggling when used consistently. When broken scanners sit unused, they communicate indifference.
- Every tool matters because every tool sends signals.

The Credibility of Tools

The power of technology is not in the tool itself but in its credibility. Inmates know the difference between a camera that works and one that does not, between a round logged electronically and one actually walked. Staff also know the difference. When tools are maintained and enforced, staff feel supported. When tools are broken or bypassed, staff feel abandoned.

The credibility of tools determines whether they reinforce or undermine Broken Windows principles.

Reflection on Signals

Technology is never neutral—it communicates culture. Functional tools communicate vigilance. Broken tools communicate neglect. Every camera, radio, tracker, and sensor is a window. When repaired and enforced, it signals staff ownership. When broken or ignored, it signals inmate opportunity.

The lesson is clear: technology must be treated as sacred. It must be maintained, enforced, and integrated into culture. Otherwise, it becomes another broken window multiplying disorder.

Case Study 1: The Silent Camera

Cameras are among the most powerful tools in a correctional facility. They extend staff presence into every corner, document incidents, and deter misconduct. But cameras are only as effective as their credibility. When they fail and remain unrepaired, they lose authority and become broken windows. Inmates quickly learn which cameras work—and which do not. Once they know, they act.

This case from a county jail in the Southeast shows how a single broken camera, left unrepaired for weeks, unraveled order and ended in violence.

The Setting

The jail housed about 1,200 inmates in pod-style housing. Each pod had two levels of cells and a central dayroom. Cameras covered every corner, feeding into a control room where officers monitored live footage. Supervisors used the recordings to review incidents and support disciplinary action.

For years, the system worked well. Inmates knew they were being watched. Staff knew misconduct would be detected, even if not witnessed directly. The constant presence of cameras reinforced Broken Windows principles: graffiti was removed immediately, contraband intercepted, and fights investigated swiftly.

Until one camera failed.

The Failure

One evening, the camera covering the rear corner of Pod C went dark. The feed disappeared from the control room. Staff logged the issue and notified maintenance, but the repair request was added to a backlog. Other projects took priority. Days passed. Then weeks.

The camera stayed broken.

At first, staff assumed the impact was minimal. The pod still had multiple cameras, and officers made regular rounds. Supervisors believed the gap was temporary. But inmates noticed almost immediately.

Inmate Awareness

Inmates see everything. Within days, they realized the rear corner of Pod C was no longer under surveillance. The lens hung uselessly, blinking red. They began gathering there—first for small things: card games, commissary trades, idle talk.

When staff told them to disperse, they complied slowly, smirking. Officers felt the shift. The corner, once neutral, had become inmate territory.

The camera had been a silent officer. With its presence gone, ownership of the space changed hands.

Escalation

The corner soon became a hub for contraband. Inmates passed tobacco, then drugs. They hid items under tables, knowing officers couldn't prove misconduct without video evidence.

Graffiti appeared on the walls. When officers intervened, inmates mocked them: "You didn't see anything. Camera's dead."

Fights followed—first quick scuffles over debts, then organized assaults. Groups staged attacks in the blind spot, confident staff couldn't see unless they walked through at the exact moment.

Supervisors noticed rising reports of disorder in Pod C but failed to connect them to the broken camera. The backlog remained. The camera stayed dark.

The Assault

The breaking point came on a Saturday afternoon. A gang dispute erupted in Pod C. Inmates lured a rival into the rear corner. Out of sight of working cameras, they attacked with makeshift weapons.

Officers in the control room saw only movement—men entering and leaving the blind spot. The assault itself was invisible. By the time floor staff realized something was wrong, the victim was bleeding on the ground. He survived but suffered severe injuries.

The aftermath was chaos. The pod was locked down. Supervisors scrambled to reconstruct the event, but without footage, accountability collapsed. Inmates denied involvement. Staff knew who was responsible, but without evidence, discipline faltered.

Administrative Response

Leadership was forced to confront the failure. One neglected camera had enabled a culture of disorder that ended in violence.

The investigation found:

- The outage was logged but never prioritized.
- Staff had grown complacent, assuming other cameras and rounds were enough.
- Supervisors failed to link rising disorder to missing surveillance.
- Maintenance delays signaled that technology was not sacred.

The message to inmates was unmistakable: staff tolerated the blind spot. Inmates claimed it.

The camera was repaired within 48 hours of the assault. Additional cameras were installed for overlapping coverage. Policy was revised to require repairs within 72 hours. Supervisors were directed to inspect pods daily and reinforce that broken cameras are security failures, not maintenance issues.

Cultural Reset

The incident changed the culture. Officers began reporting camera issues immediately. Supervisors treated outages as critical. Maintenance prioritized surveillance above all nonessential repairs.

Inmates noticed. Blind spots disappeared. Corners were cleared. Contraband declined.

The repaired camera, like a repaired window, sent a message: staff were present again. Order returned.

Lessons from the Silent Camera

- **Cameras are presence.** A broken camera is an absent officer.
- **Credibility is everything.** Inmates always know which cameras work.
- **Neglect is a signal.** A broken camera tolerated is a broken window.
- **Documentation is power.** Without footage, discipline collapses.
- **Maintenance is culture.** Repair speed equals ownership. Delay equals surrender.

Reflection

The Silent Camera shows that technology is not neutral. When functional, it reinforces the Broken Windows principles of deterring misconduct and strengthening staff authority. When broken, it communicates neglect, emboldens inmates, and spreads disorder.

Each day the camera remained dark, it was a broken window, signaling that inmates owned the space. When staff repaired it and reclaimed that corner, order followed.

The lesson is clear: treat technology as sacred. Every outage is a broken window that multiplies disorder. Every repair is a restored window that rebuilds culture.

Case Study 2: The Radio Dead Zone

Radios are lifelines in correctional facilities. They connect officers spread across housing units, yards, and corridors. They allow instant backup, coordinated movement, and rapid emergency response. A reliable radio system tells staff they are supported—and tells inmates that help is only a call away. A failing system tells staff they are isolated—and tells inmates that opportunity exists.

This case from a large state correctional facility in the Northeast shows how a persistent radio dead zone created a culture of vulnerability and nearly led to disaster.

The Setting

The prison housed more than 3,000 inmates across multiple housing blocks, work areas, and yards. The facility had been upgraded with modern radio equipment, but the thick concrete walls of certain areas created coverage gaps. The worst was the laundry building, a massive structure filled with industrial washers and dryers spread across two floors.

Staff had complained for years that radio signals in the laundry were unreliable. Messages crackled with static or dropped entirely. Calls for assistance often went unheard. Maintenance logs reflected the issue repeatedly, but funding for new repeaters was delayed. The dead zone became part of daily reality.

Early Signals

At first, the dead zone was seen as a nuisance rather than a crisis. Officers working in the laundry adapted by stepping outside to make calls or using hand signals with coworkers. Supervisors knew about the issue but considered it low priority compared to perimeter upgrades and camera installations.

Inmates, however, noticed. They watched officers leave the building to use radios. They overheard complaints about static. They realized staff working inside were effectively cut off from the rest of the facility.

The signal was clear: in the laundry, officers were alone.

Escalation

Inmates began testing the vulnerability. Minor defiance escalated when staff gave orders inside the dead zone. Inmates ignored instructions, knowing backup couldn't be summoned instantly. Contraband exchanges increased in the laundry because inmates knew discovery wouldn't trigger an immediate response.

A group of inmates began using the dead zone to intimidate weaker peers. They cornered them in areas where officers hesitated to intervene without support. Threats multiplied as staff presence weakened under the weight of poor communication.

The laundry became a pocket of inmate control inside the prison.

The Incident

The crisis came on a Tuesday afternoon. An officer assigned to the laundry confronted two inmates suspected of passing contraband. When he attempted to confiscate the item, they resisted. A fight broke out.

The officer reached for his radio and called for backup. Static answered. He repeated the call—no response. Nearby inmates realized what was happening. Some shouted encouragement. Others blocked the officer's path to the exit.

The officer was outnumbered and isolated. He fought to maintain control but sustained multiple blows. Only after another officer entered the building and physically ran outside to relay the call did backup arrive. By then, the officer had suffered serious injuries.

Administrative Response

The incident forced leadership to confront the long-ignored dead zone. The investigation revealed that:

- Staff had logged radio failures for years with no permanent fix.
- Supervisors tolerated workarounds instead of demanding resolution.
- Inmates deliberately exploited the weakness.
- The culture of neglect had communicated that safety was negotiable.

Within weeks, repeaters were installed to eliminate the dead zone. Radios were tested daily to confirm coverage. Supervisors were instructed to verify all reports of signal loss immediately.

The injured officer recovered—but the lesson was costly. A flaw tolerated for years had nearly cost a life.

Cultural Reset

Repairing the radio system changed culture overnight. Officers in the laundry reported feeling safer and more confident. Backup calls were answered instantly. Inmates, once emboldened by the dead zone, became compliant again, knowing help was only a button away.

Supervisors emphasized that technology is not background—it is survival. Training reinforced that every equipment failure must be treated as urgent. Staff were reminded that inmates see and exploit every weakness.

The repair was not just technical. It was cultural. It told staff they were supported—and told inmates that staff were united.

Lessons from the Radio Dead Zone

- **Radios are lifelines.** When they fail, staff are isolated—and inmates know it.
- **Dead zones are broken windows.** Every crackle of static communicates weakness.
- **Staff adapt, but inmates exploit.** Workarounds invite testing.
- **Neglect multiplies.** A flaw tolerated for years nearly cost a life.
- **Repair is ownership.** Fixing the system restored authority and safety.

Reflection

The Radio Dead Zone shows that technology cannot be treated as background. Radios are not conveniences—they are survival. When they fail, staff are isolated, inmates are emboldened, and safety collapses.

Broken Windows explains the danger. Each day the dead zone was tolerated was a broken window. It told inmates the laundry was theirs, and they acted accordingly. Only when leadership repaired the system did the signal shift. Staff owned the space again.

The lesson is clear: every communication tool is sacred. Every flaw is urgent. Technology is not neutral—it either reinforces presence or erodes it.

Case Study 3: The Key Tracker

Keys are the physical embodiment of authority in a correctional facility. Whoever controls the keys controls movement, access, and safety. Every locked door is only as secure as the keys that open it.

For decades, key control depended on paper sign-out sheets and staff integrity. While most officers took the responsibility seriously, the system was vulnerable to human error, shortcuts, and occasional abuse.

This case from a regional jail in the Midwest shows how adopting an electronic key-tracking system improved accountability and reshaped the facility's culture.

The Setting

The jail housed about 1,000 inmates across multiple pods, dormitories, and support areas. Key control had long been a source of tension. Officers signed keys in and out of wooden lockboxes using paper logs.

In theory, the process was strict. Keys were to be logged at the start and end of every shift, and supervisors were to review the logs daily. In practice, shortcuts were common. Officers often passed keys informally at shift change without recording it. Supervisors sometimes signed logs after the fact. Spare keys were kept in drawers or pockets rather than properly secured.

Inmates noticed. They saw officers exchange keys casually. They heard jokes about "lost keys" and witnessed staff argue about missing sets. The message was clear: authority was being mishandled.

Early Consequences

The sloppy culture around keys did not immediately cause escapes, but it created steady problems. Doors were left unlocked because officers did not know who held the keys. Contraband appeared more frequently in restricted areas. Maintenance workers complained about delays because keys were misplaced.

One incident nearly became disastrous. A key ring went missing for several hours before being found in a staff locker. The facility went into modified lockdown during the search. Inmates realized staff had lost control of their own authority. Word spread quickly, and respect for staff weakened.

Leadership recognized the system was no longer sustainable.

The Upgrade

The administration approved the purchase of an **electronic key-tracking system.** Each key ring was fitted with a unique chip and stored in a secure cabinet that required staff to log in with personal credentials. The cabinet recorded the time, date, and identity of every officer who removed or returned a key ring. If a set was not returned by the end of the shift, an alarm activated. Reports could be generated instantly to show accountability.

The rollout included training sessions and a clear message from leadership: **the new system was not optional. It was a cultural shift.** Keys represented authority, and casual handling of authority would no longer be tolerated.

Inmate Reaction

Inmates noticed the change immediately. Keys were no longer passed casually. Officers walked to the cabinet, logged in, and handled key rings with visible formality. Inmates saw that staff took the process seriously. The message was unmistakable—staff owned authority again.

Testing declined. Inmates who once lingered near staff offices to watch sloppy exchanges saw no opportunities. Gossip about "lost keys" disappeared. Doors were consistently locked and checked.

Staff Adjustment

At first, some officers complained about the added steps. Logging in and out felt slow compared to old shortcuts. Over time, however, staff adapted. The system actually saved time because supervisors no longer had to chase missing keys or fix inaccurate logs.

More importantly, officers began to feel supported. The system reinforced their credibility. When inmates complained about missing property or accused staff of mishandling keys, reports from the system provided clear evidence. Accountability was no longer dependent on memory or trust—it was documented.

Cultural Transformation

Within months, the facility noticed broader cultural changes:

- **Accountability improved.** Every officer knew their actions were recorded.
- **Confidence increased.** Staff felt supported by a transparent system.
- **Inmate respect returned.** Authority was consistent and credible again.
- **Contraband declined.** Fewer opportunities existed to move items through unsecured doors.

The electronic key-tracking system had become more than a tool. It was a cultural reset.

Long-Term Impact

Two years after implementation, the results were clear:

- No incidents of missing keys.
- Contraband incidents linked to unsecured areas dropped by 40 percent.
- Staff disciplinary actions related to key handling fell to zero.
- Surveys showed officers felt safer and more professional in their work.

Leadership used the success to reinforce a broader truth: technology supports culture, but culture sustains technology. If staff had ignored or bypassed the system, it would have failed. Because they embraced it, order multiplied.

Lessons from the Key Tracker

- **Keys represent authority.** Controlling them precisely communicates ownership.
- **Technology shapes culture.** Tools only work when used consistently.
- **Sloppiness is a signal.** Casual handling of keys communicates weakness.
- **Documentation builds credibility.** Tracking removes doubt and builds trust.
- **Culture adapts.** Resistance fades when professionalism is reinforced.

Reflection

The Key Tracker demonstrates how technology, when aligned with Broken Windows principles, can reshape culture. Mishandled keys were broken windows that signaled neglect and invited testing. The electronic system repaired those windows by making authority visible, precise, and credible.

Each casual exchange once told inmates that rules were flexible. Each logged and secured key told them authority was non-negotiable. The signal shifted because the culture shifted.

The lesson is clear: technology must be treated as sacred, but it must also be integrated into culture. Tools alone cannot fix neglect. When staff embrace them as part of ownership, they multiply order.

Analysis: Technology and Broken Windows

The three case studies—The Silent Camera, The Radio Dead Zone, and The Key Tracker—demonstrate a single truth: technology does not create order on its own. It amplifies the culture that already exists.

When tools are maintained, enforced, and used consistently, they strengthen authority and deter misconduct. When they are broken, ignored, or bypassed, they amplify neglect and invite testing. Technology in corrections is never neutral. It is either a repaired window or a broken one.

Technology as Presence

Technology extends staff presence. Cameras see what eyes cannot. Radios connect voices across walls. Key trackers log accountability across shifts. When functional, these tools communicate vigilance. Inmates know they are observed, staff know they are supported, and supervisors know they can enforce standards.

Technology also magnifies absence. A broken camera signals blindness. A failed radio signals isolation. A bypassed key tracker signals sloppiness. Inmates interpret these signals instantly. If staff tolerate failures, inmates treat them as permission to exploit.

The Silent Camera showed how a blind spot becomes inmate territory. The Radio Dead Zone showed how isolation emboldens misconduct. The Key

Tracker showed how repaired technology strengthens authority. Technology magnifies presence or absence depending on how it is maintained.

Technology as Credibility

Credibility is the real power of technology. Inmates know which cameras work, which radios transmit, and which systems are enforced. Staff know too. Credibility builds culture, while lack of credibility erodes it.

When cameras are repaired quickly, inmates believe surveillance is constant. When radios transmit clearly, inmates believe staff are united. When key trackers log every movement, inmates believe authority is precise. Credibility deters testing because the risk outweighs the reward.

Credibility collapses when broken tools are tolerated. A dark camera that remains unrepaired tells inmates surveillance is negotiable. A failing radio tells them backup is unreliable. A bypassed key-tracking system tells them authority is sloppy. Each failure multiplies disorder because it signals inconsistency.

The credibility of tools determines whether they repair or break windows.

Technology as Culture

Technology cannot replace culture. It can only reinforce it. A facility where staff are vigilant will use tools to extend vigilance. A facility where staff are complacent will use tools as excuses to avoid presence.

The Silent Camera proved this when staff relied too heavily on surveillance instead of maintaining presence. The Radio Dead Zone proved this when staff tolerated weak coverage instead of demanding repair. The Key Tracker proved this when staff embraced the system, integrated it into daily operations, and strengthened order.

Technology follows culture. If culture is strong, tools multiply strength. If culture is weak, tools multiply weakness.

Technology as Broken Windows

Each tool is a window. Repaired, it communicates ownership. Broken, it communicates neglect.

- A repaired camera tells inmates they are observed.
- A broken camera tells them there is space to act.
- A clear radio tells inmates staff are united.
- A dead zone tells them staff are vulnerable.
- A functioning tracker tells inmates authority is secure.
- A bypassed system tells them authority is negotiable.

Broken Windows Theory applies to technology as directly as it applies to graffiti or sanitation. Small cracks tolerated multiply disorder. Small repairs enforced multiply into culture.

The Cost of Neglected Technology

Neglecting technology carries steep costs. The Silent Camera enabled an assault that could have been prevented. The Radio Dead Zone left an officer injured because backup was delayed. These failures brought human, legal, and financial consequences far greater than the cost of timely repairs.

The Key Tracker demonstrated the opposite. A modest investment in a credible system reduced contraband, improved morale, and prevented crises. Prevention proved cheaper than collapse.

Leaders must calculate costs honestly. Delayed repairs do not save money. They multiply risk. Every day a tool remains broken increases the chance of crisis, lawsuit, or tragedy.

Supervisors and Technology

Supervisors are the gatekeepers of technological credibility. They decide whether a broken camera is logged and repaired or logged and ignored. They decide whether dead zones are tolerated or fixed. They decide whether systems are enforced or bypassed.

Supervisors who demand credibility create cultures of vigilance. Supervisors who tolerate neglect create cultures of disorder. The difference lies not in the equipment but in leadership.

Inmates and Technology

Inmates adapt instantly to technological signals. They test cameras, radios, and trackers daily. They know which tools work and which do not and adjust their behavior accordingly.

They also respond when credibility is restored. Misconduct multiplied when the Silent Camera was broken but declined after it was repaired. Defiance grew in the Radio Dead Zone but declined once signals were restored. Testing declined in the Key Tracker case as accountability increased.

Technology communicates constantly. Inmates read its signals faster than staff often realize.

Reflection on Technology and Broken Windows

The three case studies prove the principle: technology magnifies culture. It is never neutral. Broken tools multiply disorder. Repaired tools multiply order.

Every neglected outage is a broken window that signals absence and invites inmate ownership. Every repaired system is a repaired window that signals presence and reinforces authority.

Correctional leaders must embed this truth into culture. Technology is support, not substitute. It must be maintained with urgency, enforced with integrity, and integrated into daily practice. Otherwise, it becomes another broken window multiplying risk.

The lesson is clear. Technology cannot create ownership, but it can amplify it. When culture is strong, tools multiply strength. When culture is weak, tools multiply weakness. Leaders must decide which culture they will allow.

Tools and Takeaways

Technology is powerful but not magic. Cameras, radios, key trackers, electronic rounds, and sensors can multiply staff authority or multiply staff neglect. The difference is not in the equipment itself but in how it is used, maintained, and enforced.

Broken Windows teaches that details communicate ownership or neglect. Technology is no different. A repaired camera tells inmates staff are watching. A broken one tells them staff are blind. A clear radio call tells them staff are united. A dead zone tells them staff are vulnerable. A functioning tracker tells them authority is secure. A bypassed system tells them authority is casual.

The following tools and takeaways provide a practical framework for using technology to reinforce, not replace, staff culture.

1. Treat Technology as Sacred

- Every camera, radio, and sensor is a window. Broken tools are broken windows.
- Staff must treat technology as part of their authority, not background noise.
- Supervisors must treat outages with the same urgency as broken locks or unsecured doors.

Principle: Technology communicates culture. Treat it as sacred.

2. Repair Quickly

- ☐ Broken tools lose credibility instantly. Inmates notice failure before staff sometimes do.
- ☐ Repairs must be completed within strict timeframes, ideally 72 hours or less.
- ☐ Temporary fixes, such as extra rounds or posted staff, must cover the gap if immediate repair is not possible.

Principle: Credibility is measured by speed.

3. Maintain Proactively

- ☐ Do not wait for failure. Inspect systems daily.
- ☐ Test cameras, radios, trackers, and alarms every shift.
- ☐ Replace batteries, update software, and check connections routinely.
- ☐ Preventive maintenance communicates that staff are always ahead of disorder.

Principle: Proactive care prevents cracks from appearing.

4. Use Tools to Support, Not Replace, Presence

- ☐ Cameras do not replace rounds. Radios do not replace backup. Trackers do not replace supervision.
- ☐ Tools must extend staff vigilance, not excuse staff absence.
- ☐ Leaders must reinforce that technology is support, not substitute.

Principle: Presence is irreplaceable.

5. Enforce Credibility

- ☐ Supervisors must verify that tools are used consistently.
- ☐ Logs, recordings, and reports must match reality.
- ☐ Officers who bypass systems must be corrected immediately.
- ☐ Inmates must see that every tool is credible and enforced.

Principle: Credibility sustains deterrence.

6. Train Staff in Technology Awareness

- ☐ Staff must be trained not just in using tools but in interpreting their signals.
- ☐ Officers should understand how inmates test technology.
- ☐ Supervisors should teach staff to see lapses as signals of lost ownership.

Principle: Training turns tools into culture.

7. Integrate Technology into Inspections

- ☐ Supervisors must include technology checks in daily inspections.
- ☐ Administrators must receive weekly reports on outages and repairs.
- ☐ Technology must be part of audits, accreditation standards, and culture assessments.

Principle: Inspection enforces ownership.

8. Balance Technology with Human Authority

- ☐ Technology can track and record, but only staff can enforce.
- ☐ Leaders must ensure human presence remains primary.
- ☐ Tools should empower officers to act confidently, not withdraw.

Principle: Technology multiplies human ownership, not replaces it.

9. Document Wins and Failures

- ☐ Share examples of tools preventing contraband, fights, or escapes.
- ☐ Share cautionary tales of neglected tools leading to disorder.
- ☐ Use both to reinforce the cultural message that technology is only as strong as its credibility.

Principle: Stories sustain vigilance.

10. Budget with Broken Windows in Mind

- ☐ Technology funding must prioritize credibility over flash.
- ☐ Fewer tools maintained well are better than many tools neglected.
- ☐ Leaders must resist installing systems without plans for maintenance.

Principle: Better to have a few strong windows than many broken ones.

Sample Technology Evaluation Checklist

Cameras

- ☐ Are all cameras operational?
- ☐ Are outages repaired within 72 hours?
- ☐ Do officers trust the system to provide evidence?

Radios

- ☐ Are signals clear across all areas?
- ☐ Are dead zones identified and corrected?
- ☐ Are batteries tested before every shift?

Electronic Rounds Systems

- ☐ Do logs match actual staff presence?
- ☐ Are supervisors verifying rounds personally?
- ☐ Are false entries treated as violations?

Key Tracking Systems

- ☐ Are all keys secured in electronic systems?
- ☐ Are alarms triggered when keys are overdue?
- ☐ Are spare keys logged and inspected?

Other Tools

- ☐ Are door alarms functional?
- ☐ Are body-worn cameras used consistently?
- ☐ Are mail scanners, detectors, and sensors inspected regularly?

Reflection

Technology is a mirror of culture. The Silent Camera proved that a single outage tolerated can multiply disorder. The Radio Dead Zone proved that neglecting communication can endanger staff. The Key Tracker proved that technology aligned with culture can transform credibility and sustain order.

Broken Windows explains why. Every neglected outage is a broken window. It tells inmates the system is weak and tells staff they are unsupported. Every repaired tool is a repaired window. It tells inmates authority is constant and tells staff they are backed by leadership.

The lesson is clear. Technology is support, not substitute. It must be maintained with urgency, enforced with credibility, and integrated into daily culture. Keys, rounds, and counts form the chain of authority. Cameras, radios, and trackers extend the chain. Both staff and tools must be credible and communicate ownership.

The future of corrections will bring more technology, not less. Culture must come first. Technology follows culture.

- 11 -

STAFF PROFESSIONALISM AND DAILY STANDARDS

Broken Windows Inside the Ranks

The Broken Windows Theory is often applied to neighborhoods, communities, and inmate management, but it belongs just as strongly inside the ranks of correctional staff. Disorder does not only spread among inmates. It spreads among officers, sergeants, and supervisors when standards are tolerated instead of enforced.

Corrections professionals often focus on controlling inmate behavior, yet the foundation of authority begins with staff professionalism. Every detail of staff behavior, uniforms, punctuality, documentation, and communication sends a signal. Officers observe each other as closely as inmates observe them. When one officer cuts corners and no one corrects it, the signal spreads. Standards begin to slip and culture erodes.

The Broken Windows principle is clear: what staff tolerate in themselves, they will tolerate in inmates. If staff walk past disorder in their peers, they will walk past disorder in housing units. If staff ignore sloppy counts by a coworker, they will ignore sloppy compliance by inmates. Disorder tolerated at the staff level multiplies into disorder across the facility.

Internal standards are not just about professionalism for appearances. They are about safety. A late officer forces others to cover posts. A sloppy report hides misconduct that may resurface as violence. An untucked shirt signals lax discipline that inmates quickly notice. Small cracks tolerated among staff become wide breaches in authority.

Peer accountability is the frontline defense. Supervisors enforce policies, but staff culture is built peer to peer. When officers correct each other about uniforms, punctuality, or reports, they sustain professionalism. When they remain silent, they allow cracks to spread.

Corrections is a team profession. No officer can enforce order alone. Each relies on peers for backup, support, and credibility. That teamwork is undermined when standards are tolerated instead of enforced. A facility where officers hold each other accountable is a facility where culture thrives. A facility where officers let small cracks slide is a facility heading toward collapse.

The next sections show how this plays out. Through case studies, we will examine three common lapses — sloppy uniforms, tardiness, and falsified reports — that may appear minor but, when tolerated, become broken windows that spread disorder through the ranks.

Peer Accountability as Culture

Peer accountability is one of the most powerful forces in any correctional facility. Policies can be written, supervisors can enforce, and administrators can issue memos, but the daily culture of a jail or prison is determined by how staff treat one another. Do officers correct each other when they see lapses? Do sergeants set the expectation that standards are non-negotiable? Do supervisors model the behaviors they demand?

The Broken Windows Theory applies here as directly as it does to inmate behavior. Every small lapse among staff is a window. If it is ignored, it signals that standards are optional. If it is corrected, it signals that standards are sacred. Culture spreads from these signals.

Why Staff Do Not Correct Each Other

In many facilities, officers hesitate to hold peers accountable. The reasons vary:

- **Fear of conflict.** Correctional work is stressful, and officers often avoid tension with peers by ignoring lapses.
- **Unspoken agreements.** Staff sometimes develop a "you don't bother me, I don't bother you" approach that allows small cracks to persist.
- **Distrust of leadership.** When staff believe supervisors will not back them up, they avoid correcting peers.
- **Cultural inertia.** When sloppiness is normalized, correcting it feels abnormal.

These reasons allow small lapses to multiply. When officers see untucked shirts, late arrivals, or falsified reports go unchallenged, they learn that standards are negotiable. The signal spreads until culture itself is compromised.

Why Staff Must Correct Each Other

Peer accountability is essential because supervisors cannot see everything. Culture is shaped on the floor, not in the office. Officers spend more time with each other than with supervisors. They know immediately when standards are slipping. If they correct each other, standards are sustained. If they stay silent, cracks spread.

Peer accountability also protects credibility. Inmates watch officers closely. They notice when one officer corrects another. That correction sends a message that standards apply to everyone. When officers ignore lapses, inmates interpret it as weakness and test boundaries accordingly.

Peer accountability reinforces safety. A late officer means another must cover a post, creating vulnerabilities. A sloppy report hides risks that may surface as violence. An untucked shirt communicates lax discipline that inmates exploit. Correcting these details prevents disorder before it grows.

Ownership at the Officer Level

Ownership of standards must begin at the officer level. Administrators can set expectations, but daily ownership is built peer to peer. Officers who take pride in their appearance, punctuality, and professionalism set the tone. Officers who correct each other reinforce that pride.

Culture cannot depend on supervisors alone. If accountability comes only from above, staff develop a compliance mindset and follow rules only when watched. Peer accountability creates a culture mindset and staff follow rules because their peers expect it.

Ownership at the officer level communicates strength to inmates. When officers enforce standards among themselves, they project unity. Inmates see that rules apply universally and that cracks are closed quickly. That unity deters testing.

Supervisors as Culture Shapers

While peer accountability is essential, supervisors still play a critical role. They shape culture by modeling behaviors, supporting officers who correct peers, and refusing to tolerate silence.

Supervisors who ignore lapses communicate that accountability is optional. Supervisors who punish officers for correcting peers create fear and silence. Supervisors who model vigilance, correct lapses directly, and support officers who hold peers accountable build strong cultures.

The strongest facilities are those where officers feel empowered to correct each other because they know supervisors will support them.

Broken Windows in Staff Culture

The Broken Windows framework makes the stakes clear.

- A shirt left untucked, ignored by peers, signals that discipline is flexible.
- A late officer, unchallenged, signals that punctuality is optional.
- A falsified report, tolerated, signals that honesty is negotiable.

Each ignored lapse is a broken window. It spreads until professionalism collapses. Each corrected lapse is a repaired window. It spreads until professionalism is reinforced.

Culture as the Deciding Factor

Ultimately, peer accountability is not about policy but about culture. A facility where staff believe in standards, correct each other, and take pride in professionalism will thrive. A facility where staff remain silent, tolerate disorder, and avoid accountability will collapse.

Culture is built daily through small corrections. Every peer-to-peer interaction is a window. Closed quickly, it strengthens the structure. Ignored, it weakens it.

Reflection on Peer Accountability

Peer accountability is the frontline defense of professionalism. Supervisors cannot see every lapse. Policies cannot prevent every shortcut. Culture fills the gaps.

Broken Windows teaches that small cracks become cultural collapse when ignored. Among staff, those cracks are uniforms, punctuality, documentation, and honesty. If ignored, they multiply into corruption, abuse, and lost credibility. If corrected, they multiply into strength, unity, and authority.

The lesson is simple: staff must own standards peer to peer. Supervisors must model and reinforce, but culture is sustained by officers holding each other accountable.

Case Study 1: The Untucked Shirt

Uniforms are more than clothing in a correctional facility. They are symbols of authority. They tell inmates that staff are professional, united, and disciplined. A sharp, consistent appearance communicates ownership. A sloppy, inconsistent appearance communicates weakness.

This case from a mid-sized county jail in the Midwest demonstrates how something as small as an untucked shirt, left uncorrected, grew into larger problems of staff discipline, inmate testing, and cultural decline.

The Setting

The jail housed about 600 inmates and employed roughly 150 staff. Officers were issued navy uniforms with clear policies: shirts tucked, boots polished, nameplates visible, and gear carried consistently. The standard was designed to project professionalism and authority.

At first, enforcement was strict. Supervisors inspected uniforms at roll call. Officers took pride in their appearance. Inmates noticed and responded with compliance. The sharpness of staff communicated seriousness.

Over time, cracks appeared.

Early Signals

One officer began showing up with his shirt untucked during night shift. Supervisors noticed but said nothing. Other officers joked about it but did not correct him. Inmates, watching closely, saw that a clear violation of policy was tolerated.

The untucked shirt became a symbol. It was small, but it sent a clear message: standards were optional.

Escalation

Within weeks, other officers followed. Shirts were left partially untucked. Some officers wore sneakers instead of boots. Others removed nameplates or carried gear inconsistently. Supervisors continued to overlook these violations. The roll call inspections that once enforced standards became casual greetings.

Inmates recognized the trend. They began testing boundaries in their own ways. Some left shirts unbuttoned during inspection. Others pushed limits on cell cleanliness. When corrected, they pointed to officers with sloppy uniforms and said, "Why should we follow rules when you don't?"

The credibility of staff eroded. Authority weakened because staff failed to hold themselves accountable.

Cultural Consequences

The culture shift was significant. Staff who once took pride in appearance now shrugged off standards. Peer accountability disappeared. Officers stopped correcting each other. Supervisors, overwhelmed by other priorities, tolerated the decline.

Inmates grew bolder. Defiance increased in housing units. Minor infractions multiplied. What began with a single untucked shirt evolved into a facility-wide culture of laxness.

Graffiti appeared more frequently. Contraband increased. Officers reported more resistance to orders. The link was clear: when staff abandoned standards for themselves, inmates abandoned standards for compliance.

The Breaking Point

The cultural decline culminated during a lockdown drill. Officers were required to secure housing units quickly and present themselves for inspection. Instead of projecting authority, several officers arrived with untucked shirts, missing gear, and unshined boots. Inmates laughed openly during the drill. One shouted, "You can't even dress right, and you expect us to follow rules?"

The drill failed. Supervisors realized that the credibility of the staff had been compromised, not by inmates but by staff behavior.

Administrative Response

Leadership acted after the failed drill. They reintroduced strict uniform inspections at roll call. Officers were reminded that uniforms were not optional but symbolic. Supervisors were instructed to correct every violation immediately.

Training sessions emphasized the link between appearance and authority. Officers were reminded that inmates notice everything. The untucked shirt was not just sloppy. It was a broken window that signaled disorder.

Within weeks, standards improved. Shirts were tucked. Boots were polished. Nameplates were visible. Inmates noticed the shift and compliance improved. The signal had changed.

Cultural Reset

The renewed emphasis on uniforms created a broader cultural reset. Officers began correcting each other again. Supervisors modeled discipline by enforcing standards. Inmates, seeing staff united and consistent, adjusted behavior accordingly.

The clear lesson: discipline begins with staff appearance. Professionalism on the outside reflects discipline on the inside. Inmates respect what staff respect.

Lessons from the Untucked Shirt

- Uniforms are symbols that project professionalism or weakness based on how they are worn.
- Small cracks multiply. An untucked shirt communicated that standards were optional. Disorder followed.
- Peer accountability matters. Officers who fail to correct each other reinforce sloppiness.
- Supervisors set the tone. When supervisors ignore violations, culture erodes.
- Credibility is authority. Inmates do not respect standards that staff fail to uphold.

Reflection

The Untucked Shirt demonstrates that professionalism begins with details. Uniforms are not fashion. They are culture. A tucked shirt, polished boots, and a visible nameplate communicate order and authority. An untucked shirt communicates the opposite.

Broken Windows explains the outcome. The untucked shirt was a broken window that signaled to staff that standards were flexible and signaled to inmates that compliance was negotiable. Disorder multiplied until leadership reasserted ownership.

The lesson is simple: staff must enforce standards on themselves before they can enforce them on inmates. Professionalism is the first line of security. Discipline begins with appearance, and appearance begins with details.

Case Study 2: The Late Shift

Punctuality in corrections is more than professional courtesy. It is a matter of safety. Correctional facilities run on tight schedules: meals, counts, movement, recreation, medical appointments, and programs all depend on precise timing. When staff arrive late, they do more than inconvenience coworkers. They compromise security.

This case from a large county detention center in the South demonstrates how tolerated tardiness undermined teamwork, bred resentment, and created vulnerabilities that inmates quickly recognized.

The Setting

The detention center housed about 1,400 inmates and operated with three daily shifts. Officers rotated between housing units, intake, medical, and escort posts. Staffing was lean, and every post mattered.

Policy required staff to arrive 15 minutes before shift to receive briefing and exchange information with the outgoing officer. Supervisors emphasized this during training but rarely enforced it.

Early Signals

At first, the problem was isolated. A few officers routinely arrived five to ten minutes late. The outgoing shift covered for them, grumbling but tolerating it. Supervisors noticed but said little.

The signal spread quickly. If one officer could arrive late without consequence, others followed. Roll call became inconsistent. Briefings were rushed or skipped. Outgoing staff stayed longer to cover, building resentment. Incoming staff walked in casually, knowing they would not be corrected.

Inmates noticed. Housing units sat unattended during shift change. Escorts were delayed. Meal times slipped. The message was clear: staff discipline was negotiable.

Escalation

Tardiness began to affect safety directly. Counts were delayed because incoming staff were not ready. Recreation began late, frustrating inmates and creating tension. Medical appointments backed up, causing disputes.

In housing units, inmates tested boundaries during shift change, when coverage was weakest. They lingered in dayrooms, refused lockdowns, and challenged late-arriving officers. They knew staff were disorganized and used the gap to push limits.

Resentment grew among staff. Officers who arrived on time felt punished, covering for those who did not. Morale suffered. Complaints circulated, but supervisors still failed to enforce standards.

Thc Incident

The breaking point came one evening during second shift. An officer was assigned to intake, responsible for processing new arrests and managing detainee property. He arrived 20 minutes late. The outgoing officer, frustrated, left without briefing him.

During the gap, several new arrests arrived from local police. With no officer present, detainees waited unsecured in a holding area. One detainee, charged with violent offenses, became agitated. With no staff to monitor him, he assaulted another detainee. By the time the late officer arrived, the fight was over and both detainees needed medical care.

The incident exposed the danger of tolerated tardiness. A single late officer had left intake unsecured, resulting in violence and injuries.

Administrative Response

The administration launched an investigation. They found that tardiness had become widespread and tolerated across the facility. Logs showed consistent delays in counts, escorts, and programs. Supervisors admitted they overlooked late arrivals to avoid conflict.

The response was swift. Leadership reinstated strict roll call procedures. Officers were required to arrive 15 minutes early, and supervisors documented attendance. Tardiness became a policy violation with progressive discipline.

Training reinforced that punctuality was a safety requirement, not a courtesy. Officers were reminded that shift exchange is critical for communication, continuity, and coverage.

Cultural Reset

The renewed enforcement shifted culture. Officers began arriving early again, knowing supervisors would document attendance. Roll call became consistent, with full briefings and accountability. Outgoing staff no longer felt abandoned.

Inmates noticed the difference. Shift changes ran smoothly. Coverage was consistent. Counts and programs returned to schedule. Testing during shift change declined because the gaps were closed.

Staff morale improved. Officers who had carried the burden of covering for late peers felt supported. Resentment decreased as accountability increased. The facility regained credibility with both staff and inmates.

Lessons from the Late Shift

1. **Punctuality is safety.** Shift changes are high-risk moments that require full coverage.
2. **Tardiness is a broken window.** When tolerated, it communicates that discipline is negotiable.

3. **Peer resentment multiplies** when on-time staff cover for late staff.
4. **Inmates notice gaps.** Delays in coverage invite testing and misconduct.
5. **Supervisors set the tone.** Enforcing punctuality sustains discipline and culture.

Reflection

The Late Shift demonstrates that small lapses in staff professionalism can create major security risks. Tardiness is not a minor issue. It is a broken window that communicates disorder among staff and invites disorder among inmates.

Broken Windows explains the outcome. Each late arrival was a window left broken. It signaled to staff that discipline was flexible and to inmates that order was negotiable. The result was resentment, disorganization, and violence.

The lesson is clear: punctuality must be enforced as a matter of safety. Officers must arrive on time, supervisors must document attendance, and peers must hold each other accountable. Discipline begins with showing up.

Case Study 3: The Pencil-Whipped Report

Documentation is one of the quiet foundations of correctional work. It does not carry the urgency of breaking up a fight or the visibility of a perimeter patrol, but it sustains the credibility of the entire operation. Incident reports, logbooks, use-of-force statements, medical notes, and search records all become part of the official history of a facility. They are reviewed by supervisors, judges, lawyers, accreditation teams, auditors, and sometimes juries.

When reports are sloppy, rushed, or falsified, the entire system loses credibility. Inmates sense the weakness. Staff learn that truth is optional. Courts and outside agencies begin to doubt the integrity of the jail or prison. In corrections, pencil-whipped reports are broken windows, cracks in integrity that multiply disorder.

This case from a state correctional facility in the Midwest shows how tolerated shortcuts in documentation eroded staff culture, undermined accountability, and nearly collapsed an internal investigation.

The Setting

The prison housed about 2,200 inmates and employed more than 400 staff. Policy required every incident, use of force, and major inmate infraction to be documented within 24 hours. Shift logbooks were expected to be accurate and complete, with supervisors reviewing them daily.

In practice, shortcuts were common. Officers often copied generic phrases into reports instead of writing detailed accounts. Some left blanks in logbooks, assuming supervisors would overlook them. Supervisors, overwhelmed with administrative work, often initialed reports without thorough review.

The culture of documentation was slipping.

Early Signals

The first cracks appeared in shift logs. Officers began writing vague entries such as "rounds conducted" without detail. Supervisors accepted the logs without correction. Inmates noticed when rounds were skipped or incomplete but saw reports that said otherwise.

Next came incident reports. Instead of detailed descriptions, officers wrote short, formulaic statements: "Inmate was non-compliant. Force was necessary. Inmate was restrained without further incident." The lack of detail made it difficult to assess whether policy was followed, but supervisors tolerated it.

The message spread: paperwork was not serious.

Escalation

As the culture eroded, pencil-whipping became normal. Officers filled in logbooks after the fact. Incident reports were copied and pasted from old templates. Medical referrals were documented without inmates ever being seen.

Inmates recognized the pattern. They tested staff by refusing orders or creating disturbances, knowing officers would write vague reports that concealed details. Some began filing grievances, citing discrepancies between what actually happened and what was documented.

The credibility of staff was eroding not only internally but externally.

The Incident

The breaking point came during a use-of-force incident in one of the housing units. An inmate resisted orders, and a team of officers responded. The inmate sustained injuries requiring medical attention.

When reports were submitted, all five officers used nearly identical language: "Inmate was combative. Minimal force was used to gain compliance." The reports contained no specific details about the type of resistance, the level of force, or the sequence of events.

Supervisors accepted the reports and closed the case. But the inmate filed a grievance and later a lawsuit, claiming excessive force. When attorneys requested documentation, the vague reports undermined the facility's defense. Video footage revealed details absent from the reports, raising questions about honesty and integrity.

The investigation expanded. Auditors found widespread evidence of pencil-whipped reports across units. Supervisors had tolerated sloppy documentation for years. The credibility of the entire facility was now in question.

Administrative Response

Leadership had no choice but to act. They ordered a facility-wide review of documentation practices. Supervisors were held accountable for failing to enforce standards. Officers were retrained on report writing, with emphasis on accuracy, detail, and timeliness.

Policies were tightened:

- Reports with vague or identical language were returned for correction.
- Supervisors were required to read and sign off on every report, not just initial.
- Spot checks were conducted by administrators and auditors.
- Failure to complete accurate documentation became a disciplinary offense.

The message was reinforced: paperwork is not paperwork—it is credibility.

Cultural Reset

The shift was not easy. Officers initially resisted the stricter standards, complaining about the extra workload. Over time, however, the culture adjusted. Accurate reports protected staff from false accusations. Supervisors felt more confident defending their teams. Inmates recognized that grievances could no longer exploit sloppy documentation.

The facility's credibility improved with outside agencies. Auditors praised the reforms, and courts treated documentation with greater trust. Inside the walls, professionalism improved because officers knew they could not cut corners without consequence.

Lessons from the Pencil-Whipped Report

- **Documentation is credibility.** Reports are the official history of a facility.
- **Sloppiness is a broken window.** Vague or false reports communicate that integrity is optional.
- **Supervisors are gatekeepers.** Initialing sloppy reports reinforces disorder.
- **Credibility protects staff.** Accurate documentation is the strongest defense against accusations.
- **Culture spreads.** When pencil-whipping is tolerated, it multiplies until integrity collapses.

Reflection

The Pencil-Whipped Report demonstrates that professionalism is not just about appearance or punctuality. It is also about integrity in documentation. Reports are more than paperwork. They are evidence of credibility, accountability, and ownership.

Broken Windows explains the outcome. Each vague report was a broken window. Each tolerated shortcut communicated that truth was flexible. Disorder multiplied until an investigation exposed the collapse. Only when leadership reinforced accuracy did culture recover.

The lesson is clear: staff must own standards in documentation as much as in uniforms or punctuality. Integrity in reports is integrity in culture. Discipline begins with honesty, and honesty begins with details.

Analysis: Professionalism as Broken Windows

The case studies in this chapter point to a single truth: professionalism among staff is the foundation of order. If staff abandon standards for themselves, they cannot enforce standards on inmates. When officers tolerate small lapses in appearance, punctuality, or documentation, they communicate signals of weakness that spread quickly through the ranks and into the inmate population.

The Broken Windows Theory explains why. Every small lapse among staff is a broken window. An untucked shirt signals that discipline is flexible. A late arrival signals that punctuality is optional. A sloppy report signals that truth is negotiable. Each tolerated lapse is a signal that spreads, multiplying until culture itself begins to collapse.

Staff as the First Broken Windows

It is easy to apply Broken Windows to inmate behavior or facility conditions, but the first windows inmates see are staff. Uniforms, posture, punctuality, communication, and integrity are the daily signals inmates interpret:

- When officers walk in late, inmates know coverage is inconsistent.
- When uniforms are sloppy, inmates know discipline is casual.
- When reports are vague, inmates know accountability is weak.

Staff are the frontline representation of order. When staff standards are enforced, inmates respect authority. When staff standards are neglected, inmates exploit it.

The Untucked Shirt Revisited

The untucked shirt was more than a fashion issue. It was a cultural signal. Supervisors ignored it, peers tolerated it, and soon the entire facility reflected it. Inmates tested rules because staff no longer modeled discipline.

The untucked shirt showed how quickly professionalism erodes when peers remain silent. A single detail, left uncorrected, spread into a facility-wide culture of disorder.

The Late Shift Revisited

The late shift was more than a scheduling issue. It was a breach of safety. Officers who arrived late created coverage gaps. Supervisors tolerated it, and peers carried the burden. Resentment grew, and inmates exploited the gaps during shift change.

The late shift demonstrated how neglecting punctuality undermines teamwork and security. Inmates are most dangerous when they sense staff are disorganized.

The Pencil-Whipped Report Revisited

The pencil-whipped report was more than a paperwork shortcut. It was an integrity collapse. Officers who copied and pasted vague statements communicated that truth was flexible. Supervisors tolerated it, and soon the entire facility's credibility eroded. Inmates exploited the weakness through grievances, and courts questioned the facility's honesty.

The pencil-whipped report revealed how tolerated dishonesty destroys credibility not just inside the facility but with the public.

Patterns Across the Cases

Across the three cases, the pattern is clear:

- Small lapses tolerated multiply into major problems.
- Supervisors who ignore details undermine culture.
- Peers who remain silent reinforce disorder.
- Inmates always notice and exploit cracks.
- Professionalism cannot be optional. It must be enforced daily because it communicates authority.

Why Peer Accountability Matters Most

Supervisors cannot monitor every shirt, every clock, or every report. Culture depends on peers correcting each other. Officers must hold each other accountable, not to embarrass but to sustain professionalism:

- A peer correcting an untucked shirt reinforces pride.
- A peer reminding another to arrive on time reinforces safety.
- A peer refusing to accept a sloppy report reinforces integrity.

Peer accountability is the most powerful form of Broken Windows enforcement inside the ranks.

The Role of Supervisors

While peer accountability is critical, supervisors shape culture by what they enforce and what they tolerate. Supervisors who overlook sloppy uniforms, late arrivals, or vague reports communicate that standards are optional. Supervisors who enforce standards consistently communicate that professionalism is sacred.

The three case studies showed supervisors failing at first and then regaining control only after crises. Strong supervisors do not wait for collapse. They enforce standards daily, preventing cracks from spreading.

Professionalism as Prevention

Professionalism is prevention. A tucked shirt deters inmate defiance. An on-time shift prevents coverage gaps. An accurate report deters grievances and lawsuits. Each detail prevents disorder before it begins.

When staff abandon professionalism, they invite testing. Inmates calculate risk based on staff behavior. When staff appear disorganized, inmates increase defiance. When staff project unity and discipline, inmates reduce testing. Professionalism communicates risk to inmates. Disorder communicates opportunity.

The Cost of Neglect

Neglecting staff professionalism carries enormous costs. The Untucked Shirt led to widespread disorder and defiance. The Late Shift led to violence during a gap in coverage. The Pencil-Whipped Report nearly collapsed an internal investigation and damaged public credibility.

Each began with small cracks tolerated. Each multiplied into major consequences. The cost of neglect is always higher than the cost of correction.

Broken Windows Inside the Ranks

The Broken Windows framework applies as much to staff as to inmates. Every detail of staff professionalism is a window:

- A uniform is a window. Tucked, it communicates pride. Untucked, it communicates sloppiness.
- A clock is a window. On time, it communicates discipline. Late, it communicates disorder.
- A report is a window. Accurate, it communicates honesty. Vague, it communicates dishonesty.

Staff who repair their own windows project strength. Staff who ignore them project weakness.

Reflection

Professionalism is the first and strongest form of Broken Windows in corrections. Staff set the tone. Inmates respond to what staff model.

The three case studies show the danger of tolerated lapses: an untucked shirt spread into discipline collapse, a late shift created violence, and pencil-whipped reports undermined credibility. Each began small. Each multiplied when ignored.

The lesson is clear: professionalism is not optional. It is ownership. Staff must enforce standards on themselves and each other before they can enforce them on inmates. Supervisors must model and enforce details daily.

Broken Windows teaches us that small cracks spread quickly. Among staff, those cracks are uniforms, punctuality, and integrity. If ignored, they multiply into cultural collapse. If repaired, they multiply into strength, unity, and authority.

The lesson for corrections is simple but profound: professionalism is the foundation of authority, and peer accountability is the glue that sustains it.

Tools and Takeaways

Professionalism is the first and strongest application of the Broken Windows Theory inside a correctional facility. Before staff can enforce order on inmates, they must enforce order on themselves. Uniforms, punctuality, honesty in reports, and respect for rules are not minor issues. They are signals of culture. Inmates watch them, supervisors depend on them, and peers either reinforce or erode them.

The case studies in this chapter—the Untucked Shirt, the Late Shift, and the Pencil-Whipped Report—show how small lapses tolerated can multiply into cultural collapse. They also show how swift correction restores credibility. The following tools and takeaways offer a practical framework for embedding professionalism into staff culture.

1. **Establish Standards as Sacred**
   - Uniforms, punctuality, and documentation must be defined as sacred duties, not optional preferences.
   - Staff must be trained to understand that small lapses communicate disorder to inmates.
   - Supervisors must model strict adherence to standards every day.

   Principle: If staff do not respect standards, inmates will not respect them either.

2. **Enforce Standards Consistently**
   - ☐ Supervisors must correct every violation, no matter how small.
   - ☐ Officers must correct each other to reinforce peer accountability.
   - ☐ Consistency builds culture. Inconsistency destroys it.

   Principle: What you walk past, you accept.

3. **Build Peer Accountability**
   - ☐ Encourage officers to correct each other respectfully but firmly.
   - ☐ Reinforce that corrections are about professionalism, not personal conflict.
   - ☐ Train staff to see peer accountability as protection, not criticism.

   Principle: Peers shape culture more than policies do.

4. **Protect Punctuality**
   - ☐ Require officers to arrive early for briefing and exchange of information.
   - ☐ Document late arrivals and enforce consequences.
   - ☐ Remind staff that punctuality prevents gaps in coverage that inmates exploit.

   Principle: Time is security.

5. **Guard Documentation Integrity**
   - ☐ Train officers to write accurate, detailed reports.
   - ☐ Supervisors must read reports thoroughly and return vague or sloppy ones.
   - ☐ False or lazy reporting must be treated as a serious violation of integrity.

   Principle: Paperwork is not paper, it is credibility.

6. **Support Officers Who Correct Peers**
   - ☐ Supervisors must back officers who enforce standards on each other.
   - ☐ Retaliation against peer correction must not be tolerated.
   - ☐ Staff should know that leadership supports accountability at every level.

   Principle: Accountability must be safe to practice.

7. **Train Supervisors as Culture Shapers**
   - ☐ Supervisors must receive training in enforcing professionalism.
   - ☐ They must understand their role as the bridge between policy and practice.
   - ☐ Their silence on small issues becomes approval of disorder.

   Principle: Supervisors set the tone.

8. **Recognize Professionalism Publicly**
   - ☐ Highlight officers who model high standards.
   - ☐ Use roll call, newsletters, or recognition boards to reinforce culture.
   - ☐ Public recognition strengthens peer pressure in the right direction.

   Principle: What is praised is repeated.

9. **Create Accountability Systems**
   - ☐ Use checklists for roll call inspections.
   - ☐ Track punctuality and report-writing timeliness.
   - ☐ Share results with staff to reinforce transparency.

   Principle: What is measured becomes culture.

10. Address Culture, Not Just Policy

- ☐ Rules alone do not create professionalism. Culture does.
- ☐ Leaders must reinforce the message that details are ownership, not optional.
- ☐ Officers must believe that professionalism protects them, their peers, and the facility.

Principle: Culture sustains standards when policies cannot.

Sample Staff Professionalism Checklist

Uniforms

- ☐ Are shirts tucked, boots polished, and nameplates visible?
- ☐ Are duty belts carried consistently and completely?
- ☐ Are officers corrected immediately for violations?

Punctuality

- ☐ Do officers arrive 15 minutes early for shift briefings?
- ☐ Are late arrivals documented?
- ☐ Do supervisors enforce accountability?

Documentation

- ☐ Are reports detailed, accurate, and timely?
- ☐ Do supervisors return vague reports for correction?
- ☐ Are logbooks filled in contemporaneously, not after the fact?

Peer Accountability

- ☐ Do officers correct each other respectfully and consistently?
- ☐ Do supervisors support officers who hold peers accountable?
- ☐ Are corrections treated as professionalism, not personal attacks?

Reflection

Professionalism is the cornerstone of corrections. Without it, authority collapses. With it, authority multiplies.

The Untucked Shirt showed how a single neglected standard spread into widespread discipline collapse. The Late Shift showed how tolerated tardiness undermined teamwork and created violence. The Pencil-Whipped Report showed how sloppy documentation eroded integrity and credibility. Each began small. Each multiplied when ignored. Each was repaired only when leaders and peers reasserted ownership.

Broken Windows explains why. Every ignored lapse among staff is a broken window. It signals that standards are optional and spreads until culture collapses. Every enforced standard is a repaired window. It signals that professionalism is sacred and spreads until culture is reinforced.

The lesson is clear: staff must own professionalism as much as they own safety. Supervisors must enforce it daily, peers must hold each other accountable, and administrators must support a culture where details are sacred.

Corrections is not only about controlling inmates. It is about controlling culture. Culture begins with staff. Professionalism is not optional. It is the foundation of authority, safety, and respect.

- 12 -

CONTINUOUS TRAINING AND LEADERSHIP DEVELOPMENT

Training as Cultural Maintenance

In corrections, training is often treated as a requirement to complete rather than a process to live. New officers attend an academy, learn policies, practice defensive tactics, and pass examinations. Once certified, they return to the facility, and the focus shifts from learning to doing. But the reality is that training cannot end with the academy. Culture, like safety, must be maintained daily.

The Broken Windows Theory helps explain why. Small cracks in training and ethics grow into larger failures. A policy not reinforced becomes a policy ignored. A skill not practiced becomes a skill forgotten. An ethical standard not emphasized becomes an ethical breach tolerated. Training and ethics are windows. Repaired and reinforced, they sustain professionalism. Neglected, they weaken culture.

Corrections is not static. Inmates adapt, contraband methods evolve, and legal requirements shift. Officers must continually adapt as well. Without ongoing training, staff fall behind, and inmates notice. Gaps in staff knowledge signal weakness just as clearly as a broken door or a sloppy count.

Continuous training keeps standards alive. It reinforces that details matter. It reminds officers that professionalism is a daily practice, not a one-time certificate. Training is cultural maintenance. It repairs the cracks before they spread.

Ethics as Daily Discipline

Ethics is often discussed in terms of major violations—corruption, abuse, or misconduct—but it begins with small daily choices. The Broken Windows principle makes this clear. Just as graffiti invites vandalism, small ethical lapses invite larger breaches.

- An officer who pockets a confiscated candy bar may later pocket cash.
- A supervisor who overlooks a false report may later overlook excessive force.
- A staff member who gossips about confidential information may later leak sensitive intelligence.

Ethics is not only about avoiding scandals. It is about sustaining credibility through daily discipline. Inmates, staff, and the public watch closely. Every choice communicates whether standards are sacred or negotiable.

Ethics training must go beyond lectures on policy. It must connect directly to daily work: searches, reports, counts, and interactions. Staff must be reminded that every detail is an ethical choice. Every log entry, every decision to correct or ignore an inmate, every report is a statement of integrity.

Broken Windows applies fully here. Small ethical cracks left unaddressed become wide breaches. Ethical training is the repair process. It closes the cracks before they compromise the structure.

Training and ethics are not extras in corrections. They are the foundation of professionalism. Without continuous reinforcement, standards collapse. With it, standards hold. The following case studies will show how neglecting training and ethics creates cultural decline, and how reinforcing them creates strength.

Case Study 1: The Outdated Training Manual

Training manuals are supposed to be the backbone of correctional professionalism. They outline policies, procedures, and expectations. They give new staff a roadmap and experienced staff a reference. A current, accurate training manual signals that leadership is serious about standards. An outdated manual communicates neglect.

This case from a county jail in the Southwest shows how failing to update training materials created confusion, undermined authority, and led to a serious breach of safety.

The Setting

The jail housed around 800 inmates in pod-style housing. It operated a training academy that all new officers completed before entering the facility. Training was based on a manual last updated nearly ten years earlier. Policies had changed, but the manual had not.

Staff were well aware of the problem. Pages referenced equipment the facility no longer used. Procedures for searches and counts were written for a floor plan that had been renovated years earlier. New staff often received conflicting information: the manual said one thing, supervisors said another, and officers on the floor taught something else.

The message was clear. Training was not taken seriously.

Early Signals

New officers quietly expressed confusion. They wanted to follow policy but were unsure which version mattered: the manual, their supervisor's instructions, or the practices observed on the floor. Supervisors often dismissed questions, telling recruits to "do what everyone else does."

Inmates quickly noticed the inconsistency. One officer followed the manual's outdated pat-search procedure. Another used the current method. Some inmates exploited the differences, arguing with staff and refusing compliance. "Your partner does it differently," they said. The inconsistency became a tool for defiance.

The cracks in training were spreading into the housing units.

Escalation

As time passed, the lack of updated training created bigger problems. Contraband searches were inconsistent. Counts varied depending on who conducted them. Documentation suffered because the manual still referenced paper forms even though the facility had switched to digital reporting.

Supervisors noticed a rise in grievances. Inmates claimed staff were inconsistent and unfair. They were correct. The outdated manual created multiple standards, none applied consistently.

Professionalism eroded. New officers felt frustrated and unsupported. Veteran officers became cynical, joking that "the manual belongs in the trash." Inmates saw disorganization and pushed boundaries accordingly.

The Incident

The breaking point came during a contraband search in one of the pods. The manual instructed officers to follow a cell-search procedure that no longer matched the renovated layout. A team followed the written instructions exactly, leaving newly created areas unsearched.

Inmates knew the gaps. They had used those spaces to hide contraband for weeks. When officers declared the pod clear, inmates waited until staff left. Hours later, drugs and cell phones were retrieved from the untouched areas.

That contraband fueled a fight that evening. Several inmates under the influence attacked another inmate. Staff responded quickly, but the investigation traced the breach back to the outdated training manual. Officers had followed the written procedure, but the written procedure was wrong.

Administrative Response

Leadership faced a credibility crisis. The outdated manual had confused staff and contributed directly to disorder. The administration responded immediately:

- The manual was completely rewritten to reflect current policies and floor layouts.
- Supervisors received training to ensure consistent instruction.
- New officers were issued updated manuals on day one of the academy.
- Old manuals were collected and destroyed to eliminate conflicting information.

The message was reinforced: training materials are not suggestions. They are the foundation of credibility.

Cultural Reset

The updated manual produced immediate improvements. Officers felt supported and confident that procedures matched real conditions. Supervisors enforced consistency, knowing staff finally had accurate guidance. Inmates noticed the change as well. Procedures were applied uniformly, removing opportunities to argue or test staff.

Grievances declined. Contraband discoveries increased because searches were thorough and consistent. Staff morale improved because training was no longer a running joke. The facility once again projected professionalism.

Lessons from the Outdated Training Manual

1. **Training is culture.** Outdated manuals communicate neglect and inconsistency.
2. **Inconsistency is weakness.** Inmates exploit differences in staff practices.
3. **Credibility requires clarity.** Staff need accurate materials to enforce standards.
4. **Supervisors must enforce updates.** Even the best manual fails without leadership.
5. **Prevention is cheaper than crisis.** Updating manuals costs far less than a contraband-fueled fight.

Reflection

The Outdated Training Manual shows that neglecting training materials is not harmless. It creates confusion among staff, inconsistency in enforcement, and opportunities for inmates. Broken Windows explains the outcome. Each outdated page was a broken window. Each inconsistency signaled that training was optional and enforcement negotiable. Disorder multiplied until violence forced leadership to act.

The lesson is clear: training is cultural maintenance. Manuals, policies, and procedures must be updated regularly. Staff must see that leadership values training as the foundation of professionalism. Neglecting training is neglecting culture, and neglecting culture is neglecting safety.

Case Study 2: The Ignored Scenario

Scenario-based training is one of the most valuable tools in corrections. Unlike lectures or written tests, scenarios place staff in realistic situations where they must think, react, and apply policy under pressure. Scenarios prepare officers for the uncertainty of real events. They reinforce vigilance, teamwork, and decision-making.

But when scenario-based training is dismissed or ignored, it signals that preparation is optional. It suggests that staff can improvise rather than follow policy. This case from a state prison in the Southeast shows how supervisors who dismissed scenarios as “unnecessary” created a culture of complacency that nearly cost lives.

The Setting

The prison housed about 2,500 inmates across multiple housing units, including segregation and general population. Training was conducted quarterly and included scenarios on use of force, hostage response, contraband searches, and medical emergencies. Policy required full participation.

However, many supervisors believed scenarios were a waste of time. They argued that real-world experience was better than simulated drills. Instead of enforcing participation, they often cut scenarios short, let staff sit out, or rushed through exercises without seriousness.

The message to staff was clear: scenarios were not important.

Early Signals

Officers quickly adopted the supervisors’ attitude. Some began skipping training altogether, citing scheduling conflicts. Others attended but participated minimally, lingering in the back or joking through the exercises. Supervisors rarely corrected the behavior.

The result was predictable. Training days became unofficial breaks rather than skill-building sessions. Inmates, although not present for the training itself, noticed the effects. Officers began struggling in situations that scenario practice was meant to prepare them for.

The cracks in culture were spreading.

Escalation

Weakness appeared in daily operations. During contraband searches, officers used inconsistent techniques because they had never practiced under supervision. During minor disturbances, some staff froze while others overreacted. Reports following these events reflected confusion and poor decision-making.

Supervisors brushed off the mistakes, saying officers would "learn with experience." The message was damaging. Training was seen as optional, and vigilance continued to decline. Officers reacted to incidents rather than anticipating them.

The Incident

The breaking point came during a staged medical emergency in a segregation unit. An inmate pretended to collapse, clutching his chest and claiming he could not breathe. Officers responded but hesitated. Some believed it was a ruse. Others believed it was genuine. No one coordinated clearly.

While the confusion played out, another inmate used the distraction to pass contraband through the bars. By the time medical staff arrived, the unit was disorganized. The inmate with the medical complaint was stable, but the contraband exchange had been successful.

A later review revealed that officers had failed to follow basic emergency protocol. They had not secured the unit, coordinated roles, or communicated effectively with medical staff. All of these skills had been included in scenario training, but the training had been dismissed as unnecessary.

Administrative Response

Leadership could not overlook the failures. While no one died, the incident exposed serious vulnerabilities. Investigators confirmed that supervisors routinely dismissed or shortened scenario training, and attendance logs revealed gaps with no documentation.

The response was immediate:

- Scenario training was reinstated as mandatory, with strict attendance tracking.
- Supervisors were held accountable for unit participation.
- Training was redesigned to include stressors such as conflicting information and time limits.
- Officers were evaluated on performance, not just presence.

The message was reinforced: scenarios were essential, not optional.

Cultural Reset

The renewed emphasis on scenario training slowly reshaped culture. Officers took scenarios seriously because supervisors required it. Training days became genuine practice rather than downtime.

Confidence increased. Officers who had once hesitated responded more effectively during real emergencies. Inmates noticed. Staff appeared more coordinated and less uncertain during incidents. The culture shifted toward preparedness and unity.

Lessons from the Ignored Scenario

1. **Training is credibility.** Dismissing scenarios tells staff that preparation is optional.
2. **Supervisors set the tone.** When they downplay training, staff follow.
3. **Practice prevents panic.** Scenarios prepare officers for uncertainty that books cannot.
4. **Neglect spreads.** Once training was dismissed, vigilance across operations weakened.
5. **Culture reacts to seriousness.** When scenarios regained credibility, staff performance and the inmates noticed.

Reflection

The Ignored Scenario shows that neglecting training is not just a scheduling issue. It is a cultural signal. Supervisors who dismiss scenarios tell staff that preparation is optional. Staff who believe training is optional become reactive and inconsistent, and inmates exploit hesitation.

Broken Windows explains the pattern. Each ignored scenario was a broken window. It told staff that training was flexible and told inmates that staff were unprepared. Only when leadership reasserted seriousness did scenarios regain credibility and culture improve.

The lesson is clear: training must be treated as sacred. Scenarios are not extras. They are culture. Staff must prepare daily for uncertainty, and supervisors must model seriousness in every exercise. Preparedness is nonnegotiable.

Case Study 3: The Ethics Shortcut

Ethics in corrections is often framed in terms of big scandals—corruption, smuggling, abuse of authority. But ethical collapse rarely starts there. It begins with small shortcuts. When those shortcuts are tolerated, they spread. When they spread, they become culture. And once culture begins tolerating ethical lapses, credibility collapses.

This case from a regional correctional facility in the Midwest shows how overlooked shortcuts multiplied until they threatened the integrity of the entire institution.

The Setting

The facility housed about 1,200 inmates and employed 300 staff. Policies on ethics were clear: no personal use of confiscated items, no fraternization, accurate documentation, and zero tolerance for dishonesty.

In practice, however, small shortcuts were ignored. Officers ate food confiscated from inmates. Supervisors overlooked profanity in reports. Shift logs sometimes included "filler entries" to cover missed rounds. None of these were major scandals—but all of them were signals.

The signal was that ethics were flexible.

Early Signals

It started with confiscated commissary items. Rather than logging them and disposing of them properly, officers consumed them—a bag of chips here, a soda there. Supervisors joked about it and let it slide.

Next came unprofessional language in reports. Some officers added derogatory comments about inmates. Supervisors ignored it as "venting."

Inmates noticed everything. They saw staff eating confiscated food. They filed grievances about insults in reports. Each small crack widened.

Escalation

The shortcuts multiplied. Officers skipped rounds but logged them as complete. Supervisors, already accustomed to overlooking small lapses, accepted the logs without question. When called out, staff responded with, "Everyone does it."

Inmates recognized the inconsistency immediately. They timed contraband movements during skipped rounds. They used insulting language in reports to challenge discipline. Staff morale dipped—those who followed policy felt undermined, and those who didn't felt untouchable.

The facility's credibility eroded from every direction.

The Incident

The breaking point came during a cell search. Officers found drugs hidden in a cell. Instead of logging the contraband, they pocketed part of it. Rumors spread through the inmate population within hours.

Inmates accused staff openly. Grievances surged. Defense attorneys seized the rumors and began alleging systemic corruption.

When administrators investigated, they found a long pattern of eating confiscated food, skipping rounds, and falsifying reports. What had once been considered harmless shortcuts had grown into major breaches.

The facility's credibility collapsed.

Administrative Response

Leadership responded with sweeping reform. Officers were disciplined or terminated. Supervisors were reassigned. Ethics training was rebuilt around daily discipline rather than worst-case scenarios.

New systems were implemented:

- Confiscated items were logged, photographed, and disposed of under supervision.
- Reports were reviewed for tone and professionalism.
- Rounds were verified electronically instead of manually logged.

Leadership made the message unmistakable: shortcuts were no longer tolerated. Even small lapses would be treated seriously.

Cultural Reset

Reform was uncomfortable but effective. Officers began taking ethics seriously because leadership finally enforced standards. Supervisors corrected lapses instead of overlooking them. Inmates noticed that confiscated food wasn't being eaten and rounds weren't being skipped. Respect slowly returned.

The culture shifted from "everyone does it" to "nobody can do it." While the facility's credibility had been damaged, it began to recover.

Lessons from the Ethics Shortcut

- **Ethics erode through shortcuts.** Small tolerated lapses become systemic failures.
- **Supervisors set the tone.** Silence is approval.
- **Inmates notice everything.** They exploit hypocrisy instantly.
- **Credibility is fragile.** Years of neglect can unravel in days.
- **Culture is built in the small moments.** Ethical discipline must be reinforced daily.

Reflection

The Ethics Shortcut shows that collapse rarely begins with dramatic misconduct. It begins with tolerated shortcuts: a bag of chips from confiscated property, a skipped round covered by a pencil-whipped entry, a derogatory comment ignored in a report. Each shortcut is a broken window. Each ignored crack multiplies until credibility fails.

Broken Windows explains the pattern. Every ignored shortcut told staff that ethics were optional. Every ignored lapse told inmates that staff were inconsistent—or dishonest. Disorder grew until reform was unavoidable.

The lesson is clear: ethics is daily discipline. It is logging property correctly, completing rounds honestly, and writing reports professionally. Leaders and peers must enforce ethics at the smallest level, because small cracks spread quickly.

The culture of any facility depends on it.

Analysis: Training and Ethics as Broken Windows

Training and ethics are often treated as separate priorities in corrections, one focused on skills, the other on integrity. But the Broken Windows Theory reveals that they are deeply connected. Both are about culture. Both are about details. And both collapse when small cracks are tolerated.

The three case studies in this chapter, the Outdated Training Manual, the Ignored Scenario, and the Ethics Shortcut, all demonstrate the same principle: **neglected reinforcement becomes cultural neglect.** Training not updated becomes training ignored. Scenarios dismissed become vigilance dismissed. Shortcuts tolerated become ethics abandoned.

Broken Windows explains why. Small cracks in professionalism, whether in skills or ethics, are signals. They tell staff that discipline is optional, and they tell inmates that authority is negotiable. If ignored, the cracks multiply until culture collapses.

Training as a Window

Training communicates culture as clearly as uniforms or counts. A current, accurate manual signals professionalism. An outdated manual signals neglect. Scenarios taken seriously signal vigilance. Scenarios dismissed signal complacency.

- In the Outdated Training Manual case, every outdated page was a broken window. It told new staff that leadership did not care about consistency and told inmates that enforcement was optional. Disorder followed until leadership repaired the manual.
- In the Ignored Scenario case, every dismissed exercise was a broken window. It told staff that preparation was optional and told inmates that hesitation could be exploited. Culture collapsed until scenarios were enforced.

Training is not an event. It is maintenance. It is the daily repair of windows that would otherwise crack.

Ethics as a Window

Ethics is also communicated in daily details. A confiscated item logged properly signals integrity. One pocketed signals dishonesty. A complete round signals vigilance. A skipped round signals neglect.

- In the Ethics Shortcut case, every shortcut was a broken window. Staff who ate confiscated food, falsified rounds, or used unprofessional language in reports told inmates that ethics were negotiable. The signal multiplied until credibility collapsed.

Ethics is not just about avoiding scandal. It is about reinforcing credibility every day through details.

Training and Ethics Together

Training and ethics cannot be separated because each reinforces the other. Training teaches the standards. Ethics is the discipline to follow them. Without training, staff do not know what professionalism looks like. Without ethics, they choose shortcuts instead of standards.

The Outdated Training Manual showed how confusion eroded culture. The Ignored Scenario showed how complacency weakened vigilance. The Ethics Shortcut showed how tolerated dishonesty collapsed credibility. Together they prove that neglecting training and ethics multiplies disorder.

Why Supervisors Matter Most

In each case, supervisors were the deciding factor. They either ignored cracks or repaired them.

- Supervisors who ignored outdated manuals let disorder spread.
- Supervisors who dismissed scenarios let complacency grow.
- Supervisors who tolerated shortcuts let dishonesty become culture.

When supervisors enforce standards, cracks are repaired. When they tolerate lapses, cracks spread. The difference between collapse and professionalism lies in daily leadership.

Why Peers Are Critical

Supervisors cannot see everything. Peers fill the gaps. Officers who remind each other to update training, take scenarios seriously, and follow ethics keep culture intact. Officers who remain silent allow cracks to spread.

Peer accountability in training and ethics is as vital as in uniforms or punctuality. Culture is sustained when peers refuse to tolerate shortcuts.

Inmates Always Notice

Inmates notice lapses faster than staff. They recognized outdated procedures in the Outdated Training Manual case and exploited the gaps. They recognized hesitation from staff in the Ignored Scenario case and used it as cover for contraband. They recognized dishonesty in the Ethics Shortcut case and used it to undermine staff credibility.

Training and ethics are signals. Inmates read them instantly. Staff who neglect reinforcement send signals of weakness. Inmates exploit them without hesitation.

Professional Development as Prevention

Continuous training and ethical reinforcement are forms of prevention. They prevent confusion, complacency, and dishonesty before they spread. Just as sanitation prevents disease and counts prevent escapes, training prevents disorder.

When staff are trained continuously, they remain sharp. When ethics are reinforced daily, they remain credible. Prevention is always cheaper than collapse.

The Cost of Neglect

The costs of neglect were clear in all three cases. The Outdated Training Manual led to contraband-fueled violence. The Ignored Scenario led to medical response failures and successful inmate testing. The Ethics Shortcut led to credibility collapse and systemic scandal.

Each began small. Each multiplied when ignored. Each cost far more to repair than it would have to prevent.

Broken Windows Applied to Training and Ethics

Broken Windows teaches that every small crack is a signal. Training and ethics are windows as much as uniforms or locks.

- A current manual is a repaired window. An outdated manual is a broken one.
- A serious scenario is a repaired window. A dismissed scenario is a broken one.
- An honest report is a repaired window. A falsified one is a broken one.

Each detail is a choice. Each choice is a signal. The accumulation of signals is culture.

Reflection

Training and ethics are not extras. They are the foundation of professionalism. The Outdated Training Manual, the Ignored Scenario, and the Ethics Shortcut prove the principle: neglect spreads, reinforcement sustains.

Broken Windows explains why. Each outdated policy, ignored scenario, or tolerated shortcut was a broken window. Each told staff that discipline was optional and told inmates that authority was negotiable. Disorder multiplied until crisis forced change.

The lesson is clear: training must be continuous, and ethics must be daily. Supervisors must enforce both, peers must sustain both, and leadership must model both. Culture depends on it. Professionalism is not created once in an academy. It is repaired daily through reinforcement.

Corrections is a profession of details. Training and ethics are the details that sustain everything else. Without them, culture collapses. With them, culture thrives.

Tools and Takeaways

Training and ethics are the repair crews of corrections. They patch cracks before they become collapses. They reinforce standards before disorder multiplies. They remind staff that details matter and that professionalism is not optional.

The case studies in this chapter, the Outdated Training Manual, the Ignored Scenario, and the Ethics Shortcut, show what happens when training and ethics are neglected. The cracks spread quickly. Inmates noticed. Disorder multiplied. Only when leadership reasserted ownership did culture recover.

The following tools and takeaways provide a practical framework for administrators, supervisors, and officers to ensure that training and ethics remain central to culture.

1. Treat Training as Daily Maintenance

- ☐ Training is not a one-time academy event. It is cultural upkeep.
- ☐ Policies, procedures, and manuals must be reviewed and updated annually.
- ☐ Supervisors must communicate updates immediately and ensure consistency across shifts.

Principle: Outdated training is a broken window.

2. Make Scenarios Non-Negotiable

- ☐ Scenarios must be realistic, stressful, and mandatory.
- ☐ Staff must participate fully. Supervisors must model seriousness.
- ☐ Debriefings should connect lessons directly to daily work.

Principle: Practice prevents panic.

3. Connect Training to Daily Work

- ☐ Every training session must be tied to real-life tasks: searches, counts, documentation, and movement.
- ☐ Staff must leave training knowing how lessons apply to the floor immediately.
- ☐ Supervisors must reinforce training by coaching during real operations.

Principle: Training without application is theory.

Application sustains culture.

4. Reinforce Ethics in the Smallest Details

- Ethics is not only about avoiding corruption. It is about logging property correctly, completing rounds honestly, and writing professional reports.
- Supervisors must correct shortcuts immediately.
- Peers must refuse to tolerate dishonesty in any form.

Principle: Every shortcut is a broken window.

5. Train Supervisors as Culture Enforcers

- Supervisors must be evaluated not just on paperwork but on cultural enforcement.
- They must attend training with staff, model standards, and correct lapses consistently.
- Their silence communicates approval. Their vigilance sustains culture.

Principle: Supervisors are culture shapers.

6. Use Technology to Support Training and Ethics

- Electronic rounds systems, digital report tracking, and updated manuals online can reinforce standards.
- Technology must never replace presence, but it can verify accountability.
- Leaders must ensure that tools are credible and enforced.

Principle: Technology multiplies culture, but it cannot replace it.

7. Build Peer Accountability into Training

- ☐ Encourage officers to correct each other during scenarios.
- ☐ Recognize staff who model professionalism.
- ☐ Normalize peer corrections as support, not criticism.

Principle: Peers sustain culture when supervisors cannot see everything.

8. Evaluate Training with Broken Windows in Mind

- ☐ Ask: does this training close cracks or ignore them?
- ☐ Remove outdated or irrelevant content immediately.
- ☐ Design training to emphasize ownership of small details.

Principle: Training is about repairing windows, not checking boxes.

9. Link Ethics to Identity

- ☐ Reinforce that ethics is not just about compliance but about identity as correctional professionals.
- ☐ Use stories of past failures and successes to show that credibility depends on integrity.
- ☐ Help staff see that every decision is an ethical choice.

Principle: Ethics is who we are, not what we avoid.

10. Budget for Training and Ethics as Essentials

- ☐ Training and ethics must be prioritized in funding.
- ☐ Cutting training budgets is cutting culture.
- ☐ Leaders must recognize that prevention costs less than collapse.

Principle: Training is not extra. It is the foundation.

Sample Training and Ethics Checklist

Training

- ☐ Are manuals current and accurate?
- ☐ Are scenarios conducted quarterly and evaluated seriously?
- ☐ Are staff applying training lessons on the floor?

Ethics

- ☐ Are confiscated items logged properly?
- ☐ Are rounds completed honestly?
- ☐ Are reports written professionally and factually?

Supervisors

- ☐ Are they enforcing training and ethics consistently?
- ☐ Are they modeling standards during training?
- ☐ Are they supporting officers who hold peers accountable?

Peers

- ☐ Are officers correcting each other respectfully?
- ☐ Are shortcuts tolerated or rejected?
- ☐ Are small lapses repaired before they spread?

Reflection

Training and ethics are not paperwork requirements. They are culture. Outdated manuals, dismissed scenarios, and tolerated shortcuts are all broken windows. They signal to staff that professionalism is negotiable and to inmates that authority is weak.

The Outdated Training Manual showed how neglected materials created confusion and disorder. The Ignored Scenario showed how dismissed preparation created hesitation and opportunity for inmates. The Ethics Shortcut showed how tolerated lapses multiplied until credibility collapsed.

Broken Windows explains the pattern. Each neglected detail was a broken window. Each ignored crack spread until culture itself collapsed. Only when leaders repaired the windows, by updating manuals, enforcing scenarios, and rejecting shortcuts, did culture recover.

The lesson is clear: training and ethics are not extras. They are the foundation of corrections. Leaders must budget for them, supervisors must enforce them, and peers must live them. Training keeps staff sharp. Ethics keeps staff credible. Together they sustain culture.

Corrections is not about reacting to crises. It is about preventing them. Continuous training and ethical reinforcement are the tools of prevention. They repair cracks before they spread, sustain credibility before it collapses, and protect both staff and inmates.

The facility that invests in training and ethics invests in culture. The facility that neglects them invites collapse. The choice is daily, and the consequences are absolute.

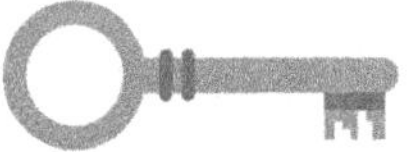

- 13 -

BUILDING STAFF RESILIENCE

Why Resilience Matters

Corrections runs on stamina. Not the kind measured by treadmills or stopwatches, but the kind that endures over years. The kind that absorbs stress, processes trauma, and keeps officers and supervisors steady in environments designed to test human limits.

Inmates study every staff member for weakness. They notice when an officer is tired, when a sergeant is irritable, when a captain seems checked out. Those moments are not just personal struggles. They are signals. And in corrections, signals spread.

Broken Windows applies here just as clearly as it does to graffiti, broken locks, or sloppy counts. Burnout, untreated stress, and unprocessed trauma are broken windows in staff culture—cracks that communicate disorder, vulnerability, and neglect. When left unaddressed, they multiply.

One officer losing his temper sends a message to peers and inmates. One sergeant brushing off staff concerns communicates that resilience is optional. One administrator ignoring wellness programs signals that longevity matters more than health. Each crack widens until morale collapses, turnover spikes, and safety erodes.

Resilience is the opposite. Resilience is repair. It means reinforcing the windows before they break. It is the ability to confront stress, absorb impact, and return to professionalism without letting the cracks spread. Resilience does not mean being unbreakable. It's knowing how to recover.

The Human Cost of Neglecting Resilience

When resilience is ignored, the staff pay the first price.

Burnout shows up as exhaustion, cynicism, and emotional detachment. Officers stop caring about details. They walk past graffiti. They tolerate minor disorder. They lose patience with inmates—and with each other. Supervisors, overwhelmed themselves, sometimes respond with discipline instead of coaching, worsening the problem.

The second cost is paid by the facility. A culture of fatigue and detachment breeds mistakes. Counts become sloppy. Contraband gets missed. Rounds go undone. The facility signals weakness, and inmates exploit it. Personal burnout becomes institutional disorder.

The final cost is paid by the community. Public trust erodes after escapes, assaults, or misconduct linked to overworked or unsupported staff. Taxpayers question leadership. Families of officers carry the weight. Communities feel the impact of cracks that were never repaired.

Resilience as Cultural Armor

Resilience in corrections is more than toughness. It is cultural armor. It protects professionalism from the constant erosion of stress. It allows officers to enforce standards without becoming brittle. It allows supervisors to hold staff accountable without crushing morale. It allows administrators to sustain order without ignoring the humanity of their workforce.

Like sanitation, design, or security protocols, resilience is not optional. A resilient staff projects ownership and stability. A fragile staff projects vulnerability. Inmates recognize the difference instantly.

Broken Windows makes the urgency clear. Each moment of unchecked burnout is a cultural crack. Each time staff are told to "suck it up" rather than given tools for recovery, another window breaks. Each time leadership ignores stress signals, inmates sense weakness and push boundaries.

But each investment in resilience is a repair. Every counseling session, peer support meeting, chaplain visit, or debrief reinforces culture and communicates that staff are valued.

Why Correctional Resilience Is Unique

Every profession needs resilience, but corrections is different. The stressors are constant and unique:

- **Constant scrutiny:** Officers have no privacy—every move is watched.
- **Unpredictable danger:** Routine can turn violent instantly.
- **Emotional labor:** Staff manage mental illness, manipulation, and trauma daily.
- **Public misunderstanding:** Few outside corrections grasp the work.
- **Shift work and fatigue:** Long hours and irregular schedules strain health and family life.

These pressures make resilience both more urgent and more fragile. Without deliberate investment, cracks appear quickly.

Signals to Staff and Inmates

Resilience sends signals like everything else in corrections. To staff, a culture invested in resilience communicates value and professionalism. Officers in such cultures take more ownership, stay longer, and hold peers accountable.

To inmates, a resilient staff communicates permanence. Officers steady under pressure are not easily manipulated or pushed. Supervisors who coach instead of collapse signal that culture is enforced consistently.

The opposite is also true. Staff who break down under stress send a clear message. Inmates exploit impatience, fatigue, or despair. Rumors spread and challenges increase. A culture that neglects resilience communicates weakness as clearly as a broken lock or a skipped round.

The Role of Leadership in Resilience

Resilience cannot be left to chance. It must be cultivated intentionally by leadership at every level. Administrators should design wellness programs that are credible and accessible. Supervisors need to model resilience by managing their own stress openly and professionally. Officers must learn to recognize cracks in themselves and in their peers and act before those cracks spread.

Leadership presence is critical. Officers who see their warden walking the floors, speaking openly about wellness, and investing in resources internalize that resilience is not weakness—it is professionalism. Conversely, leaders who dismiss resilience as "soft" or "secondary" send the opposite message. The culture follows leadership.

Resilience as Ownership

At its core, resilience is ownership of self. Just as officers are trained to own their units, supervisors to own their teams, and administrators to own their facilities, each staff member must own their mental, emotional, and physical health. Resilience is not about perfection. It is about accountability—recognizing stress, addressing it, and preventing it from spreading into culture.

Broken Windows teaches that small cracks become large failures when ignored. Resilience follows the same principle inward. Each unprocessed trauma, each ignored fatigue, each untreated stressor is a crack. Owning those details and repairing those cracks is the foundation of long-term professionalism.

Transition to the Case Studies

The impact of resilience becomes clearest in lived experience. The following case studies show:

- how burnout nearly destroyed an officer,
- how peer support programs rebuilt culture, and
- how something as simple as a chaplain visit repaired cracks before they spread.

Together, they demonstrate that resilience is not abstract. It is daily, practical, and cultural. It is the difference between sustained order and slow collapse.

Case Study 1: The Burned-Out Officer

The Setting

Officer Daniels had worked at a large county jail for over twelve years. The facility housed just over 1,400 inmates and was known for frequent overcrowding and high staff turnover. Daniels had started strong. He was steady on the floor, calm under pressure, and respected by peers. Supervisors often paired new officers with him, trusting that his professionalism would set the right tone.

By his twelfth year, cracks were showing. Overtime demands had grown as the jail struggled to fill vacant posts. Daniels often worked double shifts, sometimes logging seventy hours a week. His personal life suffered. His marriage was strained. Sleep became irregular. He coped with energy drinks, cigarettes, and silence.

To most, Daniels still looked competent. He arrived on time, submitted reports, and followed orders. But those closest to him—his partners and his sergeant—began noticing signs of burnout. His posture slumped. His voice grew sharper.

His patience shortened. What had once been a calm presence became simmering frustration.

Early Signals of Burnout

The signals were subtle at first. Daniels began skipping small details he once enforced. Shirts untucked went unnoticed. Trash left in corners stayed there. Counts were still accurate, but he walked the tiers faster, making less eye contact. Inmates noticed and began testing small things, knowing Daniels would wave them off.

Colleagues noticed too. Daniels no longer volunteered to mentor new officers. He sat alone in the break room. When peers tried to joke with him, his responses were curt. A few whispered that he was "burned out."

The sergeant observed the change but assumed experience would carry him through. "He's just tired," he said in one meeting. "He'll be fine." That assumption was the first broken window. By ignoring the signals, leadership communicated that burnout was tolerable.

The Breach

The breaking point came one evening during a tense lockdown. An inmate in Daniels' unit refused orders to return to his cell. The inmate shouted, pounded on the door, and drew a crowd. Normally, Daniels would have de-escalated calmly, using clear commands and steady presence. This time, frustration overwhelmed him.

Daniels stormed forward, shouting profanities, and shoved the inmate against the wall. Other inmates erupted, pounding on doors and shouting. Backup arrived quickly and the incident ended without serious injury, but the damage was done. Word spread that Daniels had "lost it." Inmates began testing him more aggressively, sensing weakness. Peers avoided shifts with him, worried his temper might spark another crisis.

An internal review confirmed what many suspected: Daniels was not acting out of malice but burnout. Years of stress, fatigue, and silence had cracked his resilience. His lapse was not isolated. It was the predictable result of neglect.

Administrative Response

The administration faced a choice: discipline Daniels harshly or address the root cause. The warden chose the latter. Daniels was placed on leave, not as punishment but as intervention. He was referred to counseling, enrolled in a wellness program, and paired with a peer mentor.

Supervisors underwent training to better recognize burnout in staff. A new policy required sergeants to monitor not only performance metrics but wellness indicators, sick leave patterns, overtime hours, and peer reports, and to act early.

The Recovery

Daniels resisted at first. Like many correctional officers, he saw counseling as weakness. He insisted he was fine, that he just needed a break. But the program persisted. Counselors framed resilience as professionalism, not softness. Peer mentors reinforced that needing help did not mean failing. Slowly, Daniels engaged.

He admitted his fatigue, discussed family stress, and acknowledged that his anger scared him. Over months, with support, he rebuilt balance. He returned to work with renewed perspective, speaking openly about the dangers of burnout. He became a quiet advocate for resilience, encouraging peers to seek help before cracks widened.

The Cultural Shift

Daniels' case became a teaching story within the jail. Leadership used it in training, anonymized but authentic, to show that burnout is risk, not weakness.

Officers began speaking more openly about fatigue. Supervisors asked not only "How are your reports?" but also "How are you?"

Inmates noticed the change too. When staff culture stabilized, challenges declined. Disorder had spiked when Daniels' burnout sent signals of weakness. Once resilience was rebuilt, professionalism was enforced again, and testing diminished.

Lessons from the Burned-Out Officer

1. **Burnout is visible.** Even when staff believe they are hiding it, peers and inmates see the cracks.
2. Ignoring signals is dangerous. Supervisors who dismiss burnout communicate that culture tolerates weakness.
3. **Discipline without support fails.** Correcting behavior must include addressing the cause.
4. **Resilience can be rebuilt.** Counseling, peer support, and leadership presence repair cracks.
5. **Resilience is culture.** One officer's burnout spreads signals to peers and inmates. One officer's recovery spreads signals of strength.

Reflection

The Burned-Out Officer demonstrates how resilience functions as a Broken Windows principle. Small cracks—fatigue, silence, irritability—were ignored until they multiplied into misconduct. The failure was not personal weakness but cultural neglect.

When leadership intervened, the outcome changed. Support, counseling, and mentoring repaired the windows. The message shifted from neglect to ownership. Staff learned resilience was not optional. Inmates learned professionalism was permanent.

The lesson is clear: resilience is maintenance. Staff must be cared for with the same urgency as locks, cameras, and doors. Ignored burnout collapses culture. Reinforced resilience sustains it.

Case Study 2: The Peer Team

The Setting

A mid-sized state correctional facility housed nearly 1,200 inmates and employed just over 300 staff. Like many facilities, it faced persistent staffing shortages, frequent overtime, and high stress on the floor. Annual turnover was close to 25 percent, and exit interviews consistently cited burnout and lack of support as key reasons for leaving.

Administrators had introduced wellness initiatives in the past—posters about stress management, optional yoga sessions, an Employee Assistance Program number posted in break rooms—but staff engagement was low. Officers quietly dismissed these programs as "check-the-box" gestures. Staff wanted something real, something they could trust, something owned by people who understood corrections.

The breakthrough came not from administration but from staff themselves.

The Birth of the Peer Team

It began informally. After a difficult incident in which an inmate attempted suicide, a group of officers gathered in the break room. The formal debrief was perfunctory: a sergeant summarized events, paperwork was filed, and the facility moved on. The officers did not. They talked late into the night, sharing frustrations and fears.

One officer, Alvarez, suggested forming a peer group—not therapy, not a program run by outsiders, but a team of officers who would look after each other. The idea resonated. Within weeks, with support from a forward-thinking captain, the Peer Support Team was born.

Membership was voluntary. Officers applied and were screened for credibility and professionalism. Training was provided by an outside counselor but tailored to the correctional environment. The message was clear: the team existed to support staff, not judge them.

Early Signals of Trust

At first, staff were skeptical. Many assumed the Peer Team was another administrative attempt to check a box. But credibility grew quickly when officers realized the team was made up of peers they already respected. Alvarez, known for his steady presence, was joined by Martin, a veteran sergeant, and Lopez, a young officer with strong communication skills.

The team wore no special uniforms. They carried no clipboards. They simply made themselves available. When an officer struggled after a difficult use of force, a peer team member stopped by his post during the next shift to check in. When an officer requested a quiet conversation, the Peer Team arranged space in a side office. Confidentiality was absolute. Nothing was reported to administration unless someone posed a risk to themselves or others.

The signal was clear: this was not paperwork. This was real.

The Turning Point

The Peer Team proved its value during a major incident six months after its creation. A fight in a housing unit escalated into a full-scale disturbance. Several officers were injured, and one required hospitalization. The event shook the entire facility.

In the past, staff would have received a standard debrief: a review of tactics, a reminder to write complete reports, and perhaps a visit from administration thanking them for their service. This time, the Peer Team stepped in. They organized small group discussions in break rooms, pairing officers from different shifts. They encouraged honesty, not performance. Officers spoke openly about fear, adrenaline, and frustration. For many, it was the first time they had been asked how they felt, not just what they did.

The effect was immediate. Officers reported sleeping better after sharing experiences. Tension between shifts decreased as staff realized they shared the same struggles. Injured officers returned to work sooner, encouraged by peers who stayed in touch during recovery.

Cultural Expansion

Word spread quickly. Officers began seeking out Peer Team members after stressful events. New recruits were introduced to the program during academy orientation. Supervisors began referring staff quietly, encouraging them to talk with peers instead of bottling up stress.

The administration noticed a shift. Sick leave usage declined. Turnover slowed. Morale surveys showed small but measurable improvements. Most important, the daily atmosphere in housing units changed. Officers who once carried visible frustration became steadier. Inmates, always observant, noticed the difference. They sensed that staff were less distracted, less irritable, and more consistent. Challenges decreased.

The Peer Team had become more than a support group—it had become a cultural anchor.

Broken Windows Applied

The Peer Team worked because it repaired small cracks before they spread. An officer who might have lashed out in frustration instead vented in conversation. A sergeant who might have ignored stress signals instead encouraged a Peer Team visit. Each intervention was a repaired window, preventing burnout from spreading into misconduct, turnover, or cultural collapse.

Without the team, each of those cracks might have widened. Officers might have lost their tempers. Supervisors might have dismissed concerns. Inmates might have exploited visible fatigue. The Peer Team prevented small cracks from becoming large breaches.

The Lessons of Ownership

The Peer Team succeeded because it embodied ownership at the lowest level. Staff did not wait for administration to fix culture. They owned it themselves. They built credibility through presence, consistency, and confidentiality. They demonstrated that resilience is not something handed down from above but built together from the ground up.

The Administrative Response

The warden, initially cautious, became a strong supporter. She ensured Peer Team members received overtime pay for training and relief from posts when needed. She protected confidentiality, resisting pressure from some administrators to demand reports. She recognized that the team's credibility depended on trust, and she defended it fiercely.

Eventually, the program expanded across the state system. Peer Teams were established in multiple facilities, each with its own character but bound by the same principles: credibility, confidentiality, and cultural ownership.

Lessons from the Peer Team

1. **Resilience is peer-driven.** Staff trust peers who share their experiences more than administrators or outside counselors.
2. **Credibility is everything.** Peer Team members must be respected professionals, not paper appointments.
3. **Confidentiality sustains trust.** Without it, the program collapses.
4. **Small conversations prevent big crises.** Early intervention keeps cracks from spreading.

5. **Resilience is culture, not a program.** The Peer Team succeeded because it became part of daily life, not an add-on.

Reflection

The Peer Team demonstrates how resilience can be built from within. By repairing cracks before they spread, peers reinforced professionalism, reduced turnover, and stabilized culture. They sent powerful signals to both staff and inmates: staff are supported, professionalism is valued, and culture is enforced.

Broken Windows explains why the Peer Team worked. Each conversation was a repaired window. Each act of support was a signal that cracks would not be tolerated. Over time, those signals multiplied into a culture where resilience was expected, not optional.

The lesson is clear: resilience begins with peers. Leadership must support it, but credibility grows from the ground up. When staff own resilience together, the culture becomes unbreakable.

Case Study 3: The Chaplain Visit

The Setting

The state prison sat on the edge of a rural county, housing nearly 2,400 inmates and employing just over 500 staff. The facility was old, its walls thick with history and stress. Like many prisons, staff morale ebbed and flowed with overtime demands, leadership changes, and the constant grind of life behind the walls.

Programs for inmates were visible—educational classes, religious services, and vocational training all had designated spaces. For staff, resources were thinner. Posters for the Employee Assistance Program lined the break room, but few officers called the number. The distance between leadership and line staff often felt wide.

Into this gap stepped a chaplain, not only as a minister to inmates but as a quiet presence for staff.

The Chaplain's Role

Chaplains in corrections often focus on inmate needs. They provide spiritual services, distribute reading materials, and respond to crises like deaths or family emergencies. At this facility, Chaplain Greene fulfilled all those duties faithfully. But he noticed something else: staff were struggling.

He saw officers sitting silently in break rooms, shoulders slumped. He heard sergeants speak sharply to peers, their tones edged with fatigue. He watched turnover climb, leaving young officers to shoulder more work with less support.

Instead of limiting his work to inmate ministry, Greene began stopping by officer stations. At first, he simply greeted staff, asking how their shifts were going. Then he lingered, listening. Officers began to talk—not about theology or religion, but about exhaustion, frustration, and stress.

Early Signals of Impact

The visits were brief—ten minutes here, a quarter hour there—but they made an impact. Officers began looking forward to Greene's rounds. For some, he was the only person in the facility who asked how they were doing without a hidden agenda.

One officer confided that he was considering leaving the job but had no one to talk to about the decision. Greene listened, asked questions, and encouraged him to think carefully rather than make a rushed choice. Another officer shared that she was struggling after witnessing a suicide attempt. Greene provided a listening ear and suggested counseling while reinforcing that her reaction was normal, not weakness.

Word spread. "The chaplain actually cares," officers began saying. Greene became a trusted presence—not because he had authority over them, but because he carried none.

The Breaking Point Incident

The value of the chaplain's presence became undeniable after a critical incident. An inmate assaulted an officer in a housing unit, striking him repeatedly before backup arrived. The officer survived, but the event rattled the entire shift. Anger surged. Rumors spread about retaliation. Tension between inmates and staff rose to a dangerous level.

In the hours that followed, Greene moved quietly from post to post. He checked on staff, asked how they were holding up, and let them speak. Officers voiced their anger, fear, and doubts. Greene listened, reminded them of their professionalism, and encouraged them to lean on each other.

By the next day, the anger had cooled. Rumors of retaliation died out. Officers returned to steady enforcement of rules. The incident had not disappeared, but the staff had processed it without letting cracks spread into chaos. Many credited Greene's presence as the turning point.

Cultural Expansion

Leadership noticed the impact. The warden met with Greene and encouraged him to continue his visits. Shift commanders began inviting him to roll calls—not to preach, but to remind staff they were not alone. Greene offered a brief word, often as simple as, "You matter, your work matters, and you are seen."

The visits grew into an informal wellness program. Officers began seeking Greene out proactively, catching him in hallways to talk about family stress, overtime fatigue, or the strain of working in a high-stakes environment. Greene never replaced counselors or formal programs, but he bridged a gap those resources never filled: presence.

Broken Windows Applied

The chaplain's work repaired cracks before they spread. A burned-out officer who might have lashed out at inmates found a safe space to vent. A discouraged officer who might have resigned stayed after being reminded of their value. A shift shaken by violence stabilized because staff were able to process emotions instead of suppressing them.

Without Greene's presence, those cracks might have multiplied. Burnout could have turned into misconduct. Resignation could have fueled turnover. Suppressed anger could have erupted in unprofessional behavior toward inmates. Each would have been a broken window, sending signals of weakness and disorder.

Greene's visits signaled the opposite: staff mattered, culture was cared for, and cracks would not be ignored.

The Lessons of Presence

The Chaplain Visit illustrates several truths about resilience in corrections:

- **Presence matters more than programs.** Posters and phone numbers do little if staff feel unseen. A consistent presence, even brief, communicates value.
- **Listening repairs cracks.** Staff do not always need answers—they need space to speak and be heard.
- **Support must be accessible.** Formal counseling has value, but informal support often meets needs faster.
- **Culture responds to small gestures.** A five-minute visit can shift morale more than a new policy.
- **Resilience is spiritual, emotional, and cultural.** Supporting the whole person strengthens professionalism.

The Administrative Response

The administration expanded Greene's model. Other facilities in the state added chaplains or peer support officers to serve in similar roles. Training for chaplains included modules on staff wellness, confidentiality, and cultural impact. The role was reframed not only as inmate ministry but also as staff support.

Leaders realized that resilience was not only about programs or policies. It was about daily presence, cultural ownership, and visible signals that staff were valued.

Reflection

The Chaplain Visit shows how resilience can be reinforced by something as simple as presence. Greene did not design a program or write a policy. He walked the floors, asked questions, and listened. Those small acts repaired cracks that might have spread into burnout, misconduct, or cultural collapse.

Broken Windows explains the outcome. Each visit was a repaired window. Each conversation was a signal that staff were valued and culture was protected. Over time, those signals multiplied into resilience that could withstand even the most difficult incidents.

The lesson is clear: resilience does not always require new budgets or complex systems. Sometimes it begins with presence. A single person, trusted and consistent, can shift culture. In corrections, where stress is constant and cracks appear daily, that presence can mean the difference between collapse and resilience.

Analysis: Resilience as Cultural Armor

The Pattern in the Case Studies

The three case studies in this chapter, the Burned-Out Officer, the Peer Team, and the Chaplain Visit, reveal the same truth from different angles: resilience is not optional in corrections. It is the armor that protects professionalism against the constant erosion of stress.

Each case began with small cracks. Daniels ignored his own fatigue until it erupted in misconduct. A facility tolerated turnover and stress until staff created their own Peer Team. Officers at another prison carried stress silently until a chaplain's presence gave them a safe outlet. In each case, cracks multiplied until intervention occurred. Order was restored not through punishment or policy alone, but through resilience, the deliberate repair of cracks before they spread.

Why Resilience Is Not the Same as Toughness

Corrections culture often glorifies toughness. Officers pride themselves on enduring long shifts, dangerous situations, and high stress without complaint. While toughness has value, it is not resilience. Toughness absorbs impact; resilience recovers from it.

An officer who suppresses stress may appear tough, but cracks remain. Over time, those cracks widen into burnout, misconduct, or resignation. An officer who acknowledges stress, addresses it, and resets demonstrates true resilience. Broken Windows explains why: suppression is a broken window hidden behind glass, and resilience is the repair that prevents further breakage.

How Burnout Becomes Contagious

Stress does not remain contained within one officer. Like graffiti spreading across a pod, burnout multiplies through signals. When Daniels stopped enforcing small details, inmates noticed and tested him more aggressively. Peers noticed too. Some avoided him, and others mirrored his lax standards. One officer's burnout became cultural disorder.

The same contagion appears in other facilities. When staff believe leadership does not care about wellness, they stop caring themselves. Cynicism spreads. Inmates see inconsistency and exploit it. Burnout is not private. It is contagious.

Why Peer Support Works

The Peer Team case shows why resilience cannot always be built from the top down. Staff trust those who share their burdens. Peers have credibility administrators cannot replicate. They know the shifts, the noise, the fatigue. When they speak, others listen.

Broken Windows applies here as well. Each peer conversation is a repaired window. Without it, cracks widen into misconduct or turnover. With it, cracks are contained and culture stabilizes. The Peer Team succeeded because it owned resilience at the lowest level.

The Role of Presence

The Chaplain Visit highlights a second principle: presence matters more than programs. Officers ignored posters and phone numbers because they were abstract. A chaplain walking the floors was real. His presence communicated value.

Corrections is an environment of signals. Inmates read staff presence as ownership. Staff read leadership presence as credibility. The same principle applies to resilience. Presence communicates care, and absence communicates neglect.

Resilience as Cultural Armor

Resilience is best understood as cultural armor. Just as body armor protects against physical harm, cultural armor protects against psychological erosion.

Each act of resilience, a peer conversation, a chaplain visit, a counseling session, adds a layer of protection. Each ignored crack, burnout dismissed, stress unaddressed, wellness neglected, strips armor away.

Armor is not invincibility. It does not prevent stress from occurring. It prevents stress from breaking staff or culture. Without it, professionalism collapses under pressure. With it, professionalism endures.

Leadership's Responsibility

Leadership sets the tone for resilience. When wardens, captains, and sergeants model self-care, encourage wellness, and support peer programs, they communicate that resilience is part of professionalism. When they dismiss it as weakness, they communicate the opposite.

Supervisors are especially critical. Line staff watch them closely. A sergeant who takes five minutes to ask about an officer's well-being repairs windows. A sergeant who ignores burnout spreads cracks. Leadership presence at the mid-level is the hinge on which resilience turns.

The Ethical Dimension of Resilience

Resilience is not just practical, it is ethical. Officers who fail to care for themselves risk making poor decisions that endanger inmates, peers, and the public. Supervisors who ignore stress signals fail in their duty of care. Administrators who neglect staff wellness fail in their obligation to steward the profession responsibly.

Broken Windows reinforces this ethical dimension. Each ignored crack is an ethical failure. Each repaired crack is an ethical act. Resilience is both practical maintenance and moral obligation.

Resilience Signals to Inmates

Inmates interpret staff resilience as much as they interpret staff enforcement.

A resilient officer remains calm under provocation. Inmates recognize that manipulation will not succeed. A burned-out officer loses temper quickly. Inmates recognize vulnerability and exploit it.

Resilience signals permanence. Fragility signals opportunity. Facilities that project resilience deter challenges. Facilities that project fragility invite them.

Resilience in Daily Habits

Resilience is not built in annual workshops. It is built in daily habits. Officers who sleep properly, exercise regularly, and talk through stress maintain balance. Supervisors who check on their teams build morale. Administrators who protect days off and enforce staffing balance build culture.

These habits are small but they are the windows of resilience. When enforced, they protect the structure. When ignored, they multiply cracks.

The Cost of Neglect

Neglecting resilience carries costs far beyond morale. Burnout drives turnover, which drives overtime, which drives more burnout. Misconduct tied to stress results in lawsuits, settlements, and public scrutiny. Families of officers suffer when stress turns to substance abuse or broken relationships. Communities lose trust when correctional staff collapse under pressure.

The costs of repair are far smaller. Peer programs, chaplain presence, and counseling access are inexpensive compared to lawsuits, turnover, and recruitment campaigns. Resilience is not a luxury. It is a cost-saving necessity.

Reflection

The analysis of resilience in corrections is simple but profound:

- **Burnout is contagious.** One officer's cracks spread to peers and inmates.
- **Peer support is credible.** Staff trust those who share their burdens.
- **Presence matters.** Programs succeed only when embodied by trusted people.
- **Resilience is armor.** It protects culture against the erosion of stress.
- **Neglect is costly.** Cracks ignored become breaches that damage facilities and communities.

Broken Windows frames resilience as part of the same cultural equation as sanitation, security, and professionalism. Cracks must be repaired before they spread. Presence must be constant. Ownership must begin at the lowest level.

Resilience is not separate from corrections. It is corrections. Without it, the profession collapses. With it, culture holds steady, professionalism thrives, and inmates recognize that order is permanent.

Tools and Takeaways: Embedding Resilience into Correctional Culture

Why Tools Are Necessary

Resilience is not built by slogans. It is not a matter of telling staff to "be strong" or "tough it out." It must be embedded into culture with tools that are visible, repeatable, and credible. Just as locks must be checked and counts must be exact, resilience must be practiced with discipline.

This section provides practical tools for correctional leaders, supervisors, and line staff to build resilience into daily operations. Each tool is rooted in Broken

Windows thinking: small acts, consistently enforced, prevent cracks from spreading into collapse.

1. **Supervisor Wellness Checks**

   - Include wellness checks as part of the daily routine.
   - A five-minute conversation at the start or end of a shift can reveal stress before it multiplies.
   - The question "How are you doing?" is not a courtesy. It is a leadership duty.

   Principle: Every wellness check is a repaired window. Ignored fatigue becomes cultural disorder.

2. **Protect Days Off**

   - Enforce staffing plans that allow real rest.
   - Officers forced into constant overtime lose resilience quickly.
   - Days off must be protected, not optional.

   Principle: Rest is security. A burned-out officer is a security risk.

3. **Peer Support Teams**

   - Provide credibility administrators cannot.
   - Membership should be voluntary, screened, and trained.
   - Confidentiality must be absolute.

   Principle: Staff trust peers who share their burdens. Each conversation repairs cracks.

4. **Chaplain and Counselor Presence**

- ☐ Programs succeed when embodied by trusted people.
- ☐ Chaplains and counselors should walk the floors, not wait in offices.
- ☐ Presence communicates value more than posters or phone numbers.

Principle: Presence is culture. Absence is neglect.

5. **Structured Critical Incident Debriefs**

- ☐ Debriefs must address both tactics and emotions.
- ☐ Small group discussions led by trusted peers or chaplains help staff process stress.
- ☐ Suppression of emotions leads to cracks.

Principle: Professionalism requires both performance and processing.

6. **Resilience Training Blocks**

- ☐ Annual training should include resilience modules.
- ☐ Topics include stress recognition, healthy coping strategies, sleep management, and family balance.
- ☐ Training must be realistic and tied to daily corrections life.

Principle: Training is maintenance. Each session repairs cracks before they spread.

7. Family Engagement Programs

- Families bear the weight of corrections stress.
- Orientation sessions for spouses and partners help them understand the profession.
- Family nights, newsletters, or support hotlines extend resilience beyond the walls.

Principle: Families are part of the culture. Supporting them supports staff.

8. Recognition of Resilient Behavior

- Administrators should recognize staff who model resilience.
- Awards, commendations, or simple acknowledgments reinforce culture.
- Recognition signals that resilience is valued as much as tactical skill.

Principle: What leadership praises becomes culture.

9. Anonymous Feedback Channels

- Staff often hesitate to admit burnout directly.
- Anonymous surveys or feedback systems allow concerns to surface.
- Leaders must act visibly on feedback to sustain trust.

Principle: Silence hides cracks. Feedback reveals them.

10. Crisis Support Protocols

- ☐ Staff involved in assaults, suicides, or major incidents must receive structured follow-up.
- ☐ Includes wellness checks within 24 hours, peer support within 72 hours, and counseling options within one week.
- ☐ Cracks left after crisis multiply quickly.

Principle: Crisis care is part of professionalism, not an optional courtesy.

Sample Daily Resilience Checklist

For Supervisors:

- ☐ Did I ask at least one officer about their well-being today?
- ☐ Did I check overtime hours and identify fatigue risks?
- ☐ Did I model calm presence or project stress onto staff?

For Officers:

- ☐ Did I get adequate rest before this shift?
- ☐ Did I check in with a peer honestly about how I am doing?
- ☐ Did I take five minutes to reset after a stressful incident?

For Administrators:

- ☐ Did we enforce protected days off this week?
- ☐ Did peer teams or chaplains have visible presence on the floor?
- ☐ Did we recognize at least one act of resilience publicly?

How Broken Windows Shapes Resilience Tools

Broken Windows explains why resilience tools must be daily, visible, and enforced. Each ignored crack multiplies. Each enforced habit repairs.

- ☐ A supervisor ignoring overtime hours communicates that fatigue is tolerated.
- ☐ A sergeant asking about well-being communicates that resilience is enforced.
- ☐ An administrator cutting wellness programs communicates that staff are expendable.
- ☐ A warden protecting days off communicates that staff are valued.

Signals are constant. Tools ensure consistency with culture.

The Cost of Neglect vs. the Cost of Repair

Neglecting resilience carries enormous costs:

- ☐ Higher turnover and recruitment expenses
- ☐ Increased overtime and budget strain
- ☐ Misconduct, lawsuits, and liability tied to stress
- ☐ Public trust erosion after burnout-related crises

The cost of resilience tools is far smaller:

- ☐ Chaplain salary
- ☐ Overtime pay for peer team training
- ☐ Time for structured debriefs
- ☐ Protected days off

The comparison is stark. Neglect dwarfs repair costs.

Reflection

Resilience is not soft. It is security, professionalism, and culture. Without it, cracks multiply until facilities collapse under stress. With it, staff endure, professionalism thrives, and inmates recognize that order is permanent.

Broken Windows frames resilience as part of the same cultural logic as cleanliness, counts, and locks. Each small act of support is a repaired window. Each ignored signal of burnout is a broken window. The culture either strengthens or erodes.

The lesson is clear: resilience must be enforced with the same discipline as security protocols. Supervisors must model it. Officers must practice it. Administrators must protect it. Families must be included. When resilience is embedded in daily culture, correctional facilities are not just staffed, they are armored.

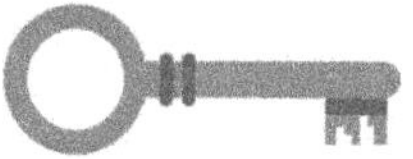

- 14 -

INTERNAL ACCOUNTABILITY AND PEER STANDARDS

Why Accountability Defines Culture

Every correctional facility is built on rules. Policies govern movement, counts, searches, meals, and recreation. Procedures dictate how staff document incidents, respond to emergencies, and interact with inmates. But rules and procedures mean little without accountability.

Accountability is the difference between words on paper and culture in practice. It is what transforms a policy from a suggestion into a standard. Without accountability, rules erode. Without accountability, professionalism weakens. Without accountability, inmates recognize inconsistency and exploit it.

Broken Windows explains why. Each ignored violation is a broken window. Each officer who cuts corners without consequence communicates that standards are negotiable. Each supervisor who looks the other way signals that rules are optional. Each administrator who tolerates misconduct communicates that professionalism is expendable. Cracks spread quickly. In corrections, those cracks are not abstract. They result in violence, escapes, and loss of public trust.

By contrast, accountability repairs windows. An officer correcting a peer's sloppy count reinforces culture. A sergeant documenting misconduct consistently signals that rules are enforced. An administrator disciplining fairly but firmly communicates that professionalism is permanent. Each act of accountability repairs cracks and prevents collapse.

The Difference Between External and Internal Accountability

External accountability comes from outside: courts, inspectors, accreditation bodies, legislatures, and the media. It matters, but it often comes late, after cracks have spread. A lawsuit is accountability after failure. An inspector's report is accountability after disorder.

Internal accountability is proactive. It begins with staff holding themselves and each other to standards daily. It is sergeants refusing to pencil-whip logs. It is officers speaking up when peers cut corners. It is administrators walking floors and asking hard questions. Internal accountability is culture. External accountability is consequence.

Facilities that rely only on external accountability are reactive. Facilities that build internal accountability are resilient.

Peer Standards as the Backbone of Culture

Internal accountability begins with peer standards. Officers spend more time with each other than with supervisors. They notice when someone cuts corners, ignores policy, or slips into burnout. When peers correct each other, culture is enforced instantly. When peers remain silent, cracks spread unchecked.

Peer standards are powerful because they communicate credibility. An officer may dismiss a supervisor's criticism as politics, but a peer's correction carries weight. "We do not do that here" spoken by a respected colleague reinforces culture more strongly than any memo.

Broken Windows applies here as well. A single peer refusing to let a corner be cut repairs a window. A single peer ignoring misconduct breaks one. Each peer act sends a signal to the entire team.

The Cost of Silence

Silence is one of the most dangerous cultural signals in corrections. When staff ignore misconduct, when peers refuse to speak up, and when supervisors look the other way, silence communicates tolerance. Inmates see it and exploit it. The public eventually learns of it, and trust erodes.

Silence is a broken window. Each time staff fail to hold each other accountable, culture weakens. The damage is not only immediate, it is generational. New officers entering the profession learn quickly what is tolerated. If silence is the norm, they adapt to it. If accountability is the norm, they adapt to that.

The Ethical Dimension of Accountability

Accountability is not only practical. It is ethical. Officers who ignore misconduct fail in their duty of care to inmates, peers, and the public. Supervisors who pencil-whip reports fail in their obligation to enforce truth. Administrators who tolerate misconduct fail in their responsibility to steward the profession.

Broken Windows frames accountability as a moral obligation. Each ignored crack is an ethical failure. Each repaired crack is an ethical act. Accountability is not only about compliance. It is about integrity.

Leadership's Role in Internal Accountability

Leadership presence determines whether accountability thrives or fails. A warden who walks floors, asks direct questions, and acts on what is seen communicates that standards matter. A captain who overlooks misconduct communicates that culture is negotiable.

Supervisors play a unique role. They are the bridge between policy and practice. If they model accountability, staff follow. If they avoid conflict, staff adapt. Peer standards reinforce culture, but supervisors sustain it. Leadership at every level must communicate that accountability is not optional.

Signals to Staff and Inmates

Accountability sends signals to both staff and inmates. To staff, it communicates that professionalism is real, that culture is enforced, and that integrity matters. To inmates, it communicates that staff are united, that rules are consistent, and that testing is futile.

The absence of accountability sends the opposite message. To staff, it communicates that professionalism is a slogan. To inmates, it communicates that staff are divided, that rules are negotiable, and that testing is rewarded.

Broken Windows explains why signals matter. Accountability is not abstract. It is visible. It is communicated in every correction, every report, and every act of enforcement.

Why Internal Accountability Is Hard

Holding others accountable is difficult. Officers fear being labeled disloyal. Supervisors fear conflict with subordinates. Administrators fear backlash from unions or politics. Silence often feels safer.

But silence is never safer in the long term. Cracks spread. Disorder grows. Public trust erodes. The price of silence always exceeds the discomfort of accountability.

Facilities that normalize accountability overcome fear by building trust. Officers know that corrections from peers are not betrayal but professionalism. Supervisors know that enforcing standards is expected, not optional. Administrators know that discipline, applied fairly, strengthens credibility.

Transition to the Case Studies

The importance of accountability becomes clear in lived experience. The following case studies illustrate how ignored misconduct eroded culture, how peer correction rebuilt standards, and how a supervisor's silence nearly collapsed professionalism.

Together, they reinforce the truth that accountability is culture. Broken Windows explains why: every act of accountability is a repaired window, and every failure is a broken one.

Case Study 1: The Ignored Misconduct

The Setting

A large urban jail housed over 2,000 inmates and employed nearly 700 staff. The facility faced constant challenges: gang rivalries, chronic overcrowding, and high turnover among officers. The jail had a strong written policy manual. It was thick, detailed, and updated annually. On paper, accountability was clear. In practice, cracks spread quickly.

The culture tolerated silence. Officers often looked the other way when peers cut corners. Supervisors signed reports without verifying accuracy. Administrators avoided difficult confrontations with unions or influential staff. Small acts of misconduct were ignored. Over time, those small cracks widened into cultural disorder.

Early Signals of Misconduct

It began with minor infractions. Officers skipped rounds but marked them complete on logs. Supervisors knew but did not challenge them. Radios went unchecked, leaving dead batteries in circulation. A sergeant noticed but shrugged. Counts were occasionally cleared without visual confirmation. Staff justified it as efficiency.

Inmates noticed. They began to test boundaries. Some slipped contraband into cells during skipped rounds. Others manipulated counts by hiding in blind spots. Small cracks in accountability communicated that standards were negotiable.

Among staff, silence became the norm. New officers quickly learned that speaking up was risky. Veterans told them to mind their business and avoid making enemies. Peer correction was absent. Internal accountability collapsed.

The Escalation

The cracks widened into serious misconduct. Officers were caught sleeping during shifts. Contraband flowed more freely into the facility, fueling gambling and gang activity. A group of officers developed a reputation for excessive force, retaliating against inmates without documentation. Supervisors heard rumors but avoided formal investigations, fearing conflict.

One incident revealed the depth of the problem. An officer assaulted an inmate during a lockdown, using force far beyond policy. Several peers witnessed it. None reported it. The inmate filed a grievance, but it was dismissed for lack of evidence. Word spread among inmates that staff could act with impunity. Word spread among officers that silence was safer than truth.

The culture was broken. Accountability was absent.

The Breaking Point

The turning point came when external accountability arrived. A video of the assault surfaced, recorded on a contraband phone and smuggled to the media. The footage showed the officer's misconduct clearly. It also revealed that other staff were present and did nothing.

Public outrage followed. Headlines accused the jail of brutality and cover-up. Civil rights groups demanded investigation. The county commission ordered an external audit. Lawsuits were filed.

The audit revealed systemic failure. Rounds were falsified. Reports were incomplete. Supervisors admitted they avoided confronting misconduct. Administrators conceded they tolerated silence to keep the peace with staff. Internal accountability had collapsed, and external accountability was forced to intervene.

Administrative Response

Under public pressure, the administration launched reforms. Several officers were terminated. The sergeant who ignored misconduct was demoted. The warden resigned. Policies were rewritten to emphasize peer reporting and supervisor responsibility. Training sessions stressed that silence was complicity.

New leadership communicated a different message: misconduct, no matter how small, would be addressed. Officers were encouraged to report peers, with protections against retaliation. Supervisors were required to verify rounds and counts in person. Audits were conducted monthly.

The facility began to stabilize, but the damage to credibility lingered. Staff morale suffered. Inmates remained skeptical. Public trust had been eroded.

Broken Windows Applied

The case illustrates Broken Windows with stark clarity. Each ignored act of misconduct was a broken window. Each falsified round, each unchecked radio, and each unchallenged use of force communicated that standards were optional. Inmates saw the signals and exploited them. Staff saw the signals and adapted to silence. Culture collapsed.

External accountability repaired the windows only after they had shattered. Internal accountability could have prevented collapse if peers, supervisors, or administrators had acted earlier.

Lessons from the Ignored Misconduct

1. **Silence is complicity.** Ignoring misconduct communicates tolerance.
2. **Small cracks widen.** Skipped rounds and falsified logs lead to serious violations.
3. **Inmates see everything.** Weakness in staff culture is exploited instantly.
4. **External accountability is late.** Audits and lawsuits arrive after collapse. Internal accountability prevents collapse.
5. **Leadership sets the tone.** Administrators who avoid confrontation communicate that misconduct is acceptable.

Reflection

The Ignored Misconduct shows how silence destroys culture. Small cracks in accountability multiplied until external forces intervened. The cost was high: lawsuits, resignations, damaged trust.

Broken Windows provides the lesson. Each ignored act was a broken window. Each failure to act signaled that culture was negotiable. Facilities cannot rely on external accountability to repair cracks. They must build internal accountability daily, peer to peer, supervisor to officer, administrator to staff.

The lesson is clear: silence is never safer. Accountability, enforced daily, sustains culture.

Case Study 2: The Peer Correction

The Setting

A medium-sized county jail housed around 1,100 inmates with a staff of just over 250. The facility faced typical challenges: staffing shortages, occasional spikes in violence, and aging infrastructure. Yet compared to many urban jails, it maintained a steadier culture. The difference was not in funding or facilities. The difference was in peer standards.

From the academy forward, staff were told, “We hold each other accountable here.” It wasn’t a slogan on a poster but a lived expectation. Officers who cut corners were corrected by peers before supervisors ever had to step in. Small cracks were repaired immediately, signaling to inmates and staff that details mattered.

The Early Test

Officer Rivera had been on the job for less than a year. He was energetic and eager to prove himself. At times, he moved too quickly and skipped steps in order to keep pace with experienced officers. During a busy evening count, he called numbers rapidly and glanced at doors without pausing to confirm each inmate was present and upright.

Officer Lewis, a veteran with fifteen years of service, stood beside him. He could have ignored the sloppiness. The sergeant on duty was across the unit and unlikely to catch it. Instead, Lewis stopped Rivera mid-count.

“Slow down,” Lewis said quietly but firmly. “We don’t rush this. Look in each cell. Eyes on every inmate. Start again.”

Rivera looked embarrassed, and a few inmates smirked. Lewis didn’t back down. Rivera restarted the count and completed it correctly.

Signals to the Unit

That small moment sent immediate signals.

- To Rivera, it made clear that shortcuts were not acceptable.
- To inmates, it showed that officers corrected each other right away, leaving no cracks to exploit.
- To other officers, it reinforced that peer correction was expected, not a betrayal.

The sergeant noticed and later praised Lewis during briefing. "That's how we do it here." The message was reinforced across the shift.

The Cultural Pattern

This was not a one-time incident. In this facility, officers corrected each other on everything from sanitation to communication to professionalism. If someone left a radio uncharged, a peer reminded them. If someone spoke disrespectfully to an inmate, a peer pulled them aside after the shift. If someone hesitated to enforce a minor rule, a peer encouraged consistency.

The culture was reinforced daily, not through memos but through action. Supervisors supported the practice, yet the real weight of accountability rested with the officers.

The Major Incident

The strength of peer accountability showed itself during a serious event. A fight broke out in a dayroom involving several inmates. The first responding officer, under stress, raised his baton in violation of policy. Before he swung, another officer shouted, "Holster it!" The officer froze, lowered the baton, and regained control. Backup arrived, and the incident ended with minimal force.

During the debrief, the supervisor highlighted the peer correction as the turning point. If the baton had been used, the situation could have escalated into allegations of excessive force, legal issues, and disciplinary action. Instead, professionalism was maintained because one officer stepped in at the right moment.

Why Peer Correction Worked

Several factors made peer correction effective:

1. **Clear expectation.** Officers were taught early that accountability among peers was part of the job.

2. **Supervisor support.** Sergeants praised officers who corrected each other.
3. **No retaliation.** Corrections were about professionalism, not politics, and retaliation was not tolerated.
4. **Daily consistency.** Corrections happened regularly, which normalized the practice.

Broken Windows applies here. Every peer correction was a repaired window. Every uncorrected lapse would have been a crack. The consistent corrections kept cracks from spreading.

The Impact on Inmates

Inmates recognized the consistency. They knew officers would not let each other cut corners. This reduced testing. There was no point in exploiting weaknesses because peers closed those gaps immediately. The facility stayed more stable than other jails of similar size not because of budgets but because of culture.

The Impact on Staff

New officers like Rivera adapted quickly. They learned that accountability wasn't personal but professional. Correction wasn't humiliation; it was part of the job. Over time, they became the ones doing the correcting.

Veterans like Lewis gained credibility with both peers and supervisors. Their willingness to hold standards made them cultural anchors. Supervisors relied on officers like Lewis to model the expectations of the facility.

Lessons from the Peer Correction

- ☐ Peer correction works faster than supervisor discipline.
- ☐ Correction must be normal, not reserved for crises.
- ☐ Supervisors must support it or the practice collapses.

- Consistency reduces inmate testing.
- Peer correction builds future leaders.

Reflection

The Peer Correction shows how accountability can thrive at the lowest level. One veteran officer who refused to let a junior officer cut corners repaired a window before it broke. The facility's culture stayed strong because peers enforced standards daily.

Broken Windows gives the lesson. Every peer correction repairs a window. Every moment of silence breaks one. Facilities that build peer accountability are strong. Facilities that tolerate silence are fragile.

The takeaway is simple: accountability has to begin with peers. Supervisors can reinforce it. Administrators can support it. But only peers, present in the moment, can repair cracks before they spread.

Case Study 3: The Supervisor Who Looked Away

The Setting

A state correctional institution housed just under 1,800 inmates and employed about 400 staff. The facility had a mixed reputation. Some units ran smoothly under steady leadership, while others struggled with disorder and low morale. The difference often traced back to the supervisors assigned to each area.

On one shift, a sergeant named Collins commanded a housing unit of nearly 200 inmates. Collins had been promoted for his length of service rather than for leadership ability. He was known as easygoing and conflict-averse. Staff liked him personally, but inmates quickly sensed his reluctance to enforce standards.

The First Signals

Cracks appeared early. Officers on Collins' shift occasionally arrived late to briefing. Instead of addressing it, Collins shrugged. Radios went unchecked and batteries died mid-shift. Collins overlooked it. Counts were completed sloppily, with doors glanced at instead of inmates confirmed. Collins signed the paperwork anyway.

Officers learned quickly that Collins would not challenge them. Small acts of neglect multiplied. Inmates noticed too. Trash lingered in corners. Rules on uniforms and lockdown became inconsistent. Discipline weakened.

Each overlooked detail was a broken window. Collins' silence communicated that standards were optional.

The Escalation

As cracks spread, misconduct increased. Some officers cut corners intentionally, confident Collins would ignore it. A few began fraternizing with inmates, exchanging favors for small perks. Gossip about contraband grew. Collins heard rumors but avoided confrontation. "It'll work itself out," he said once.

One evening, an officer on Collins' shift allowed inmates extra time out of cells during lockdown. The violation was obvious, visible on cameras. Collins was informed but did nothing. "No harm done," he said. Word spread quickly. The sergeant looked the other way. Inmates pushed limits more aggressively. Officers cut corners more boldly.

The Breaking Point

The collapse came during a routine shakedown. A team from another unit entered Collins' pod to conduct a search. Within minutes, they uncovered cell phones, homemade weapons, and large quantities of contraband.

The discovery shocked administrators. How had so much contraband accumulated? The answer became clear during the investigation. Officers admitted that standards had been lax for months. Rounds were skipped. Searches were rare. Rules were inconsistently enforced. Inmates took advantage, smuggling and hiding contraband freely.

At the center of it all was Collins. He had seen the cracks. He had heard the rumors. He had witnessed the lapses. But he looked away. His silence allowed disorder to spread until it was uncontrollable.

Administrative Response

The fallout was severe. Several officers were disciplined for misconduct. Collins was demoted. Administrators implemented a corrective action plan that required supervisors to document enforcement of rules daily and report misconduct immediately. Training reinforced the principle that silence is complicity.

The warden addressed staff directly. "Every ignored detail is a signal. Every time we look away, inmates see weakness. Every time we enforce standards, inmates see strength. This facility will not tolerate silence."

Broken Windows Applied

The case demonstrates Broken Windows clearly. Each act of silence by Collins was a broken window. Each ignored detail — late staff, unchecked radios, sloppy counts, extra time out — was a crack. Inmates interpreted those cracks as signals of weakness. Disorder multiplied until contraband flooded the unit.

Had Collins corrected small lapses early, the culture could have been preserved. His silence communicated tolerance, and the culture collapsed.

The Impact on Staff

Staff under Collins adapted to his silence. Some enjoyed the lax standards and cut corners without fear. Others grew frustrated, knowing professionalism was eroding. Morale fractured. Resentment grew between those who cared about standards and those who did not.

When the shakedown revealed the contraband, even officers who had stayed professional felt betrayed. They had warned Collins, but he looked away. His failure damaged trust not only with staff but with leadership.

The Impact on Inmates

Inmates exploited the cracks quickly. They recognized Collins' reluctance to enforce rules. They pushed boundaries and found space to smuggle contraband. Gang leaders gained leverage. Violence increased as contraband fueled gambling and debt. Inmate respect for staff declined, replaced by confidence that officers could be manipulated.

Inmates did not need to overpower staff. They simply waited for silence to multiply.

Lessons from the Supervisor Who Looked Away

- **Silence is leadership failure.** A supervisor who avoids conflict communicates that rules are optional.
- **Cracks multiply quickly.** Inconsistent enforcement invites contraband and disorder.
- **Supervisors shape culture.** Officers mirror the standards their sergeant enforces or ignores.
- **Inmates read silence instantly.** What staff avoid, inmates exploit.
- **Leadership credibility depends on presence.** Absent or silent supervisors damage morale and trust.

Reflection

The Supervisor Who Looked Away shows how leadership silence destroys culture. Collins did not commit misconduct himself. He did something more dangerous. He allowed it. Each overlooked detail was a broken window. Each act of silence was a signal. Inmates interpreted weakness. Staff adapted to neglect. Culture collapsed.

Broken Windows explains the failure. Supervisors must enforce standards daily. Looking away is never neutral. It is complicity. Accountability requires presence, courage, and consistency.

The lesson is clear. Supervisors who remain silent become broken windows themselves. They signal that cracks are tolerated. To preserve culture, supervisors must repair cracks immediately. Silence is never safer. Accountability is always the standard.

Analysis: Accountability as the Core of Correctional Culture

The Pattern in the Case Studies

The three case studies in this chapter—the Ignored Misconduct, the Peer Correction, and the Supervisor Who Looked Away—reflect the same principle from different angles. Accountability is the foundation of correctional culture. Without it, professionalism erodes. With it, order is sustained.

In the first case, silence allowed small cracks to multiply until external accountability arrived through lawsuits and media exposure. In the second, peer accountability repaired cracks immediately, preventing disorder from spreading. In the third, a supervisor's silence created an environment where contraband flooded a unit and credibility collapsed.

Together, the cases reveal the truth: accountability is not optional. It must be enforced at every level, peer to peer, supervisor to staff, and administrator to team. Broken Windows explains why. Each act of accountability repairs a window. Each failure to act breaks one.

Why Silence Is the Enemy of Accountability

Silence is one of the most destructive forces in corrections. When staff see misconduct but say nothing, when supervisors ignore violations, or when administrators avoid conflict, silence communicates tolerance. Inmates see it. They exploit it. Staff adapt to it. Culture erodes.

Silence spreads because it feels safer in the short term. Officers fear being labeled disloyal if they correct peers. Supervisors fear conflict with subordinates. Administrators fear political fallout. But silence is never safer in the long term. It always leads to cracks multiplying until collapse.

Broken Windows frames silence as a broken window itself. Each unspoken correction, each unsigned report, each avoided confrontation is a crack. Once silence becomes the norm, accountability is impossible.

Why Peer Standards Matter Most

Peers spend more time with each other than with supervisors. They see the small cracks first: the skipped round, the sloppy count, the disrespectful word. When they correct each other, culture is reinforced instantly.

Peer standards carry unique credibility. An officer may dismiss a sergeant's correction as politics, but a respected peer's words carry weight. "We don't do that here" from a colleague strengthens professionalism more effectively than any memo.

Facilities that normalize peer accountability build resilience. Facilities that discourage it encourage silence. Peer correction is the fastest, most credible form of accountability.

The Role of Supervisors

Supervisors shape accountability more than anyone else. They bridge the gap between policy and practice. When supervisors enforce standards consistently, staff follow. When supervisors look away, staff adapt to silence.

The case of Sergeant Collins shows the danger of supervisor silence. Even without committing misconduct, his failure to act created an environment where rules collapsed and contraband spread. Supervisors are never neutral. Their silence is complicity.

Conversely, supervisors who reinforce peer corrections amplify culture. When a sergeant praises a veteran officer for correcting a rookie, it communicates that accountability is expected, not punished. Supervisors who back peer standards strengthen professionalism across the shift.

The Role of Administrators

Administrators set the outer frame of accountability. They design policies, establish expectations, and discipline misconduct. When administrators enforce accountability fairly and consistently, staff believe professionalism matters. When they tolerate silence or protect favored employees, culture collapses.

External accountability arrives when administrators fail. Lawsuits, audits, and media scrutiny fill the gap left by absent leadership. The cost is always high in money, morale, and credibility. Internal accountability led by administrators prevents these failures.

Why Accountability Is Ethical as Well as Practical

Accountability is not only about rules. It is about integrity. Officers who ignore misconduct fail in their duty of care to inmates, peers, and the public. Supervisors who look away abandon their obligation to enforce standards.

Administrators who tolerate silence fail in their responsibility to support the profession.

Broken Windows frames accountability as an ethical duty. Each ignored crack is an ethical failure. Each repaired crack is an ethical act. Accountability is not just compliance. It is moral leadership.

Signals to Inmates and Staff

Accountability sends visible signals. To staff, it communicates that professionalism is real and standards matter. To inmates, it communicates that staff are united and consistent, and that testing is pointless.

The absence of accountability sends the opposite signals. To staff, it suggests professionalism is optional. To inmates, it suggests rules are negotiable and staff are divided.

In corrections, signals matter as much as locks. Inmates interpret staff culture immediately. Accountability projects strength. Silence projects weakness.

The Cost of Neglecting Accountability

Neglecting accountability is costly. It leads to misconduct, contraband, violence, lawsuits, turnover, and loss of public trust. The Ignored Misconduct case showed how silence resulted in external accountability through lawsuits and media attention. The Supervisor Who Looked Away case showed how silence allowed contraband to flood a unit, endangering staff and inmates.

The cost of accountability is far lower. Peer corrections require no budget. Supervisor presence requires no new equipment. Administrator consistency requires courage, not money. The comparison is not close. Neglecting accountability is expensive. Enforcing it is efficient.

How to Normalize Accountability

Facilities that thrive normalize accountability through daily habits:

- **Train peer correction as professionalism.** From the academy forward, new officers should learn that correcting peers is a duty, not betrayal.
- **Supervisors must model accountability.** When sergeants enforce rules consistently, staff see that silence is not tolerated.
- **Administrators must discipline fairly.** Consistent discipline builds credibility. Favoritism destroys it.
- **Celebrate peer corrections.** When officers correct each other respectfully, supervisors should acknowledge it as strength.
- **Protect whistleblowers.** Staff who report misconduct must be shielded from retaliation. Without protection, silence wins.

Reflection

The analysis of accountability is simple but unavoidable. Silence destroys culture. Peer correction sustains it. Supervisors shape it. Administrators frame it. Broken Windows explains why: each act of accountability repairs a window. Each failure to act breaks one.

Correctional facilities that build internal accountability thrive. They prevent cracks from spreading, deter inmate testing, and preserve professionalism. Facilities that tolerate silence collapse, forcing external oversight through lawsuits and audits.

The lesson is clear: accountability is culture. It is not optional or external. It begins with peers, is reinforced by supervisors, and is sustained by administrators. Without it, cracks spread until collapse. With it, order holds steady and professionalism endures.

- 15 -

SUSTAINING BROKEN WINDOWS PRINCIPLES LONG TERM

Why Sustainability Matters

Correctional facilities often succeed in the short term. A new warden arrives with energy and sharp standards. A reform program launches with enthusiasm. A training cycle instills professionalism for a season. The facility improves for a while. Then slowly, cracks return. Standards drift. Programs fade. The energy of reform diminishes, replaced by old habits.

This cycle is common in corrections. Leaders come and go. Initiatives rise and fall. Culture shifts forward and backward like a tide. What remains is inconsistency, bursts of order followed by returns to disorder.

Sustainability is the antidote. To sustain Broken Windows principles long term means embedding them so deeply into culture, training, supervision, and daily practice that they survive leadership changes, budget cycles, and staff turnover. Sustainability transforms Broken Windows from a program into a profession.

Broken Windows as a Long-Term Framework

Broken Windows is often misunderstood as a short-term enforcement strategy. In its earliest policing applications, critics accused it of being zero tolerance or temporary quality-of-life sweeps. But the principle is broader. Broken Windows is about signals. It is about repairing cracks before they spread. Signals cannot be temporary. They must be constant.

In corrections, Broken Windows cannot be seasonal. It cannot rise with one leader and fade with the next. It must be institutionalized. The standard that every broken latch is a security breach, that every sloppy count is a cultural crack, and that every act of silence is complicity must be permanent. Without permanence, culture collapses as soon as attention shifts.

Why Corrections Struggles with Sustainability

Several realities make sustainability difficult in jails and prisons:

- **Leadership turnover.** Wardens, sheriffs, and administrators often serve limited terms. Each brings new priorities. Without continuity, reforms collapse.
- **Staff fatigue.** Even strong reforms can wear staff down if not reinforced. Enthusiasm fades. Old habits return.
- **Budget cycles.** Funding rises and falls with politics. Programs start strong but end when money disappears.
- **Cultural resistance.** Staff sometimes see reforms as fads, waiting them out rather than embracing them.
- **External pressure.** Crises, lawsuits, or political shifts can pull focus away from internal culture.

Broken Windows must be sustained in spite of these forces. Otherwise, every reform will be temporary, and every culture fragile.

Signals of Sustainability

A facility sustains Broken Windows principles when:

- Standards remain consistent across shifts and years, not dependent on one supervisor.
- Peer correction is normalized so new officers learn it from day one.
- Training embeds Broken Windows principles into every module, not only electives.
- Administrators reinforce culture even when budgets tighten.
- External accountability validates internal accountability, not replaces it.

Sustainability is visible when culture does not collapse during leadership transitions, staffing shortages, or crises.

The Role of Institutional Memory

Facilities that sustain Broken Windows build institutional memory. They do not reinvent culture every five years. Instead, they preserve lessons, train new staff in them, and adapt them to changing conditions.

Institutional memory is built through:

- Documentation of policies and case studies.
- Mentorship between veterans and rookies.
- Integration of Broken Windows into training academies.
- Celebrating long-term cultural anchors, peer standards, supervisor presence, and inmate compliance.

Without institutional memory, every reform starts from scratch. With it, reforms accumulate, building strength over decades.

The Ethical Dimension of Sustainability

Sustainability is not only practical. It is ethical. Correctional facilities exist to protect the public, uphold safety, and enforce lawful order. Allowing culture to collapse every few years fails that mission. It endangers staff, destabilizes inmates, and erodes community trust.

Broken Windows explains why sustainability is an ethical duty. Each ignored lapse in sustainability is a broken window. Each facility that reverts to disorder communicates that professionalism is negotiable. The public deserves better. Staff deserve better. Inmates deserve better.

Sustainability Through Ownership

The only way to sustain Broken Windows long term is to embed ownership at every level. Programs run from the top fade when leaders leave. Culture owned by peers endures.

- Officers must own details in their housing units.
- Supervisors must own standards in their shifts.
- Administrators must own the framework across the facility.
- Training staff must embed it into every lesson.
- Peer teams must normalize corrections and resilience.

Ownership transforms Broken Windows from a reform into a way of life.

Transition to the Case Studies

Sustainability can sound abstract, but it becomes real in stories. The following case studies show how facilities failed when reforms faded, how others succeeded when culture was embedded, and how accreditation became a tool to preserve order across generations.

Together, they reveal the truth: Broken Windows can be sustained, but only if embedded deeply enough to survive turnover, fatigue, and change.

Sustainability is the difference between temporary improvement and permanent culture.

Case Study 1: The Short-Lived Program

The Setting

A county jail in the Midwest housed around 900 inmates and employed roughly 220 staff. The facility was known for its cycles of reform. Every few years, a new sheriff or jail administrator would launch a program designed to "fix the culture." Posters would go up, new slogans would be introduced, and training sessions would be scheduled. For a while, enthusiasm would grow. But within months, cracks always appeared. Staff would return to old habits, programs would fade, and the cycle would begin again.

One such program was called Operation Clean Slate. Launched with enthusiasm, it was designed to improve sanitation, professionalism, and morale. On paper, it reflected Broken Windows principles. In practice, it failed to sustain itself.

The Launch

Operation Clean Slate began with energy. The new jail administrator held a press conference announcing the program. He spoke about the importance of cleanliness, order, and professionalism. Staff were issued new uniforms. Housing units were deep-cleaned. Maintenance crews repaired broken locks and painted walls. Training sessions emphasized the importance of attention to detail.

The first few weeks saw real improvements. Inmates noticed the changes. Showers were cleaner, graffiti disappeared, and officers enforced small rules more consistently. Staff morale rose. The facility looked sharper, and the atmosphere steadied.

The Cracks Appear

But within weeks, cracks began to show. Officers complained that cleaning assignments interfered with routine security tasks. Supervisors grumbled about increased paperwork tied to sanitation checks. The administrator who had championed the program was frequently away at county meetings, leaving deputies to carry the load.

Inmates tested the system by scribbling graffiti in corners and leaving trash in common areas. When officers failed to correct it immediately, the signals shifted, and disorder crept back.

Staff began to view Operation Clean Slate as "another program" rather than culture. Old habits re-emerged. Rounds were skipped. Paperwork was pencil-whipped. Trash accumulated.

The Collapse

Within six months, the program had all but disappeared. Posters about professionalism faded on bulletin boards. Sanitation inspections became sporadic. Supervisors stopped asking about Clean Slate in roll call. Staff dismissed it as another "flavor of the month."

Inmates noticed the collapse. Graffiti reappeared in pods. Contraband incidents rose. Fights increased. What had begun with enthusiasm ended in disorder.

Operation Clean Slate had been a short-lived program because it was never embedded into culture. It relied on leadership energy, not institutional ownership. When leadership attention shifted, the program died.

Why the Program Failed

Several factors explain the collapse:

1. **Leadership Absence.** The administrator who launched Clean Slate failed to stay present. Without visible ownership, the program lost momentum.
2. **Supervisor Resistance.** Middle managers saw Clean Slate as extra work, not culture. Their reluctance undermined enforcement.
3. **Staff Fatigue.** Officers viewed Clean Slate as temporary. They waited it out, assuming it would fade, and they were right.
4. **Inmate Testing.** Inmates challenged the new standards. Staff failed to enforce consistency, sending signals that reform was negotiable.
5. **No Embedding.** Clean Slate was never integrated into policy, training, or daily habits. It remained an add-on, not a foundation.

Broken Windows Applied

Operation Clean Slate illustrates Broken Windows clearly. In its early days, the program repaired windows. Clean walls, painted doors, sharp uniforms, and consistent enforcement sent strong signals. But cracks soon appeared. Supervisors resisted. Officers cut corners. Inmates tested. Leadership disappeared. Each ignored crack was a broken window. Disorder multiplied until the program collapsed.

The lesson is not that Broken Windows principles failed. The lesson is that sustainability failed. A program cannot repair windows if it is temporary. To succeed, Broken Windows must be embedded into culture, not rolled out as a campaign.

The Aftermath

After Operation Clean Slate collapsed, the facility returned to its cycle. A few years later, a new sheriff launched a different initiative. Staff responded with skepticism. "We've seen this before," they said. Inmates recognized the cycle too, testing the system early and often.

Public trust eroded. Local media reported on recurring fights and sanitation problems. The facility became a symbol of inconsistency. What could have been a lasting cultural reform became another example of temporary enthusiasm.

Lessons from the Short-Lived Program

- **Programs fade, culture endures.** Without embedding into daily life, reforms collapse.
- **Leadership presence matters.** Launching a program without sustaining it signals weakness.
- **Supervisors must buy in.** Without mid-level enforcement, reforms die.
- **Inmates test reform.** If staff fail to enforce consistently, inmates expose cracks.
- **Embedding is essential.** Reforms must be part of policy, training, and peer standards.

Reflection

The Short-Lived Program demonstrates why sustainability is essential. Operation Clean Slate began with enthusiasm but collapsed because it was never embedded into culture. Each ignored crack multiplied until order was lost.

Broken Windows explains the failure. Repaired windows remain whole only if maintained. Left alone, they break again. Sustainability is maintenance. Without it, every program becomes a temporary fix, every reform a short-lived gesture.

The lesson is clear: programs are temporary. Culture is permanent. To sustain Broken Windows principles long term, facilities must embed them into every policy, every shift, and every peer correction. Otherwise, reforms will fade like posters on a wall.

Case Study 2: The Lasting Culture

The Setting

In the Southeast, a regional detention center held just over 1,300 inmates and employed 320 staff. Unlike many facilities that lurched from reform to reform, this jail had a reputation for steadiness. Staff turnover was lower than the state average. Inmate incidents occurred, but they were managed without spirals of disorder. Inspectors routinely praised the facility's professionalism.

The secret was not money. The building was old. The budget was modest. The secret was culture. Broken Windows principles were not rolled out as a campaign. They were embedded into daily operations so deeply that they endured leadership changes, staffing shortages, and political pressure.

The Origins of Culture

Fifteen years earlier, the jail had faced crisis. Inmate violence was high, sanitation was poor, and morale was low. A new warden, Miller, arrived with a focus on details. He walked the tiers daily, correcting officers, addressing inmates, and enforcing standards. At first, staff resisted, viewing his presence as micromanagement. Over time, Miller's consistency created credibility.

He emphasized three principles:

1. **Details matter.** No corner was too small to correct.
2. **Peers own culture.** Officers were expected to correct each other daily.
3. **Supervisors must be present.** Sergeants were on the floor, not in offices.

Miller framed these principles as Broken Windows applied to corrections. He did not launch a program. He built habits.

Leadership Transition

After eight years, Miller retired. Staff feared the culture would collapse. A new warden, Rodriguez, arrived with her own style. But instead of changing course, she reinforced what Miller had built. She made adjustments for technology and training but left the foundation intact: details, peers, supervisors.

The culture survived the transition because it no longer belonged to one leader. It belonged to the staff. Officers expected each other to enforce standards. Sergeants enforced consistency. Administrators reinforced presence. Inmates recognized the permanence.

The Test of Crisis

Five years into Rodriguez's tenure, the jail faced a budget crisis. Overtime soared as positions went unfilled. Tensions rose. In many facilities, these conditions would have collapsed culture. At this jail, Broken Windows principles held.

Even when short-staffed, officers conducted rounds and counts with precision. Supervisors doubled their presence on floors to reassure staff. Peer correction increased, with officers reminding each other not to cut corners under pressure. Inmates tested, but staff stayed consistent. The culture held because it was embedded, not dependent on resources.

The Signal to Inmates

Inmates noticed. They remarked to each other that "nothing changes here." Even during staff shortages, rules were enforced. Sanitation was maintained. Counts were accurate. Uniforms were sharp.

The signal was powerful. Inmates realized that testing the system was futile. Order was not seasonal. It was permanent.

The Test of Politics

Another test came when a new sheriff was elected. Campaigning on promises of reform, he suggested the jail was "stale" and needed change. When he toured the facility, however, he found professionalism intact. Inspectors praised the consistency. Community leaders reported fewer complaints about the jail. The sheriff wisely chose not to dismantle the culture and took credit for sustaining it.

The culture survived again because it was not dependent on one warden, one sheriff, or one program. It had become institutional memory.

Broken Windows Applied

The lasting culture illustrates Broken Windows in its strongest form. Each detail was a repaired window. Each peer correction was a reinforcement. Each supervisor presence was a signal. Over time, these habits accumulated into culture so steady that leadership changes and crises could not undo it.

The difference from the Short-Lived Program was embedding. Broken Windows was not a campaign. It was daily life. That permanence sustained order.

Lessons from the Lasting Culture

1. **Programs fade, culture endures.** Embedding principles into daily operations makes them permanent.
2. **Leadership transitions matter less when culture is owned by staff.** When staff expect accountability, new leaders reinforce rather than replace.

3. **Crises test culture.** When resources shrink, embedded principles hold stronger than programs.
4. **Signals shape inmate behavior.** Consistency over years communicates permanence.
5. **Institutional memory sustains professionalism.** Case studies, training, and mentorship carry culture forward.

Reflection

The Lasting Culture shows how Broken Windows can be sustained across decades. Details enforced, peers correcting, supervisors present, leaders consistent, together, these habits created a culture that outlived individuals and crises.

Broken Windows explains the success. Each repaired window was maintained. Each act of ownership reinforced permanence. Sustainability was not an initiative but a way of life.

The lesson is clear: lasting culture requires embedding. Programs fade. Leaders change. Budgets shrink. But embedded habits endure. Broken Windows must be more than reform. It must be the profession itself.

Case Study 3: The Accreditation Standard

The Setting

A state prison housing 2,200 inmates with a staff of nearly 500 had a history of inconsistency. Leadership changes were frequent. Wardens averaged only three years before retiring, resigning, or transferring. Each new leader arrived with energy, introduced reforms, and left. Culture shifted with each transition. Staff joked that policies were rewritten more often than they were enforced.

When the prison sought national accreditation, skepticism was high. Staff assumed it would be another program, thick binders of policies created for inspectors, then forgotten. Over time, accreditation became more than paperwork. It became the framework that sustained Broken Windows principles across leadership changes.

The Push for Accreditation

The push came after a series of lawsuits. Families of inmates sued over medical neglect and use-of-force incidents. Settlements cost the state millions. Lawmakers demanded reform. The Department of Corrections committed to accreditation as a way to restore public trust.

The accreditation process required compliance with hundreds of standards: sanitation, safety, security, medical care, and staff professionalism. At first, staff saw it as overwhelming. Leadership framed it differently. "This is not about binders," the warden said. "This is about culture. These standards are windows. We keep them whole."

The First Cycle

The first audit was grueling. Inspectors identified dozens of deficiencies: incomplete logs, sloppy counts, unsanitary showers, inconsistent training records. Staff worked overtime to correct them before the final inspection. Accreditation was achieved, but many dismissed it as a one-time event.

The turning point came when the warden left. A new warden arrived, but the standards remained. The facility had to prepare for another audit in three years. Staff realized the expectations were not temporary. Compliance was not optional. The culture began to shift.

Embedding Standards

Over time, accreditation standards became embedded into daily operations:

- Sanitation checks were built into daily supervisor walkthroughs.
- Training requirements were enforced annually, not just before audits.
- Documentation was verified weekly by administrators, not just filed.
- Peer accountability was reinforced, as staff reminded each other to maintain compliance.

Broken Windows principles aligned perfectly with accreditation. Each standard was a window. Each small detail mattered. Sustaining compliance required constant repair of cracks.

The Test of Leadership Change

Five years into accreditation, the facility faced another leadership change. A new warden arrived with a different philosophy. Unlike past transitions, culture did not collapse. Staff explained the standards. "This is how we do it," they said. The warden adapted to the culture rather than reshaping it.

This marked a reversal. Instead of leadership defining culture, culture defined leadership. Accreditation provided continuity across transitions. Broken Windows principles, embedded in standards, survived leadership turnover.

The Test of Crisis

The ultimate test came during a staffing crisis. Overtime soared. Vacancies left posts uncovered. In many facilities, such strain would have collapsed culture. Accreditation standards held. Supervisors enforced sanitation. Officers conducted rounds and counts with precision. Training continued on schedule.

Inspectors returned during the crisis and found compliance intact. "This facility has institutionalized its culture," the audit report stated. "Standards are not dependent on leadership or resources. They are embedded."

The Signal to Staff and Inmates

Accreditation signaled permanence. To staff, it communicated that professionalism was expected regardless of leadership changes. To inmates, it communicated that rules were enforced consistently, not subject to politics.

Inmates stopped testing reforms, recognizing they would not fade. Officers took pride in sustaining standards, knowing their work would be validated by external inspectors. Culture was reinforced both internally and externally.

Why Accreditation Worked Here

Not all accreditation processes sustain culture. Some facilities create binders for auditors and then return to disorder. This prison succeeded because it treated accreditation as culture, not compliance:

- Leadership framed standards as Broken Windows. Each was a window to be kept whole.
- Supervisors embedded standards into daily routines. Inspections were not events but habits.
- Staff ownership grew. Officers corrected each other to sustain compliance.
- External accountability reinforced internal accountability. Audits validated daily professionalism.

Lessons from the Accreditation Standard

1. **Standards are windows.** Each one communicates professionalism or neglect.
2. **Accreditation is sustainable only if embedded.** Binders do not repair cracks; habits do.
3. **Leadership transitions matter less when standards are cultural.** Leaders adapt to culture, not the reverse.

4. **Crises test sustainability.** If standards collapse under stress, they were never embedded.
5. **External accountability strengthens internal accountability.** Accreditation validates professionalism to staff, inmates, and the public.

Reflection

The Accreditation Standard shows how Broken Windows principles can be sustained long term through structured frameworks. By treating accreditation as culture, not paperwork, a facility institutionalized professionalism across leadership changes and crises.

Broken Windows explains the success. Each standard was a window. Sustaining them required constant repair of cracks. Because staff owned the standards, culture endured beyond leaders, politics, and crises.

The lesson is clear: sustainability requires embedding. Programs fade. Leaders change. Crises strike. Accreditation, when taken seriously, preserves culture by institutionalizing Broken Windows principles across time.

Analysis: Sustainability as the Measure of Culture

The Pattern in the Case Studies

The three case studies in this chapter—The Short-Lived Program, The Lasting Culture, and The Accreditation Standard—highlight the difference between reform that fades and reform that endures. Each facility faced similar pressures: leadership changes, staff fatigue, budget strain, and inmate testing. The difference was whether Broken Windows principles were embedded into daily operations or treated as temporary campaigns.

- The Short-Lived Program failed because it relied on enthusiasm rather than ownership. It was a campaign, not culture.

- The Lasting Culture succeeded because Broken Windows principles became daily habits enforced by peers, supervisors, and leaders.
- The Accreditation Standard endured because it institutionalized Broken Windows through external validation, embedding professionalism beyond leadership cycles.

Together, the cases reveal the truth: sustainability is not optional. Without it, every reform collapses, every gain is temporary, and every cycle returns to disorder. Sustainability is the difference between seasonal improvement and permanent culture.

Why Programs Fail and Cultures Endure

Programs fail because they rely on top-down energy. They depend on a leader's presence, posters, or training sessions that fade when leadership attention shifts. Programs are fragile and collapse when leaders leave, staff resist, or budgets tighten.

Cultures endure because they are owned at every level. They are enforced by peers, sustained by supervisors, reinforced by administrators, and recognized by inmates. Cultures do not depend on one person. They depend on daily habits. Broken Windows explains why: programs repair windows temporarily, but only cultures maintain them permanently.

Why Leadership Turnover Tests Sustainability

Corrections leadership is inherently unstable. Sheriffs are elected. Wardens are appointed. Administrators transfer, retire, or resign. Each brings new priorities. Without sustainability, culture shifts dramatically with each change.

- The Short-Lived Program collapsed when leadership attention disappeared.
- The Lasting Culture survived because staff owned the principles, so new leaders adapted rather than dismantled.

- The Accreditation Standard endured because standards were institutionalized, making leadership transitions less disruptive.

The lesson is clear: sustainability requires embedding principles so deeply that leadership transitions do not collapse them. Leaders should strengthen culture, not reinvent it.

Why Crises Test Sustainability

Budget shortages, staffing vacancies, or violent incidents expose whether culture is real or cosmetic. In crises, staff naturally look for shortcuts. If professionalism is only a program, cracks widen instantly. If professionalism is culture, staff enforce standards even under strain.

- The Short-Lived Program collapsed under inmate testing because standards were not embedded.
- The Lasting Culture endured a budget crisis because peers and supervisors enforced standards despite shortages.
- The Accreditation Standard survived a staffing crisis because compliance was institutionalized.

Crises reveal the truth: sustainability is tested under stress. Only embedded culture survives.

Why Inmates Test Sustainability

Inmates are expert observers. They know when programs are cosmetic. They test reforms early, waiting to see whether staff enforce consistently. If staff falter, inmates exploit weakness. If staff remain consistent, inmates adjust behavior.

- In the Short-Lived Program, inmates scribbled graffiti and left trash, and staff failed to respond. The program collapsed.
- In the Lasting Culture, inmates tested during staff shortages, but staff remained consistent, and order held.

- In the Accreditation Standard, inmates recognized that standards were permanent, not political, and adjusted accordingly.

Broken Windows explains why: inmates test every crack. Sustainability means cracks are repaired instantly, regardless of circumstances.

Why Institutional Memory Sustains Broken Windows

Institutional memory preserves culture across generations. Without it, every reform starts over. With it, reforms accumulate. Staff pass lessons to rookies. Supervisors enforce habits learned from veterans. Administrators build on standards rather than discarding them.

- The Short-Lived Program lacked memory. Each new initiative was a clean slate, unrelated to the past, destined to fade.
- The Lasting Culture preserved memory through mentorship, training, and shared habits.
- The Accreditation Standard preserved memory through documented compliance and regular audits.

Sustainability requires memory. Without it, reforms fade. With it, culture compounds.

The Ethical Duty of Sustainability

Sustainability is not only practical. It is ethical. Correctional facilities exist to protect the public, ensure safety, and uphold lawful order. Allowing culture to collapse every few years endangers staff, destabilizes inmates, and erodes public trust.

Broken Windows frames sustainability as moral responsibility. Each ignored lapse is a broken window. Each facility that reverts to disorder communicates that professionalism is negotiable. The public deserves better. Staff deserve better. Inmates deserve better.

How to Build Sustainable Culture

Facilities that sustain Broken Windows principles share common practices:

1. Embed, don't announce. Culture is built through habits, not slogans.
2. Empower peers. Peer correction must be normalized and praised.
3. Ensure supervisor presence. Sergeants must enforce standards daily.
4. Institutionalize training. Broken Windows must be integrated into academy, in-service, and supervisor development.
5. Protect against turnover. Policies must preserve standards through leadership changes.
6. Document memory. Case studies, training manuals, and inspections must capture lessons.
7. Validate externally. Accreditation or audits reinforce internal accountability.

Each practice repairs windows consistently, ensuring cracks do not return.

Why Sustainability Costs Less

Neglecting sustainability is expensive. Programs that collapse waste money. Lawsuits from disorder cost millions. Public trust lost after scandals takes decades to rebuild.

Sustainability costs little. Supervisor presence requires time, not money. Peer correction requires courage, not budgets. Training requires reinforcement, not reinvention. Accreditation requires effort, but its cost is far lower than the price of collapse.

The comparison is stark: neglect drains resources. Sustainability preserves them.

Reflection

The analysis of sustainability is unavoidable. Programs fade. Culture endures. Leadership turnover tests it. Crises expose it. Inmates challenge it. Institutional memory preserves it. Sustainability is the difference between reform that collapses and reform that becomes profession.

Broken Windows provides the framework. Each act of sustainability repairs a window. Each ignored lapse breaks one. Facilities that embed Broken Windows into daily life survive leadership changes, budget cuts, and crises. Facilities that treat Broken Windows as a campaign collapse as soon as attention shifts.

The lesson is clear: sustainability is culture. It must be embedded, enforced, and preserved across generations. Broken Windows is not a program. It is the profession itself.

Analysis: Why Sustainability Separates Programs from Culture

The Pattern in the Case Studies

The three case studies in this chapter—The Short-Lived Program, The Lasting Culture, and The Accreditation Standard—show different paths correctional facilities take when applying Broken Windows principles.

- In the Short-Lived Program, enthusiasm and slogans sparked short-term improvements, but without embedding into daily culture, the program faded and disorder returned.
- In the Lasting Culture, principles were embedded through peer correction, supervisor presence, and leadership consistency, creating professionalism that endured across leadership transitions and crises.
- In the Accreditation Standard, external accountability became internal culture when staff treated standards as windows to keep whole, not binders for auditors.

Together, these cases reveal the truth: sustainability is the difference between temporary reform and permanent professionalism. Broken Windows is only effective when it is sustained over time.

Why Programs Fade

Programs fade for predictable reasons:

1. **Leadership absence.** Leaders launch initiatives but fail to stay present. Staff interpret this as a signal that the program is temporary.
2. **Supervisor resistance.** Middle managers see reforms as extra work. Their reluctance undermines enforcement.
3. **Staff fatigue.** Officers wait out reforms, knowing old habits will return if they resist long enough.
4. **Inmate testing.** Inmates challenge reforms. If staff fail to enforce consistently, the signals collapse.
5. **Lack of embedding.** Programs remain separate from daily habits, policies, and peer standards.

Broken Windows explains why these failures occur. Each ignored detail is a broken window. Programs fail when they repair windows once but stop maintaining them.

Why Culture Endures

By contrast, culture endures because it embeds Broken Windows principles into daily operations.

- **Peer correction becomes normal.** Officers enforce standards on each other, not waiting for supervisors.
- **Supervisors stay present.** They walk the floors, enforce consistency, and model accountability.
- **Leadership consistency.** Administrators reinforce culture across years, not just campaigns.

- **Institutional memory.** Lessons are preserved through training, mentorship, and documentation.
- **Signals to inmates.** Consistent enforcement communicates permanence, deterring testing.

Broken Windows explains why culture succeeds. Each detail repaired daily prevents cracks from multiplying. Culture is not an event but a cycle of maintenance.

The Role of Accreditation

Accreditation shows how sustainability can be institutionalized. When treated as paperwork, accreditation fails. When treated as culture, it sustains professionalism across leadership changes.

Accreditation works when:

- Standards are embedded into daily routines.
- Supervisors enforce them continuously, not just before audits.
- Staff see audits as validation, not punishment.
- Leadership frames standards as cultural windows, not compliance checklists.

Broken Windows aligns perfectly with accreditation. Each standard is a window. Sustaining them requires constant repair. Accreditation provides external validation, but sustainability depends on internal ownership.

Why Sustainability Is Hard

Sustainability requires overcoming several barriers:

- **Leadership turnover.** Each new leader brings new ideas. Sustainability requires culture so strong that leaders adapt to it.
- **Staff skepticism.** Officers, after seeing many programs fail, distrust reforms. Sustainability requires proving permanence.

- **Budget cycles.** When money disappears, programs collapse. Sustainability requires embedding principles into low-cost daily habits.
- **Cultural resistance.** Some staff resist accountability, preferring silence. Sustainability requires peer standards to overcome resistance.
- **External crises.** Lawsuits, politics, and public scrutiny can derail reforms. Sustainability requires culture resilient enough to endure pressure.

Broken Windows helps overcome these barriers by framing sustainability as constant repair. Crises and changes will always create cracks. Sustainability requires repairing them daily.

Signals of Sustainable Culture

Facilities that sustain Broken Windows principles long term display visible signals:

- Staff correct each other daily without hesitation.
- Supervisors enforce standards consistently across shifts and years.
- Administrators reinforce culture during leadership transitions.
- Training academies embed Broken Windows into every module.
- Inmates recognize that rules are enforced permanently, not seasonally.

When these signals are present, culture is sustainable. When they are absent, programs fade.

The Ethical Duty of Sustainability

Sustainability is not only practical. It is ethical. Correctional facilities exist to protect the public, safeguard staff, and provide lawful order for inmates. Allowing culture to collapse every few years is a failure of duty. It endangers staff, destabilizes inmates, and erodes public trust.

Broken Windows frames sustainability as an ethical responsibility. Each ignored lapse is a broken window. Each reversion to disorder is an ethical failure. The public deserves more than temporary reforms. Staff deserve stability. Inmates deserve consistency.

The Cost of Failing to Sustain

Failing to sustain Broken Windows principles carries enormous costs:

- **Financial costs.** Lawsuits, overtime, and turnover drain budgets.
- **Operational costs.** Disorder increases violence, contraband, and escapes.
- **Cultural costs.** Staff lose faith in reforms. Inmates exploit inconsistency.
- **Reputational costs.** Public trust collapses after scandals.

The cost of sustaining principles is far smaller. Supervisor presence, peer correction, honest documentation, and consistent discipline are inexpensive. They require ownership, not money.

How to Sustain Broken Windows Principles

1. **Embed in policy.** Every rule should reflect Broken Windows logic: details matter, cracks spread, standards must be enforced.
2. **Embed in training.** From academy to in-service, Broken Windows must be taught as culture, not theory.
3. **Embed in supervision.** Supervisors must model accountability daily, not seasonally.
4. **Embed in peer standards.** Officers must normalize correction as duty.
5. **Embed in institutional memory.** Case studies, training modules, and mentorship must preserve lessons across generations.
6. **Embed in accreditation.** Use external standards to reinforce internal culture.

Sustainability requires embedding at every level. Without embedding, reforms fade. With embedding, culture endures.

Reflection

The analysis of sustainability is clear. Programs fade. Culture endures. Accreditation sustains when treated as culture, not paperwork. Broken Windows explains why. Each ignored lapse is a broken window. Each act of embedding is a repair.

Correctional facilities must choose: pursue temporary programs that fade, or embed Broken Windows principles as permanent culture. The cost of programs is waste. The cost of sustainability is consistency. The benefit is safety, professionalism, and trust.

The lesson is clear: sustainability is not optional. It is the profession itself. Broken Windows principles must be sustained across years, leaders, and crises. Only then can corrections move from temporary reform to lasting culture.

Tools and Takeaways: Making Broken Windows Permanent

Why Sustainability Requires Tools

Reform is easy to start and hard to sustain. Correctional history is filled with well-meaning initiatives that began with enthusiasm but ended in neglect. Posters faded, policies gathered dust, and staff returned to old habits. The difference between short-lived programs and lasting culture is tools.

Broken Windows teaches that every crack, if ignored, spreads. Sustainability requires tools that repair cracks consistently. These tools must survive leadership transitions, staff turnover, budget cuts, and crises. They must be simple, visible, and repeatable.

1. **Institutionalizing Peer Correction**
   - Normalize correction. Train new officers that correcting peers is not betrayal but professionalism.
   - Reward corrections. Supervisors should publicly acknowledge officers who correct peers respectfully.
   - Document corrections. Facilities can track informal corrections in brief logs to reinforce culture.

Principle: Peer correction sustains culture daily. Without it, reforms collapse between audits.

2. **Embedding Standards into Policy**
   - Policies should frame every standard in Broken Windows terms: details matter, cracks spread, enforcement is constant.
   - Avoid vague language. Policies must require action, not suggest it.
   - Update policies regularly, and tie them to daily practice, not just leadership memos.

Principle: Policies sustain culture when they require daily repair of cracks.

3. **Training for Permanence**
   - Every academy class should teach Broken Windows principles as culture, not theory.
   - In-service should reinforce details: counts, rounds, searches, sanitation.
   - Scenario-based training should simulate cracks and require immediate repair.

Principle: Training must prepare staff for culture, not just compliance.

4. Supervisor Standards of Presence

- ☐ Supervisors must walk floors daily, asking questions and enforcing standards.
- ☐ Facilities should require documented supervisor rounds, with administrators verifying.
- ☐ Presence must be framed as leadership, not punishment.

Principle: Supervisors sustain culture by being visible windows themselves.

5. Accreditation as a Framework, Not a Binder

- ☐ Accreditation standards must be embedded into daily operations, not performed for audits.
- ☐ Supervisors must treat every standard as a window to keep whole.
- ☐ Administrators must frame accreditation as culture validation, not paperwork.

Principle: Accreditation sustains culture when treated as permanent accountability.

6. Leadership Continuity Plans

- ☐ Facilities should create written continuity plans that preserve culture during leadership transitions.
- ☐ Outgoing leaders should document practices, lessons, and standards for successors.
- ☐ Staff should be trained to maintain standards regardless of leadership changes.

Principle: Leadership changes should adapt to culture, not erase it.

7. **Resilience in Budget Crises**
   - Facilities must design Broken Windows practices that require minimal resources.
   - Sanitation, rounds, and counts cost time, not money.
   - Supervisors must reinforce that culture holds even during staff shortages.

Principle: Sustainability must survive budget cuts.

8. **Institutional Memory Systems**
   - Facilities should preserve case studies, lessons, and cultural victories in training archives.
   - Mentorship programs should pair veterans with rookies to pass on culture.
   - Annual reviews should include reflection on culture, not just incidents.

Principle: Memory sustains culture across generations.

9. **Data as Cultural Feedback**
   - Track and share metrics that reflect Broken Windows culture: sanitation scores, contraband finds, count accuracy, peer corrections logged.
   - Transparency communicates seriousness. Hidden data communicates weakness.
   - Use data in roll call to reinforce ownership.

Principle: Culture sustained is culture measured.

10. Celebrate Longevity, Not Just Crisis

- Most facilities only reward staff after crises. Sustainability requires celebrating staff who preserve order daily.
- Annual awards can highlight officers who sustained standards consistently, not only heroics in emergencies.
- Recognition reinforces that quiet professionalism is valued.

Principle: Culture sustains when routine excellence is honored.

Practical Framework for Sustainability

For Officers:

- Own your housing unit. Correct peers and inmates daily.
- Treat every detail as a signal: uniforms, counts, sanitation, rounds.
- Remember: silence breaks windows. Correction repairs them.

For Supervisors:

- Be present on floors daily. Absence communicates weakness.
- Praise peer corrections publicly. Discipline misconduct consistently.
- Verify, don't just sign. Paperwork must reflect truth.

For Administrators:

- Preserve culture across leadership transitions.
- Use accreditation as cultural reinforcement, not paperwork.
- Protect whistleblowers and reward professionalism.

Broken Windows Applied to Sustainability

Sustainability is cultural maintenance. Programs are temporary repairs. Culture is permanent repair. Broken Windows explains the difference.

- **Short-lived programs** repair windows once, then walk away. They always collapse.
- **Lasting culture** repairs windows daily, embedding standards so deeply that they survive change.
- **Accreditation** sustains culture when standards are treated as permanent windows, not binders.

Each ignored lapse is a broken window. Each embedded standard is a repaired one.

The Cost of Sustainability vs. the Cost of Collapse

Sustaining Broken Windows principles costs little:

- Peer correction is free.
- Supervisor presence costs time, not money.
- Policy updates require effort, not budgets.
- Accreditation costs investment, but saves millions in lawsuits.

The cost of collapse is enormous:

- Lawsuits drain budgets.
- Contraband fuels violence.
- Disorder raises turnover.
- Public trust evaporates.

The comparison is not close. Sustainability is cheaper, safer, and more credible.

Reflection

Broken Windows Behind Bars is not about temporary reform. It is about permanent culture. Sustainability is the difference. Programs fade. Culture endures.

The tools are simple: peer correction, supervisor presence, honest policies, embedded training, accreditation as culture, continuity across leadership, institutional memory, resilience in crises, transparency in data, and recognition of consistency.

Broken Windows explains why each matters. Every detail is a signal. Every ignored crack spreads. Every repaired crack sustains culture. Sustainability is not optional. It is the profession itself.

The lesson is clear: corrections cannot rely on short-term programs or external audits to sustain order. Broken Windows principles must be embedded so deeply that they outlive leaders, crises, and politics. Only then can facilities sustain professionalism, protect staff, stabilize inmates, and preserve public trust.

- 16 -

SUSTAINING ORDER THROUGH BROKEN WINDOWS

The Power of Details

Corrections is a profession of details. A shirt tucked in, a door properly latched, a count done with precision, a shower kept clean. To outsiders, these may appear minor. To those who live and work inside jails and prisons, they are everything. Details are the signals that define culture.

The Broken Windows Theory explains why details matter. Each small crack, if ignored, spreads. Each detail enforced repairs the crack before it widens. Order and professionalism are built in small acts, not grand gestures.

Throughout this book, we have seen that the power of details is universal. Graffiti on a wall, if left uncorrected, becomes a gang marker. A skipped round signals opportunity. A sloppy count invites escape. A silent supervisor communicates complicity. These details are not cosmetic—they are cultural.

The lesson is clear: in corrections, there are no small things. Everything is a signal. Everything matters.

The Role of Staff Ownership

Correctional culture cannot be sustained by administrators alone. Programs launched from the top fade when leaders leave. Sustainability depends on staff ownership.

- When officers correct each other, culture is preserved.
- When supervisors walk the floor, standards are reinforced.
- When administrators embed Broken Windows principles into policy, training, and accreditation, culture becomes permanent.

Ownership is the difference between temporary compliance and lasting professionalism. Ownership turns Broken Windows from theory into a way of life.

- Officers own housing units. Their presence, corrections, and consistency define culture where inmates live.
- Supervisors own shifts. Their visibility and corrections communicate whether rules matter.
- Administrators own the framework. Their policies, discipline, and presence sustain culture across time.

Sustainability requires ownership at every level.

The Future of Broken Windows in Corrections

Corrections is entering a new era. Facilities face challenges unimaginable in earlier decades: digital contraband, staffing shortages, mental health crises, and political scrutiny. These challenges make Broken Windows principles more urgent, not less.

Technology will never replace staff presence. Policy will never replace peer correction. Accreditation will never replace culture. The foundation of professionalism will always be the daily enforcement of details.

The future requires:

- Embedding principles into every academy curriculum.
- Training supervisors to correct culture, not just manage paperwork.
- Using accreditation as a tool of sustainability, not compliance.
- Building resilience so staff can sustain professionalism under stress.
- Preserving institutional memory through mentorship and documentation.

The challenges are real, but the path forward is clear. Broken Windows provides a framework for culture that endures.

What This Means for Correctional Leaders

Leaders' greatest responsibility is culture. Policies, budgets, and programs matter, but without culture, they collapse. Broken Windows provides the framework to sustain culture long term.

Leaders must:

- **Be visible.** Presence is leadership.
- **Correct small cracks.** Every ignored detail spreads.
- **Reinforce peer standards.** Officers who correct peers must be praised, not punished.
- **Discipline fairly.** Favoritism destroys credibility.
- **Protect whistleblowers.** Silence erodes culture.
- **Sustain memory.** Preserve lessons across leadership transitions.

Leadership is not about slogans. It is about signals. Leaders must send daily signals that professionalism is permanent.

What This Means for Line Staff

Line staff are the culture. They walk the tiers, conduct counts, enforce rules, and interact with inmates daily. Their presence or absence, corrections or silences, consistency or shortcuts define culture instantly.

Line staff must:

- Own their units. Every detail is their responsibility.
- Correct peers respectfully and consistently.
- Enforce small rules with fairness and firmness.
- Maintain professionalism in dress, speech, and conduct.
- Recognize that inmates watch every detail.

Line staff are not passive actors. They are the profession. Broken Windows sustains only when officers own culture daily.

What This Means for Inmates

Broken Windows is not about punishment—it is about signals. When staff enforce details, inmates experience stability. Rules are consistent. Order is predictable. Even discipline, when firm and fair, creates safety.

When staff neglect details, inmates experience chaos. Rules are inconsistent. Order is negotiable. Discipline is arbitrary. Chaos fuels violence, fear, and instability.

Broken Windows provides inmates with a stable environment. Stability creates the conditions for rehabilitation, education, and personal growth. Broken Windows does not deny these goals—it enables them.

The Ethical Dimension of Broken Windows

Corrections is not only about custody—it is about ethics. Staff owe a duty of care to the public, to each other, and to inmates. Broken Windows is an ethical framework because it enforces integrity.

- Ignoring cracks is an ethical failure.
- Enforcing standards is an ethical act.
- Sustaining culture is an ethical responsibility.

The public entrusts correctional professionals with authority over lives. That authority requires professionalism at all times. Broken Windows provides the map to enforce that duty ethically.

Sustainability Across Generations

The ultimate test of Broken Windows in corrections is generational. Programs last months. Leaders last years. Culture must last decades.

Facilities that sustain Broken Windows pass professionalism from one generation of staff to the next. Veterans teach rookies. Supervisors mentor officers. Administrators preserve memory. Inmates recognize permanence.

This generational transfer is the essence of sustainability. Broken Windows must become institutional DNA.

Final Call to Action

Corrections is a profession defined by challenges. Inmates test limits. Staff face stress. Leaders balance politics, budgets, and public scrutiny. Crises are inevitable.

But culture is a choice. Every facility chooses daily whether to enforce details or ignore them. Every staff member chooses daily whether to correct cracks or look away. Every leader chooses daily whether to sustain culture or let it collapse.

Broken Windows teaches that every choice is a signal. Every signal shapes culture.

The final call is simple but urgent:

- Do not ignore cracks. Repair them daily.
- Do not tolerate silence. Correct it with presence.
- Do not rely on programs. Embed culture permanently.
- Do not wait for external accountability. Enforce standards internally.
- Do not let leadership changes erase culture. Preserve professionalism across generations.

Corrections is not about slogans. It is about signals. Broken Windows provides the framework to sustain those signals long term.

Reflection

This book has shown that corrections is not about bricks and bars, budgets, and politics. It is about culture. And culture is built in details.

Broken Windows explains why every detail matters. Every count. Every round. Every report. Every word. Each one is a signal. Each one either sustains order or spreads disorder.

Sustaining Broken Windows principles long term is the profession itself. Programs fade. Leaders change. Budgets shrink. Crises strike. But culture, when embedded, endures.

The future of corrections depends on this endurance. Facilities that sustain Broken Windows will protect staff, stabilize inmates, and preserve public trust. Facilities that neglect it will collapse into disorder, scandal, and failure.

The choice is clear. The path is available. The profession is ready.

The lesson is permanent: repair every crack, enforce every detail, sustain every standard.

Broken Windows is not theory. It is the culture of corrections. It is the path to safety, professionalism, and resilience. It is the map for today and for generations to come.

ABOUT THE AUTHOR

Shaun Klucznik is a career corrections professional with nearly three decades of experience in jail administration and public safety leadership. He currently serves as Jail Administrator for the Hernando County Sheriff's Office in Florida and as President of the American Jail Association (2025–2026), where he works to strengthen professional standards, training, and support for correctional staff across the nation.

Beginning his career as a correctional officer, Shaun rose through the ranks to command one of Florida's most recognized detention facilities. His leadership emphasizes accountability, professionalism, and the principle that correctional safety begins with attention to detail.

Shaun is also an educator, serving as adjunct faculty in philosophy and ethics, where he brings the lessons of leadership, responsibility, and resilience to students entering careers in public service, healthcare, and criminal justice. His academic background includes a master's degree in philosophy, with a focus on ethics and decision-making.

Drawing from his personal journey, professional command experience, and years of training officers and supervisors, Shaun developed *Broken Windows Behind Bars* to provide a framework for correctional leaders and line staff alike. The book combines theory with practical application, using real-world case studies to illustrate how small details create—or collapse—order in a correctional facility.

Dedicated to those who serve in jails and prisons every day, Shaun's work champions the belief that corrections is not only about custody; it is about culture. Order, professionalism, and accountability begin with staff ownership of the smallest details.

www.ingramcontent.com/pod-product-compliance
Ingram Content Group UK Ltd.
Pitfield, Milton Keynes, MK11 3LW, UK
UKHW022028190726
13853UKWH00005B/2166

9 798993 792453